Eng 102-
Library test

Power and Violence

The personal aggressiveness of the governors who administer punishment may be matched by the counter aggressiveness of those who are punished; and, when this is true, the oppressed may derive as much satisfaction from their side of the experience as do the power group from theirs. The rebel and the resistant build up their own . . . symbolism of action. In secrecy and darkness they may develop their own world of satisfactions; and from within this inner world of resistance they hurl defiance at authority. Paul and Silas sing in chains at midnight, and masses acclaim the great prisoners as leaders or martyrs if need be. These groups may either thrust power back in defeat or force excess that in turn defeats authority by its atrocity.

Power is not strongest when it uses violence, but weakest. It is strongest when it employs the instruments of substitution and counter attraction, of allurement, of participation rather than of exclusion, of education rather than of annihilation. Rape is not an evidence of irresistible power in politics or in sex.

—From Chapter 6, "The Poverty of Power"

CHARLES E. MERRIA

POLITICAL

POWER

With a New Introduction by

HAROLD D. LASSWELL

COLLIER BOOKS, New York, N.Y.
Collier-Macmillan Ltd., London

This Collier Books edition is published by arrangement with The Free Press, a Division of The Macmillan Company

Collier Books is a division of The Crowell-Collier Publishing Company

First Collier Books Edition 1964

Library of Congress Catalog Card Number: 63-10946

Published simultaneously by Collier-Macmillan Limited, London

Hecho en los E.E.U.U.
Printed in the United States of America

Acknowledgments

I WISH TO acknowledge deep obligation to my two colleagues, Professors T. V. Smith and Harold D. Lasswell, whose comment and critique have been invaluable to me in the prosecution of this study; to many other colleagues who have taken time to pass upon the manuscript; and particularly to Dr. H. E. Cohen for valuable services in collection of data and preparation of material.

Introduction

DESPITE THE YEARS that have intervened it is possible without difficulty to recapture the circumstances in which the late Professor Merriam composed and delivered the lectures reprinted in this volume. During the busy and booming 1920's the initiative of Professor Merriam had been decisive in bringing the Social Science Research Council into existence at the national level, and in [illegible] political [illegible] [illegible] [illegible] [illegible] [illegible] [illegible] [illegible]

[illegible] of graduate student that one [illegible] is a curious compound of cupidity and curiosity. The factor of cupidity is always obvious in a society where it is (or was) comparatively [illegible] [illegible] [illegible] [illegible] [illegible] of course is [illegible] [illegible] [illegible] fellowships travel with the speed of [illegible]. The University of Chicago was [illegible] [illegible] the time.

The element of curiosity must never be overlooked or downgraded no matter how amusing the pose of cynical comment upon the foibles of academe. More exciting than [illegible] quotations is the [illegible] that something [illegible] and intellectually [illegible] [illegible] did indeed travel that Chicago was the place to go for [illegible] challenge in the field of political science (to which my present comment is restricted). [illegible] turned down [illegible] and fellowships to try their luck at Chicago. (In confirmation, by the way, of any [illegible] [illegible] [illegible]

Introduction

DESPITE THE YEARS that have intervened it is possible without difficulty to recapture the circumstances in which the late Professor Merriam composed and delivered the lectures reprinted in this volume. During the busy and booming 1920's the initiative of Professor Merriam had been decisive in bringing the Social Science Research Council into existence at the national level, and in founding a Local Community Research Committee at The University of Chicago. At the same time Professor Merriam transformed his own department into a center for the cultivation of the "new aspects" of politics, by which was meant the interplay of theory and empirical research.

It is well known that the grapevine that connects the world of graduate students with one another is a curious compound of cupidity and curiosity. The factor of cupidity is always obvious in a society where it is (or was) comparatively rare for the offspring of wealthy families to devote themselves to fields like political science, sociology and the collateral social sciences whose deference accreditation, particularly in terms of respect is (or was) lower than law or medicine, or various branches of humanistic study. Hence the glad tidings of good fellowships travel with the speed of pecuniary exigency; and The University of Chicago was moderately well provided at the time.

The element of curiosity must never be overlooked or downgraded no matter how amusing the pose of cynical comment upon the foibles of academia. More exciting than market quotations is the glowing news that something original and intellectually exciting is going on. News did indeed travel that Chicago was the place to go for something challenging in the field of political science (to which my present comment is restricted). Students turned down scholarships and fellowships to try their luck at Chicago. (In confirmation, by the way, of my remark about curiosity overcoming cupidity

I might cite the case of a distinguished eastern university whose fat fellowships in this subject went begging for years. The prospect of utter boredom was too much to contemplate.)

As the graduate group at Chicago grew the pressures on Professor Merriam rose. The principal burden was his to provide a sufficiently comprehensive and explicit introduction to the as yet largely hypothetical "new aspects." The principal task of a teacher and scholar of vision is to create men in other than his own image. He is himself an imperfect model of the image of greater perfection to which his experience and creativity have led him to aspire. It is out of the question to turn to the next university and recruit a colleague who conforms in every particular to the model; in fact, he may not approximate the image as adequately as the originator himself.

However, it is possible to assemble a few men of common aspiration who exemplify, in part, at least, the result intended. Then come the years during which some students begin to approach the image of the dream. The early products of the new environment are likely to be very imperfect outcomes indeed since in some degree they are cut off from ready identification with more traditional perspectives and competences, and usually lack familiar mastery of the new.

Professor Merriam was abundantly aware of the fact that he was inaugurating a set of transformations that would take many years to exemplify and complete. He took with complete seriousness—and with characteristic lack of solemnity—his responsibility to point the way as best he could to students. His seminars were germinating beds where many seeds were sprouted for eventual transplantation and ripening into full-blown monographs and treatises. There was always a quiet preference for a project that depended upon directly observing politics since Merriam was convinced that too many political scientists had been too closely tied to the bookshelves. He wanted a less chair-borne profession, and he proposed to get it, not by abolishing cushions, but by encouraging motility.

What was the place of the book in all this? In one sense it

was mothered by pedagogical necessity. When the emphasis in the study of government and law moves toward the facts of life, the focus is upon power. At the time, however, no treatise dealt with the phenomenon of political power in a context sufficiently contemporary yet informed by history and traditional analysis, to clarify the scope of the subject.

Merriam wanted to exhibit the full range of political relationships. In his lectures he was groping for a mode of presenting the phenomenology of power, of saying to the student, "Look, this is the sort of thing I mean; here is what we need to explain and if possible to control for worthy purposes." And for once he wanted to take the purposes for granted—that is, all purposes save enlightenment—and to present a map or a photograph gallery of the political process.

He was strongly committed to the importance of finding successful ways of communicating his conception of the distinguishing characteristics of the political. It seemed intellectually scandalous to Merriam—although he was too shrewd and worldy wise to "emote" about it—that so many able thinkers past and contemporary seemed incapable of grasping the political frame of reference.

It is undeniable that the elusive character of the political process puts a strain upon obsessional thinkers who are deeply driven to orderly rigidity. As Merriam understood the political it was irremovable from any social process or human personality. Politics cannot be extirpated because wherever there is interaction there is interdependence; and whenever there is interdependence there are adjustments to be made that implicate and affect all or many of those who are constitutive of the context. Whatever the object of intelligent inquiry, wrote Merriam in his Preface, "the significance of the central integrating power becomes more apparent."

The aim of the lecturer was to drive this point home with as much finality as richness of example can provide. The author wanted to make it impossible for any reflective mind to confound the political function with any specific organization that in the conventional usage of any community happens to carry the label of government. True government might or might not involve the officials of the moment or the official class as a whole. This is to be revealed by appropriate methods of empirical investigation; it is inadmissible to take it for granted that function and structure are congruent with one another.

The competent observer can find integrative activity by discovering the working arrangements among important economic, ethnic and other groups within a given territory; plus similar arrangements with groups beyond the boundaries of a given community. The observer can locate part of the integrative process if he examines individual interrelationships. Granted that in any social setting personalities are usually adapted to one another without the aid of government—through the family, the church, the occupation, the gang, for example—yet "many adjustments require the assistance of the political power to affect the reconciliation of competing claims and interests" (Chapter 1).

No qualified observer will close his eyes to the "power hungry" who are ready to utilize any "situation in which a form of arrangement and understanding is ripe for development" (Chapter 1).

Merriam chose a collection of "marginal" instances that exhibit the role of politics with great clarity and vividness. Witness the famous chapters on "Law among the Outlaws" and the "Poverty of Power," the latter covering nonviolent strategies of exercising power.

Many readers have detected differences in the pace and tonicity of Merriam's exposition in the several chapters of the published lectures. That the author was enjoying himself, and gladly shared his enthusiasm with others, shines through such chapters as I have mentioned. Yet it is an undeniable advantage to be able to summon the figure and voice of the speaker into one's mind as a reader moves through the book as a whole. Many pages betray a plodding, unaccented quality that loses both the intonation of Merriam's personality and the inner tension appropriate to the magnitude and dignity of the undertaking. In the lecture hall of the Social Science Research Building these pages did not sound pedestrian: they shared the aura of the man. Merriam looked like a Roman Senator and spoke with unhurried authority. On second thought, the Old Roman image must be retouched. Merriam's full lips did not purse into the thin and biting line of the later Empire.

If one may hazard a surmise about the subterranean sources upon which Merriam drew in the most interesting chapters of *Political Power* I should offer this interpretation. He wanted to de-parochialize the contents of the book by drawing little if at all upon certain kinds of material. There is very little about Chicago politics, or political parties, or the stirring events of the then contemporary Great Depression. Merriam sought to universalize the spatial frame of the lectures by selecting cases from many countries at many times. He was aware that in the minds of many students political power was too much identified with political parties. This is comprehensible in the light of the conspicuous part that the parties play in American public life. And a more strictly academic reason was involved. In the movement to broaden the study of political science beyond philosophy, public law and structures of government, the most promising step had been to concentrate upon the party system; this was, in fact, a field in which Merriam had consistently pioneered.

But Merriam wanted to put political parties in the frame of a total theory of politics; and this meant de-emphasizing the data of parties and elections. He hoped to make it easier for colleagues in political science to perceive the contribution that can be made to the central theory of the subject by studies that range from international to national to local affairs, and from the causes of war to the causes of political personality.

Though denied public avowal the fires of personal experience betray their presence in the temperature of certain lectures. After all, "Law among the Outlaws" is the work of the former chairman of one of Chicago's intermittent crime commissions, and of an ex-alderman who knew the inner knavery of active politics at first hand. In fact Merriam had been "counted out" of election as Mayor of Chicago (as I heard in gaudy detail from the son of the man who did the dirty work. I refer to Chicago when I knew it. It may be that in supervening years the still small voice of conscience has shamed the city into virtue). When the lecturer referred to the "organized gangs of the upperworld" (Chapter 3) there are undertones from the Progressive Republican whose active political career was blocked by the public and especially the covert opposition of the bankers, public utility owners, and real estate operators who preferred "a crook you can deal with" to a "reformer" who might open the gate to "socialism."

In these lectures Merriam deliberately chose to abstain from strict definition. This I knew because I offered to go through the manuscript and prepare a glossary of terms and definitions. He preferred the broad, evocative canvass at this stage, deferring systematic treatment until some years afterward. One result of Merriam's choice was to cancel a plan to make more explicit and less cryptic the characterizations of power that were offered by the three lecturers in the series (Merriam, Lasswell, T.V. Smith).

The diverse terminologies of the authors concealed no fundamental difference of approach. On the contrary. For instance, Merriam took the pursuit of values for granted, and left the details for future discussion. His chief integrator of a latent political situation was described as value "hungry"; he pursued power more intensely than most men. The many groups and individuals whose integration is the task of politics are obviously assumed to be adjusting their value demands with one another, including the demand to use power as a base for other values than power, and for power itself.

Merriam clearly assumed that value demands were affected by matter of fact expectations about the conditions and probabilities that they would be realized. The emphasis put upon individuals as total personalities or as role takers within a group implied that the primary ego symbol ("I," "me") could be bracketed with others to constitute a self (an identity through the mechanism of identification). Many common perspectives were shared among group participants. In *Political Power* Merriam described the common myth largely in terms of "miranda" and "credenda." At a later date I split the credenda in two—the "doctrine" (philosophy) and the "formula" (legal prescriptions).

In presenting the integrative function of politics Merriam spoke of the entire range of hypothetical involvement from nearly none to totality. It was implied that the scientific observer must take responsibility for choosing the degree and character of the involvement to which he attaches the label "political." By stressing value analysis I made it explicit that involvement was a matter of the relative number of participants in a given context who were implicated, and the importance of the values at stake. I deliberately left for later treatment the "finalizing" of my recommended categories, referring to "safety, income, and deference" as "representative values." Eventually I found it convenient to employ eight basic categories, and to treat "power" (one of the "deference" values) as "decision." (The other deference values are called "respect," "affection" and "rectitude." The "welfare" values become "wealth," "well-being," "enlightenment" and "skill.") I also deferred to a later stage the systematic doubling of reference to a given context of events by adding the consideration of "institutions" to "values." Institutions are defined as patterns of shaping and sharing that are relatively specialized to the principal value outcomes.

Enough for the present. The main point is to indicate something of the frame of reference among us at the time, and to emphasize the willingness to allow formal categories to remain partially explicit until disciplined by further experience.

Among the many important distinctions latent in Merriam's treatment of power is a contrast that I now prefer to phrase in terms of the complementarity of *public order* and *civic order*. In some situations it is apparent to any observer that officials who are authorized to speak in the name of the whole are using the base values at their disposal in an authorized manner to defend the integrity of the whole against challengers; and that the defense is a strategy that imposes severe, rather than mild, value deprivations upon a challenger. Perhaps this is the most generally admitted case of political power in active application, since the participants in the process are generally agreed that officials have authority to act in the circumstances. Further, the challengers are blocked and damaged; hence power is both authoritative and controlling.

To generalize in terms of public order: The public order is composed of the basic value patterns and institutions protected by the legal order; the legal order has at its disposal enough authority and control to impose severe deprivations upon challengers.

Turn now to the other extreme and consider a case where only mild deprivations are expected to be imposed upon anyone who deviates from the accepted prescriptions of the community. Complicate the situation by imagining that the individuals who are generally perceived as acting on behalf of the community hold no legal authority conferred by an organization conventionally called government. Or assume that the active leaders are accredited officials and that the "letter of the law" (the manifest content of a statute) purports to authorize them to use severe sanctions against deviants; yet there is no expectation or demand that an occasional aberrant case is to be exposed to other than mild remonstrance. What have we here?

This is civic order. It complements public order inside conventional organs of government and in the surrounding social context. Qualified observers can detect the degree of interpenetration between the public and civic order as a whole. In Merriam's words, "The monopoly of force, which is so often declared to be the chief characteristic of the political association, is not meant for daily use, but as a last resort when all other measures of persuasion and conciliation have failed" (Chapter 1).

October 1962

HAROLD D. LASSWELL
Yale University Law School
New Haven, Connecticut

Contents

Preface

WHAT DO WE KNOW about political power? One may point to mountains of books and masses of answers. Some have deified and worshiped power. Others have defied it, or torn it from the lexicon of life. Others again have woven webs of intricate interpretations, apologies, and justifications, juristic, ethical, ethical-juristic, historical, economic, psychological, scientific. Still others have busied themselves with setting metes and bounds for the treatment [illegible] the theory of sovereignty, and now I begin this essay in the midst of a furious struggle for the possession of the symbols and the substance of political power (the German Reichstag elections of [illegible]) [illegible] my years of reading, reflection, and [illegible] experience.

No one may be [illegible] but my hope is that this [illegible] with due allowance made for a democratic and [illegible] environment of the first third of the twentieth century in America.

I shall not be concerned primarily with the question whether power, as Rousseau thought, must have a moral basis or whether it is essentially [illegible], as some have inferred from Machiavelli and others from Nietzsche, or whether the state is the irresistible Leviathan constructed by Hobbes and Austin; or whether the state should do much, very little, or nothing [illegible] whether the many or the few

Preface

WHAT DO WE know about political power? One may point to mountains of books and masses of answers. Some have deified and worshiped power. Others have defied it, or torn it from the lexicon of life. Others again have woven webs of intricate interpretations, apologies, and justifications, juristic, ethical, ethical-juristic, historical, economic, psychological, scientific. Still others have busied themselves with setting metes and bounds for the great Leviathan, cunningly devising ways and means of holding in check the arrogance of authority. I write now almost across the street from the halls where once the voice of Hegel expounded the logic and moral basis of the state, where Treitschke glorified the beauty of power. Years ago I began here in Berlin a monograph of the theory of sovereignty and now I begin this study in the midst of a furious struggle for the possession of the symbols and the substance of political power (the German Reichstag election of 1932).

It is not my purpose to repeat or refute the conclusions of the masters of political dialectics. Acknowledging my deep obligation to such thinkers, I propose to set forth what I have found out about the nature of political power during my years of reading, reflection, observation, experience.

No one may be accepted as wholly impartial and detached, but my hope is that this inquiry may be relatively objective, with due allowance made for a democratic and bourgeois environment of the first third of the twentieth century in America.

I shall not be concerned primarily with the question whether power, as Rousseau declared, must have a moral basis; or whether it is essentially immoral, as some have inferred from Machiavelli and others from Nietzsche; or whether the state is the irresistible Leviathan constructed by Hobbes and Austin; or whether the state should do much, very little, or nothing at all; or whether the many or the few should rule—the center or the circumference: or the traders, the technologists, the warriors, the priests, or the proletariat.

My purpose is to set forth what role political power plays in the process of social control. And this with perhaps more realism than is usual with those who seek to attack or defend some form or phase of government. I shall endeavor to show the situations in which power comes into being; the plurality of competing loyalties; the shame of power and some of the credenda, miranda, and agenda of authority; some of the techniques of power holders who survive; and some of the defense mechanisms of those upon whom power is exercised; the poverty of power; the disintegration, decline, and overthrow of authority; the emerging trends of power in our time.

Since many erudite and penetrating volumes have been written on the nature of political power, one may well inquire, what has been left unsaid? The answer is that the nature of power must be reconsidered from time to time in the light of the trends of social organization and of the human intelligence playing upon it. In recent years great masses of new material have been discovered in the fields of economics, anthropology, history, sociology, government, and these facts challenge the attention of those who are concerned with political authority. New doctrines of social environment, of social heritage, of personality are appearing to upset older conceptions and conclusions. Emerging psychiatric data, psychological, psychobiological facts regarding the nature of human personality are closely related to power complexes and attitudes.

Institutional changes of great meaning are also occurring under the influence of science, technology, invention, both social and mechanical. The family, the church, the school, industry, agriculture, labor, are undergoing profound modification, fundamentally affecting the basis of political power, and its external forms and manifestations, and compelling a reconsideration of earlier conclusions reached in the light of less adequate data.

Some of the basic features in power situations may be observed in lower orders of life than the human; among worms even, among bees and ants, among birds and sheep, among chimpanzees.[1] One cannot observe or read about the achievements in order and organization of these subhuman groups without being profoundly impressed. The phenomena of sub-, super-, and coordination are especially exemplified in the life of ants, where all evidences of external order are marvelously displayed.[2] Leaders, followers, warriors, slaves, mass formations of many types, exhibit a pattern of action, amazingly like that of political action in the human world.

The civil government of these numerous and varied groups has never been thoroughly studied by persons familiar with the forms and processes of politics, but chiefly by natural scientists, whose interest and special equipment are of an admirable but quite other description. Crude similarities have already been pointed out between the phenomena of masses, of childhood, of primitives, and of certain subhuman groups, notably the chimpanzees.

Some of these analogies have not been especially helpful, it is true, as in the case of the defense of slavery by one who observed the triumph of the red ants over the black, or the alleged discovery that the communism of ants indicates the low level upon which this type of social organization must always be found. But a more penetrating and less prejudiced study might reveal relations of genuine importance for the understanding of political behavior.[3]

Observations of the social processes among the preliterate groups, such as those projected by the anthropologists, may also be expected to yield facts and interpretations of great value in the understanding of the life and behavior of more mature social groupings, as anthropology advances from the

[1] R. M. Yerkes and A. W. Yerkes, *The Great Apes, A Study of Anthropoid Life*.

[2] Cf. W. M. Wheeler, *Social Life among Insects*.

[3] Interesting fanciful types are Anatole France, *Penguin Island;* C. S. Day, *This Simian World*. An interesting topic is the technique of the intercommunication of authority in such groups as wolves, chimpanzees, wild horses, bees, etc.

museum stage to a sharper assumption of responsibility for the interpretation of current forms of social and political life.[4]

Likewise many of the secrets of political power may be found in the penetralia of the human personality, which we are just beginning to explore, and from which we may hope to return with far deeper insight into the riddles of human behavior. Psychology, psychiatry, psychoanalysis, the study of the human constitution in its physiological and psychological aspects will unlock the door to many inner chambers of life hitherto barred to the observer and give us a new basis for the understanding and interpretation of human activity in the political and social realms. Until these data have been gathered and interpreted, our knowledge must remain fragmentary and incomplete, but this will always be true as long as the quest for wider and deeper knowledge goes forward.

The study of mass psychology may be expected to provide us with far more accurate knowledge of the movements of aggregations of persons acting in loosely formed crowds or closely integrated groups and associations. A social psychology may be expected to emerge as well as an individual psychology, and in the combination of these two types of knowledge and insight, there may be found material of the very greatest significance for the student of political power and political association.

It may be asked, first of all, what is political power, or perhaps even what is power? Or are such concepts so broad and vague that from the outset we may see that no definite observation or conclusions may emerge from the most persistent and acute inquiry?[5]

Whether it would be profitable to linger over the definition

[4] Works like those of W. H. R. Rivers, Clark Wissler, and many others are important contributions not merely to the understanding of the primitive process, but to the comprehension of the meaning of modern patterns of political association and action.

[5] See Charles E. Merriam, *History of the Theory of Sovereignty since Rousseau* (1900); Hymen E. Cohen, *Recent Theories of Sovereignty.*

of power in general[6] may well be questioned in the domain of social relations, as well as in the field of natural science where discussion of the definition of electricity, or gravity or energy, would be relatively unpromising and unprofitable. In political power situations, there appears a type of force through which masses of human beings are manipulated as if by some magnetic attraction or aversion. They drive hither and yon; their lives, their liberties, their fortunes, are subject to organized command and control. Life and death may be in the scales. We may not be able to define or escape this power, but the common-sense manifestations of it are on every hand.

One observation only may be made in passing. The power does not lie in the guns, or the ships, or the walls of stone, or the lines of steel. Important as these are, the real political power lies in a definite common pattern of impulse. If the soldiers choose to disobey or even shoot their officers, if the guns are turned against the government, if the citizenry connives at disobedience of the law, and makes of it even a virtue, then authority is impotent and may drag its bearer down to doom.

Power withdraws from its physical externals, beyond its symbols, lurking somewhere behind its material defenses. It is a creature of habits, of culture patterns woven deeply into the lives of men; subjective it might well be termed, were this term not employed at times to the exclusion of the emotional and psychobiological, as if epi- or para-phenomenal, as if apart somewhat from the central drive of life.

To the rationalization and derationalization of this mystery of command, obedience, cooperation, many of the world's keenest minds have devoted their intelligence. There have been conjured up such powerful and combative genii that

[6] Significant titles would include: Robert M. MacIver, *The Modern State;* Harold J. Laski, *The Grammar of Politics;* Benjamin Kidd, *The Science of Power;* Hans Kelsen, *Allgemeine Staatslehre;* Karl Mannheim, *Ideologie und Utopie;* Jacob Wackernagel, *Der Wert des Staates;* and Friedrich von Wieser, *Das Gesetz der Macht.*

their struggle and noise have often led us to forget the essence of authority in the battle over its competing justifications, intimately related as they have been to the social interests and advantages of divers types and times.

But how among men is political power distinguished from other forms of power in social situations, from the authority exercised by the church, the chamber of commerce, the labor union? How shall we define the "political" so clearly and sharply as to set it apart from all other and competing forms of social control?[7] What is the difference between economic power and political power, between ecclesiastical and political, between group authority in many forms and the more strictly political? Does not one shade over so gradually into the other that there is little room for clear lines of distinction? Does not one at times assume the functions of the other in such a manner as to blur all definitions hopelessly?

The truth is that only confusion will be created by trying to draw too sharp and exclusive a line between political and all other forms of organization. The governmental, the legal, the political, all have their analogues in other organizations, where similar phenomena of sub-, super- and co-ordination may be discovered, and nothing is to be gained by attempting to trace impossible lines between them. On the contrary, a clearer view is gained by frankly recognizing the fundamental similarity between them, and the parallelism and even frequent interchangeability of functions. Indeed if this were not so, the world would be far more difficult to govern, for the habits and ways learned in one group would not be transferable to another and reinforced by additional experience and observation. It is indeed not far from the truth to assert that much of the contemporary confusion regarding the scope of government is caused by the insistence of some one specific difference between the political and all other forms of associated life.

But this is not to say that there do not exist marks of distinction between the political and other organizations, usually

[7] See Carl Schmitt, *Das Wesen des Politischen,* as an attempt at such definition.

observable and cumulatively effective as characteristic marks, even though these too are more readily interchangeable than is often supposed. Still, the modern political group has a territorial basis, evident in boundary lines. It is true that there have been forms of nomadic states, as well as sessile states. It is also true that the growth of modern intercommunication and of modern interrelations has disturbed many of these lines and may still more rudely alter them in the future. A world state would remove the territorial boundaries of the political group and make the opposite true, namely that the political association had no boundaries at all, as distinguished from other groups with narrower limits.

The political association has a generality of purpose, falling to no other group in so broad a fashion. The maintenance of the group defense against external force is a specific function of the political agency, and the preservation of some form of external order and justice in which the other processes of social living may be set. The type of this general framework may vary widely, but the special significance of it is less subject to change.

The residual quality of the political relationships, while apparently vague in its scope, is nevertheless characteristic and is of vital importance. Famine, fire, and flood, or in more modern days disease and industrial security challenge the political group to leadership with or without apparatus or equipment, which if not at hand must be improvised. In any case, responsibility must be assumed. The leaders must lead, or give way to others who will.

Political power possesses a peculiar and indefinable integrating quality, important for the individual personality and for the social group of which he is a part. The concepts of order, of justice, of leadership, of responsibility, of trusteeship, of coordination, and of cooperation are rooted deep in the inner life of the individual and the association of individuals which we term society; and the adequate functioning of political powers is essential to the fullest and richest development of the individual no less than of the group life. Whichever way the inquiring mind of modern intelligence turns this becomes more evident. Whether in the study of personalities, of associations, of social forms and institutions, of competing ideologies and interests, the significance of the central integrating power becomes more apparent, and the possibilities of the regulator for good or evil take on a deeper meaning. It is not so much the scope of power that is vital, as the quality of it, the characteristics of equilibrator, stabilizer, general director, or, coming back to the old word, governor.

By common consent the political relation is permitted a wider latitude in the direction of pains and penalties than any other group in the social organization. These "sanctions," as they are called, may in fact be juristically without limit, although in practice subject to sharp check by those who are presumably in a habit of obedience, but who may fall out of the habit when it becomes convenient. These penalties include control over persons and property, restraint, immobilization, limitation of status, and coercion in innumerable forms, and extend to the loss of life itself in peace and war. This blanket power is recognized in the political relationship alone, although its forms may be employed by other groups as well, under certain conditions, as in secret societies and various other organizations springing up from time to time, and wielding powers more commonly administered by the formal political organization.[8]

This difference in penalties may, however, readily be exaggerated, for all groups possess penalties of their own, powerful and effective in their respective domains. The church has weapons with which it may punish both in this world and with threats of the hereafter. The fraternal associations may make life uncomfortable and indeed unendurable for those who refuse to comply with their canons of conduct. The economic organization may impose the loss of labor, of opportunity, of livelihood upon those who fail to conform to its rules of action or incur its displeasure for one reason or another. Hell, coventry, the poorhouse, may be as effective as the prison or the gallows or the tax.

Thus the political differs not merely in the type of penalty, but in the universality or generality of penalties available for

[8] See Chap. 3, "Law among the Outlaws."

the regulation of conduct. There are few penalties which the state may not employ although specific forms of punishment have been weighed and found wanting by the common judgment, as in the case of torture of various types—or the prohibition of the death penalty in times of peace. But of course new types of tortures may be invented with the growing complexity of life and the increasing possibilities of personality disturbance revealed through modern scientific analysis.

What the political group possesses is sometimes termed "a monopoly of legality," but this is a slippery term and may in effect amount to a definition of the political in terms of itself; in other words, the political has a monopoly of the political, which carries us nowhere toward an understanding of the nature of the political process itself. If we look only at the instrumentation of politics through institutions, we may observe the special position of the governmental mechanism in the social order, seen in the large. But if we look at the border lines of institutions political and otherwise, the view is no longer clear. The very question that arises is again the characteristic of the political.

But if we keep away from the more narrowly juristic point of view, we may attribute to this phrase the content of a general understanding that the so-called political group is conceded the privilege of proceeding, within the customary forms and through the accepted mechanisms, and within the generally accepted purposes of the group, to order and arrange affairs without appeal to any other formally constituted and recognized body, except upon border-line questions—an inevitable and perplexing reservation. And these decisions, arrangements, and penalties may cut squarely across the lines of other groups in the community, who, however, possess their own instruments of resistance, some within the domain of legality and others entirely outside.[9]

But is there not rather a competition of legalities in which the fittest survives? In a sense this is so. But there is in "legality" a symbolic value of high importance in social relations. To be "legal" is to bear the proud banner which rallies

[9] See Chap. 6, "The Poverty of Power."

to its support great numbers of almost any community or tends to do so. To be "illegal" is to deter many from support of a position or a personality otherwise acceptable or expedient. The legal is likely to emerge with the crown of victory, other things being equal.

Thus in transition or tension periods the symbolic value of the legality which in some ways seems so vague and empty becomes rich and full of meaning and power. The insurgent, the revolutionary (anarchists excepted) do not really scoff at legality as such, but at the particular holders of it, who abuse the authority vested in them, betray their trust, are unworthy, and should be replaced by those who understand better the use of the community authority. The King of England was first unkinged and then executed as a private citizen; in like manner, the King of France went to his death; and the Czar of all the Russias. It is not authority that is executed or imprisoned, but the betrayers of authority. The old symbols of departing rulers may be discarded, but new forms and colors will promptly appear, reminders of the new holders of the old power.[10]

Finally, I may say that I do not profess to present on this occasion a new synthesis of power woven from the strands of fact and reflection in our time. I have reserved such a task for another occasion, hoping in this particular study to direct attention to some of the neglected essentials in the political process. What I am setting down here are notes on political power, observations as I have journeyed along, sometimes, it is true, stopping to engage in battle or assume the role of counselor of state.

I have not invented a new set of terms, distressing as this may be to those who look for a glittering vocabulary unintelligible to the layman. I should be the first to recognize the high values of precision in definition and terminology, but on the other hand there are dangers in confusing science with mere terms or insight with verbal invention. If new relations are discovered, it will be easy to christen them with becom-

[10] The old distinction was that between *tyrannus absque titulo* and *tyrannus ab exercitio*.

ing names. Perhaps indeed I should have shown greater deference to the terminology of the orthodox churches of Marx, Mussolini, Pareto, Plato, and Freud. I trust that none of their followers who may chance to cast their eyes upon these lines will consider the use of my own poor patois as evidence of intentional disrespect to any other student of government or society.

To those who deal only with finalities, these comments may seem very ephemeral and may be ignored. But to those who look for the evolution of knowledge—to the general accumulation of successive increments of fact, reflection, experience, observation, generalization—these comments may have value as hypotheses if not as conclusions.

In any case it is true that in the new world into which we are madly rushing no single factor in life will be more important than the composition and incidence of political power, and no task more urgent than the understanding and utilization of a force whose mastery may mean light or darkness for individuals and for civilization.

1934

C. E. M.

Political Power

Chapter 1

The Birth of Power

How does political power come into the world? Of what situation is it born?

Many answers to this question have been made. The fatherhood of power is found in violence, in the raw will to dominate; in some divine sanction which makes of power a second religion; in some agreement or contract between members of the incipient political society. These answers are [illegible] and important [illegible] in the life of [illegible] the [illegible] power [illegible] relations?

The busy ant, the [illegible] bull, the neighing stallion, the primitive chief, the hoary elders, all had leadership long before reason or [illegible] appeared. There was power long before [illegible] word [illegible].

What then [illegible] power [illegible]? They may be [illegible] but without [illegible] fication, under three main heads:

1. The social group situations which give rise to the need for organized political action.

2. The personality types to be adjusted and adapted to social living.

3. The power hungry, the leaders, who are ripe for these group situations and these personality arrangements.

In the interplay of these factors, the birth of power may be observed, and its essential characteristics and processes discovered. Power is first of all a phenomenon of group cohesion and aggregation, a child of group necessity or utility, a function of the social relations of men. Perhaps the sociologist may say that the social situation is a matter for his

Chapter 1

The Birth of Power

HOW DOES POLITICAL power come into the world? Of what situation is it born?

Many answers to this question have been made. The fatherhood of power is found in violence, in the raw will to dominate; in some divine sanction which makes of power a second religion; in some moment of contract between members of the incipient political society. These answers are impressive and important. I do not underestimate their importance in the life of mankind. But for the moment I address myself to the somewhat different problem; what are the situations under which political power develops in human relations?

The busy ant, the chesty ape, the massive bull, the squealing stallion, the primitive chief, the hoary elders, all had leadership long before systems of philosophy appeared. There was power long before there was a written word for it.

What then are these situations from which authority emerges? They may be grouped for purposes of convenience, but without too great emphasis on this special form of classification, under three main heads:

1. The social group tensions which give rise to the need for organized political action.
2. The personality types to be adjusted and adapted in social living.
3. The power hungry, the leaders, who are ripe for these group situations and these personality arrangements.

In the interplay of these factors, the birth of power may be observed, and its essential characteristics and processes discovered. Power is first of all a phenomenon of group cohesion and aggregation, a child of group necessity or utility, a function of the social relations of men. Perhaps the sociologist may say that the social situation is a matter for his technique to analyze and interpret; and perhaps the psychoanalyst may declare that the individual relation falls within his *fach.* I may cheerfully concede that they are both right, but that the interrelationship between these intensive and extensive factors is precisely the political; and I welcome the much needed aid of both the sociologist and the psychoanalyst in the understanding of this complex problem, so long a puzzle to mankind.[1]

The social situation constantly involves the maintenance of equilibrium between groups, classes, factions, by whatever term denominated. These groups are held in combination by custom projected through time, by living interests, by symbols and associations of divers colors and force, by physical proximity and familiarity, by violence, by all the bonds that may draw men together in communities of interest. In broad terms these groups may be classified as: ethnic, religious, economic, regional, cultural.[2]

The problem of cohesion in the modern state involves the relationships between, say, two or three ethnic groups, two or three religions, three or more economic classes, several well-defined geographical regions, and a mass of cultural groups of innumerable types. Even if there were a community with only one ethnic stock or culture, one common religion or none at all, one economic class, there would still be regions no matter how small the state, and a wide variety of cultural groups, and there would be sharp clashes of interest

[1] Valuable contributions have been made at just this point by Ratzenhofer, *Wesen und Zweck der Politik;* von Ihering in *Zweck im Recht;* by Durkheim, Spencer, Simmel, Sombart, Max Weber, Wallas—in general, however, without knowledge of the more recent developments in the fields either of personality or of social control in the most recent manifestations of mass phenomena. Interesting doctrines have been advanced by Freud, but without a sure touch in the field of governmental or social relations. My colleague, Dr. H. D. Lasswell, has developed important aspects of this subject in his *Psychopathology and Politics* and is engaged in other similar studies of great importance to the understanding of the sociopolitical process.

[2] For fuller treatment of this subject, see my discussion in *The Making of Citizens,* Chap. I, and the various volumes in that series of studies of civic education in various countries.

among producers and consumers regarding the equitable intervaluation of their services. There is the possibility within the groups themselves of further differentiation into many minor groups which break up *ad infinitum* into yet more minute splinters. And if there were no groups there would still be individuals, as aggressive and *difficile* as groups themselves.

The accommodation of these groups (and of the individuals within them) produces a situation from which political authority emerges, either in dire distress as a last resort, or as a constructive adjustment of a cooperative type, perhaps rationalized as the optimum condition of life.

Sometimes this adjustment may be brought about through the instrumentality of a single class or group, and sometimes by combination cutting through the group lines quite sharply, or, of course, by a combination of groups, religious, ethnic, economic, cultural, regional. In a modern state there are major combinations which may be formed for purposes of party or political control, as the following simple table shows:

Ethnic	Religious	Economic	Cultural	Regional	
X	Catholic	Business	....	North	Urban
Y	Protestant	Labor	....	South	Rural
Z	Jewish	Agriculture	....	East	
Etc.	Mohammedan,				
	Buddhist, etc.		....	West	

The most diverse combinations are formed from time to times as the balance of social interests oscillates.

Out of these combinations emerges the power situation, which involves association for some common purpose, and the emergence of the government and the rulers, equipped now with power in the form of violence, or prestige or interest, that in turn cuts across class lines and individual dispositions. Could these groups amicably adjust their grievances and compose their differences as they indeed frequently do, there need be no central authority called government, with its broad possibilities of positive and negative action, unwelcome often to those who are the parents of the power. For government is often an unruly child, unmindful of its forbears, and disposed to differentiate itself from the groups out of which it sprang, even as other children with more clearly marked inheritance.

Conceivably there might be a long series of self-determining, autonomous groups, each a law unto itself and harmoniously revolving through space without collision, in a state of cosmic combination without the intervention of any law except that of social gravity. Both the communistic anarchists and the guild socialists have played with this idea as a possibility and as eminently desirable in the reorganization of human relations. The problem of the interrelation of these groups was once held by G. D. H. Cole as soluble through the establishment of "a democratic supreme court of functional equity," an imposing phrase of wide sweeping prestige value, hopefully designed to meet the stern requirements of the situation.

Once the need or advantage of a power situation is generally recognized, whether through consent, duress, prestige, or what not as an element of cohesion, the governmental power comes into being, and its personnel and its functions are regularized. If a parliamentary situation is set up, the group struggle may be continued with some vigor but broadly, within the boundaries of the legal order. If the type of cohesion is not so developed as to warrant such forms of pressure, there remain the roads of war and violence, until separate states are set up or some common authority wins its way to the generally accepted status of government.

When once the power situation is set up, the incidents of authority already described in previous paragraphs come into life: the generality of a residual common purpose, the defense against external groups, the maintenance of a state of order and justice, the monopoly of legality, the prestige and symbolism of political power. All forms of government, whether paternal, maternal, or fraternal, profess these broad purposes and employ forms of instrumentation and symbolism. The inner content of power does not vary so much as the tension situation and the special form of the social malaise or milieu or utopia arousing general interest and concern.

It may also prove true that the profession of general interest and responsibility is merely a verbalism to cover selfish exploitation. In any case, deference to the "common interest" is a tribute to the basis of authority. It will be paid by the tyrant as well as by the demagogue, by the patrimonial ruler who must care for his people as for his cattle as well as by the popular courtier who flatters and fawns as a part of a play for prestige and domination. The tyrant will not admit that he is a tyrant, at least not an experienced one, or that he is arbitrary or irresponsible, for he is always the vicar of someone or something, God or the nation or the class or the mass or the customs of his folk. And, indeed, however arrogant he may be, he finds it difficult to escape from the world of law which he himself and his system have invoked.[3] The most arrant impostor may thus find himself irrevocably committed to a system which no longer allows him that untrammeled liberty of choice and action, which he may dearly love but which by virtue of his very power escapes him. His sense of power is once more reduced to the dream world from which it came, and its earthly shape eludes him. So it may be said, the price of power is limitation. The ruler is ruled by his own rules.

Nor will a dominant class think itself as other than a trustee for the community over which its scepter extends. It will be a guardian of inferior peoples, of backward regions, of undeveloped classes, of groups who require some form of tutelage for their own best and highest interests. Every other group will receive exact justice, all to which it is entitled, in the judgment of those who hold the power. In point of fact the dominant group may from any objective point of view be correct in principle and in practical plans; but it may also be sadly wrong, as many bitter experiences of subject peoples attest. From every century there rise the cries of those who fell victims to the ruthlessness of a dominating group.

It cannot be concluded, however, as many have, that the essence of the power situation is force, in the sense of vio-

[3] Georg Jellinek, *Allgemeine Staatslehre,* Book III, Chap. XV, pp. 461 ff., on self-limitation of law.

lence and physical brutality. It was curiously enough an avowed anarchist who made one of the greatest contributions to the science of government in the nineteenth century. It was none other than Prince Kropotkin who pointed out the importance of mutual aid as a factor in human evolution in his famous discussion of that topic. Altruism as well as egoism has a place in human relations and organization, and cooperation has as genuine a position as coercion. The race advances not merely by the devouring of the unfit by the stronger, but by the triumph of the groups which have acquired the techniques of cooperation and mutual aid as over against those in which egoism and unrestrained individualism are regnant. This reasoning of the eminent philosopher and geographer was substantially sound and has a permanent value in the evolution of the understanding of the state. The conclusion which he drew, namely the elimination of government, does not follow, for the very reason he discovered but would not apply, namely the admixture of coercion and cooperation in the modern social and political *entourage*. It is conceivable that there might be a form of political order in which there was no force (violence) exercised, or exercised at very rare intervals, either because the power of custom had been so firmly established that violence became unnecessary, or, perhaps, because there was so high a degree of intelligent appreciation of the utility of the rules of the community that the same result was reached. In most communities the use of force is relatively uncommon in proportion to the number of regulations, and the success of the organization is not measured by the amount of violence in specific cases, but by the extent to which violence is avoided and other substitutes discovered. The monopoly of force, which is so often declared to be the chief characteristic of the political association, is not meant for daily use, but as a last resort when all other measures of persuasion and conciliation have failed.

The functional situation out of which the political arises is not the demand for force as such, but the need for some form of equilibrium, adjustment, *modus vivendi* between the various groups and individuals of the community, as a substitute indeed for force in many cases. Not only the anarchist but many others, individualists so-called, make the same fundamental error in analysis of the power situation in society,[4] of overstating the role of violence.[5]

The distinguished apostle of socialism, Karl Marx, likewise gravely erred in his conception of the essential nature of the meaning of the political in human association. The state he looked upon as the result of the war between economic classes, in this case the bourgeoisie and the proletariat. "The state is the official form of the antagonism between classes," and when the class war ends and there appears a one-class society, proletarian in composition, the state will disappear, since the occasion for its existence has gone. True, if one defines the state in this manner, the conclusion follows. But what shall we call what remains, as in Soviet Russia at the present moment?[6] The political association or situation is far older than the "class" under capitalism, and arises under a wide variety of conditions. Many of these are instances of other forms of exploitation under different forms of economic organization from the present, but it is as difficult to think of the state as arising solely from these relations as it is to imagine the disappearance of the function of the political order when the present economic crisis is adjusted in some different manner. But in general the political acumen of Marx is far less penetrating than his insight into economic relations, and his avoidance of the organizational implications of the principles he expounded is evident throughout his writings. Certainly there is nothing in the contemporary activities of socialists or communists, or in earlier experiments of the same type, to indicate the withering away of the political aspects of association; and there can remain only the faint-hearted expression of the distant

[4] Some of the followers of Kropotkin, however, have been less under the influence of the earlier idea. Se also Emma Goldman, *Living My Life*.

[5] Cf. W. C. MacLeod, *Origin and History of Politics*.

[6] See the interesting analysis of Marx's ideas in S. H. M. Chang, *The Marxian Theory of the State*.

expectation that at some time in the vaguely unspecified future the element of government may disappear from social organization.[7]

From one point of view, then, the power situation involves a series of intergroup relations, calling for a balance and ordering of some type, which will be preferable to the distress caused by lack of common arrangements and understandings. There are also, however, the relations of a group of external political groups; and by this road we come into the field of interstate or international arrangements and understandings, seriously complicating the symmetry of the simpler local situations.[8] This becomes all the more intricate when we observe that many of the local intrastate groups have extensions outside the boundaries of the political association, as ethnic, cultural, religious, etc., and the web is correspondingly more involved as the number of possible interrelations increases. The task of political association is thus a manifold one, of reconciling the interests of the internal groups and at the same time the external groups, and simultaneously the internal projected into the external interrelationship. This may be illustrated by observing the difficulties of a multiethnic or other group state, such as Switzerland, when it undertakes to deal with other powers as represented, let us say in the League of Nations.

But there are also types of social situations in which power becomes necessary or desirable which are not balances or adjustments among existing groups, but are the adaptation of interests and attitudes not reflected or represented in any existing and crystallized association. These may be attitudes and interests cutting across the lines of existing cultural associations and finding need of adjudication, or expression through some political power agency which they invoke. Then the power group itself may initiate lines of social action which meet the approval of all or important groups of association throughout the political society. In the more developed forms of political life, the political becomes an interest in itself; and on its own begins to reach out into the

[7] Cf. Chang, *op. cit.*

[8] On this point see the following chapter.

domain of social activities, perhaps in unexpected directions —a broad frame of reference for cooperative action.

Personalities and Power Situations

Significant as are the group accommodations just discussed, the adjustments of personalities in the general framework of social milieu are of equal meaning. If one looks objectively at government he may observe a mass of personality reconciliations which must somehow be effected, somehow reconciled to the general set of understandings, experiences, institutions which make up society. The biological and social heritage of the group throws forward a broad variety of different types of individuals who must in one way or another be set in the whirling web of social and political relations, without tearing it or themselves or too many of them to pieces.

If we can lose sight for a moment of the social interests and ideologies upon which governments and societies are ostensibly constructed, democracy, fascism, communism, absolutism, we may see that the basic political problem may be viewed in quite a different light from that of the common institutional mechanisms or the historic and traditional group power struggles.

The aristocrat, the democrat, the communist, the nationalist, after the noise and shouting of the battle die away and victory makes possible responsible direction, each finds the problems of personal claims, values, modes of life springing up. The same problems remain for every victor to consider and perpetually balance in the unending series of adjustments arising out of the differing personality patterns of the citizenry. The special form of social interest or the special type of ideology will supply the key to various forms of action, but there will remain the perennial problems of millions of varying personalities struggling for expression and recognition; for the realization of the special values in life which they cherish and adore.

Types of personalities must be adapted and adjusted under all systems by whatever means are available—by force, custom, persuasion, social pressure, individual reorientation;

otherwise the concern will not go forward, will not function. And this adaptation of value systems constitutes one of the great tasks of social control, and more specifically of political organization and control. This lies at the heart of the power problem under all forms of political and other social organization—the staple of their activities, after the argument over the ideologies and the group interests has been for the moment disposed of.

What then are the main types of personality from the point of view of the power problem? In the older terminology there were good men and bad men; there were just and unjust; there were docile and insubordinate; patriots and traitors; dreamers and doers; there were power hungry and power indifferent persons; masters and slaves.

In later terms there are introverts and extraverts; there are those with high and low and medium I.Q.'s; there are differentials determined by long "batteries" of tests technically administered by psychologists, biochemists, gland specialists, physiologists, constitutionalists; there are those with father and mother complexes; there are those with superiority and inferiority complexes; there are sadists and masochists; there are narcists and exhibitionists; there are obsessives and hystericals; paranoiacs, manic-depressives; acid and alkali types; psychotics and neurotics. Some of these types become or tend to become mild deviates; others criminals; others patriots, martyrs, slackers, traitors, with high or low civic morale.

These multifarious types of personalities, centers of their little worlds, whirling among millions of others at lightning speed, carry infinite possibilities of collision, confusion, destruction. There is in gregariousness, especially as observed in subhuman groups, an automatic form of tropism which seems to protect them against each other and to organize itself in working patterns, although rival groups seem more disposed to struggle and destruction. And perhaps underneath the surface and all unknown to us, there are similar basic social tropisms which take care of humans, as of the distant nebulae.

Not only are there many widely varying types of men

amongst whom the conduct and objectives of the government must be adjusted; but the attitudes of the same persons change from day to day and still more from one mode of experience to other modes and shades of social contact. There are those who cling to life as if shipwrecked in some great storm, concerned only with the problem of holding on to a thin rope of existence which may at any moment part. Others are full of the *joie de vivre,* with every step and every breath a joy that radiates throughout the being and which questions nothing in such a world of sheer delight of existence.

There are great groups entirely indifferent to affairs of state; not consciously irresponsible, but blind and deaf to the affairs of such a world. They wake from time to time to challenge the great outside forces with which they do not usually concern themselves. There are those who resist and rebel with and without reason; some in one form and others in another mood. There are the rivals unrecognized by authority, the temperamentals who may be radical or conservative as far as economic class is concerned, but are fundamentally difficult of adjustment in any case. There are those who fear all power; and those who bow and scrape to leaders who bring them security.

Judgment upon government is rendered by a great mass of citizens, upon the basis of such facts or fancies as they may at the moment possess and which may be merely the reflection of some narrow personal experience. Men tend toward either unusual criticism or unusual conformity. At one moment they complain unreasonably of the acts of government, and in the next moment they are enthusiastically applauding the events and persons whose life typifies the essence of the state.

Much of the personality adjustment is indeed effected without the aid of government, some through other members of the family of power—the family, the church, the occupation, the gang—others through less organized forms of orderly association. But many adjustments require the assistance of the political power group to effect the reconciliation of competing claims and interests. The values of the producers as against those of the consumer, of seniority and youth, of ins and outs, the secure and the insecure—these are balanced by a variety of methods. But one of them is the political, in which are embedded many of the main elements in adjustment, as in the case of inheritance, trade regulation, minimum standards of existence, boundary lines not only of land, but of reputation, privacy, rewards of invention and enterprise, interchange of values in a wide-ranging series of instances. The standards of responsibility, the limits of permitted deviation, the care for a wide group of defectives, dependents, delinquents, without special regard to the group from which they hail—these are tasks often devolved upon the government; and this whether it is bourgeois, proletarian, tribal, theocratic, or otherwise.

The governor views the situation as a whole, having in mind all the interests involved, as modified by his class interest and his own personal advantage and interest. The subject views the situation from the side of his personal interest and advantage as modified by that of his group and by that of the state as a whole. Between the extremes of docility and of criticism the mass oscillates from time to time, as determined by temperament, social experience, social tensions, advantages, and the impact of power influences playing upon them.

Governments of course prefer conformity to criticism, and docility to the spirit of challenge. For the losses from lack of docility are nearer at hand and easier to observe than the losses from uncritical conformity, which are more remote and always seem less real. The immediate problems of statesmanship are always urgent and imperative, and what is remote or postponable may be thrust aside for concentration on the direct emergency which must be settled at any cost. Conformity is almost always more agreeable to the governor, and he will cultivate the attitude and the types which encourage this trait, even when he is aware of the dangers of too great docility in the long run.

Every power system is adjusted, delicately or indelicately as the case may be, to these type situations which require the cooperative control of the community for their effective adaptation. If this cannot be done, then the group cannot be defended, the law cannot be enforced, the taxes cannot be collected, both order and justice sicken and fade, the morale of the community wanes, and the power group dissolves or gives way to another.

To this the apparatus of governmental lures and threats must be adapted, and the survivors are those who best understand how to deal with these delicate personal relationships, deep down beneath the surface of political activity. Rule of thumb has answered the purpose of control for centuries, but now with deeper understanding and with the sharper instrumentation of social education, there comes an important and new stage in the ordering of power. In a rough way, results have been achieved through such devices as the sonorous and rhetorical appeals made to the youth by the military group, regard for the maturity of the elders in the state or community, sundry provisions for seniority in rank and command, efforts to conciliate the discontented on the one hand and the vested rights of establishment on the other; by the oratorical appeals to various types of personality groups as diagnosed by the manipulators of crowd opinion; and more than all by the steady reliance upon fear, upon recognition, upon security, upon hope as great driving impulses of human organization, by the organized play upon the primitive emotions which have been unveiled from time immemorial by those with the hunger for power.

But more than this is possible through the study and application of the more recent developments in the field of human personality, even now with the subject imperfectly developed, and still more in the not distant future with the further progress of social science. The power problem involves the relationship of widely different types in a form of so-called order, a frame within which social life may be carried out without too great inconvenience for too many people.

The understanding of these types waits upon fuller knowledge of the developing studies of human personality, or whatever other axis the study of humans may revolve about as times goes on; and we may look forward confidently to much more complete and systematic knowledge of the "constitutional" bases of human behavior, including the biological and the psychological, in the interrelations which yet defy the inquiring eye of the scientific observer and baffle the student of behavior.[9]

Not only is this true, but the governmental mechanism must further take account of the development of the personality through various stages of growth and change, the varying age groupings, the changes that take place as the individual advances from one stage to another of the great life drama. The problem of the child in relation to association and authority, the shift to adolescence and its vital implications for social adjustment or maladjustment, maturity, and senescence; these represent important variations of the personality with direct bearings upon the problem of adjustment and adaptation in a political and social framework. Each stage and group must be carefully considered with reference to the position of the power situation and the growth of sub-, super-, and co-ordination in the political association. The genetics and the dynamics of personality must be brought into view for the finer adjustment of the governing function in a community.

Here we find the birth of power, apart from the world of ideologies and interests in one sense, although in another inseparably united with them; for what we know is that all of these factors are parts of one indivisible problem, however they may be differentiated in ordinary observation and thinking.

Economic, religious, racial issues come and go, but these personality types and problems of adjustment recur through the centuries and linger far beyond the life of any ordinary social issue, however revolutionary its implications may be.

[9] A summary of the significant literature in this field may be found in Appendix C of *Proceedings, Second Colloquium on Personality Investigation,* pp. 170–206. On constitutional studies, G. E. Coghill, *Anatomy and Problems of Behaviour;* George Draper, *Diseases and the Man;* E. Kretschmer, *Physique and Character;* Nicola Pende, *Constitutional Inadequacies,* and others. For bibliographies of psychiatry and psychoanalysis, psychology and sociology, see *Proceedings,* pp. 189 ff.; pp. 192 ff.; pp. 196 ff.; and pp. 202 ff.

The struggles and wars which are the outcome of the clash of group interests and the brutality of their solution, the valiant efforts of the power hungry, are in a real sense only episodes in the long struggle for the adjustment and adaptation of the conflicting types of human personalities which spring from our social and biological inheritance and from their modifications by social experiences of infinite variety. They are the eternal stuff of which government is constructed; the continuing factors in a world of changing forms, leaders, and processes political.

The Power Hungry and the Power Situation

But the birth of power presumes not merely a situation in which a form of arrangement and understanding is ripe for development, but likewise individuals or groups of individuals who are ready to utilize the opportunity afforded by this conjunction of circumstances. Out of this whirl of events there come leaders, governors, specialists in the art demanded or made possible by the social environment of the moment: those who know how and have the urge to act. I do not raise here the age-old question whether the situation makes the man or the man makes the situation. It is sufficient for my present purposes to find that they work together in the formation of a power complex, without deciding which of them came first or whether there is any general rule of precedence.

But what manner of men are these governors? It is not a satisfactory answer to say, as has often been asserted, that we are ordained, or that we are elected, or that we are the élite, as determined by ourselves. We already know that you are, but we raise the query what manner of persons you are or how you came to be; or how your special faculties and dispositions were adapted to the *entourage* in which they are found.

In this attention to the interrelationship between the social situation and the qualities of the leaders lies our surest safeguard against the pitfalls that mark the way toward objective knowledge of the power complex. Otherwise we may fall ready victims to the common forms of dogmatism regarding types and capacities of leaders and governors, which may be little more than the projection of the selfish interests of those who advance them as generalizations. That men hold power because they are of divine descent or special divine authorization may satisfy the Lord's anointed, but not the scientist; or that they come of a special pedigree of family or tribe, eugenically anointed as it were; or that seniority or wealth or other status has raised them where they are; for from these same interesting backgrounds there emerge asses as well as lions in a frequency distribution which raises serious doubts in the mind of the skeptical as to the infallibility of the process. These apologia are important as propaganda tools, but not as serious credentials. They are projections of prestige in the hope of mass acceptance, and it must be said in many cases they serve their purposes well as measured by pragmatic standards.

But what shall we say of the obvious fact that not infrequently the ass does actually have the power, or at any rate wears the lion's skin? The nominal power holder may be by common consent a fool or an incompetent, apparently incapable of defending himself against any aggressor except as he is surrounded by a system. Outside the walls, he becomes a harmless old gentleman, to be viewed with reminiscent interest rather than with fear or adoration, a lion we may touch without fear.

If we examine our rulers more carefully, it becomes evident that the qualities of leadership are found in a group of individuals who together are able to function as a politicizing instrument for the community and for themselves. The nominal bearer of the externalia of power may be in fact powerful per se, or he may be the representative of a larger group of persons better qualified to understand and execute. Councils, courts, cabinets may contain the wisdom which really rules through a prestige instrument, a sounding board rather than a voice.

But why do not the real leaders overturn the nominal and substitute themselves for their dummies? This ignores the whole basis of power which lies in a social situation, conditioning the actions of the leaders, and making it difficult or impossible for them to operate against the very basis of their own authority. They are not merely leaders per se, but they function in a total situation of which they are parts. As servants of the crown they may largely direct the crown, but as claimants of the crown they may become traitors.

But still the question may and should be raised, what manner of men are these who are found within the inner circle if not always at the technical apex of authority? Give us a sign by which we may infallibly identify them. Give us a test that will not fail. Well, then, history is full of them, is it not? Are not all leaders lions, or eagles, or wolves, or bulls, or bears, browbeaters with raucous voices, glaring eyes, and fierce scowls, preeminent in size or weight or speed or skill in combat, looking like kings or grand dukes or little gods? Look around you, or historically perhaps. No? Well, then, are they not all orators with booming or seductive voices, mob masters, taming the crowds with their irresistible wiles, prophets, demagogues, crowd compellers, full of *empressement?* As, for example, shall we say the imposing Gandhi, or the towering Lenin, or the massive Hitler? No, something seems awry here and we must go back to more careful analysis of the problem.

Types of leaders differ with the social relationship in which they are set, with the tensions within these types, with the varying requirements of prestige and of ideology. The leader is a function of the social pattern and cannot be understood apart from it. And as there are many types of situations, and many degrees of tension, and many different ways of meeting the same problem; as, further, there are distinctions to be drawn between those who hold the power nominally and those who function through them, the conclusion is inevitable that there are many kinds of leaders and many qualities, dispositions, aptitudes, characteristic of these power possessors.[10]

We must further reckon with the fact that the scientific knowledge of human personality is only in its infancy. The proper study of mankind is man, but the more intimate study of human personality in the light of and with the aid of

[10] This topic will be more fully considered in a forthcoming monograph, *Leadership,* by C. E. Merriam and H. E. Cohen.

modern scientific techniques has barely begun, and none are more modest in judgment upon personality than those who have penetrated farthest into the dimly explored domains of psychiatry, psychoanalysis, psychobiology, psychology, psychophysical constitutionalism, social psychology, in which there seems to lie so much of the secrets of human life. Psychoanalysis alone has already even in its infancy revealed truths of basic importance for the complete understanding of the processes of social control, and its scroll is not yet unfolded. When the "constitutional" background and the social experience of the individual are more fully understood and more expertly related than now, it may be possible to comprehend more fully the predispositions toward politics which now obsess so many individuals.

What do they seek, those with this power hunger, in this field of government, consciously or without appreciation of what they strive toward? And what types most readily find expression and satisfaction in varying situations? And what may we seek in them to satisfy the different equations in human political behavior most effectively? What modifications of the splendid description of guardians made by Plato in the dawn of political inquiry will be made by modern science?[11] To these fundamental queries only the most tentative answers may be given.

What we now know is that leader types vary widely:

1. With the social situations and tensions they serve.

2. With their specific function in what special situation, as general, drill sergeant, judge, parliamentarian, dictator, king.

And what we further know is:

3. That a distinction must be observed between the prestige projectors and those ruling through the prestige agencies.

4. That potential leadership is not uncommonly distributed through society, available either for the old or for new types of situations and tensions.

It is not generally recognized that leadership is not something wholly unusual and amazing. Quite the contrary, political leadership is conditioned upon the prevalence of like

[11] *Republic* (Jowett ed.), Book II, pp. 375 ff.; Book III, pp. 389, 412, 413, 414; Book V, pp. 462–466.

qualities within the community in which it is exercised. This is evident enough when we consider that a great general does not commonly emerge from a nonmilitary people, or a great parliamentarian from a people not habituated to such procedure, or a great judge where there is no refinement of the juristic techniques. The leader is original, perhaps, but not too original, otherwise he cannot be understood or followed or supported by his potential group. He leads by and through a set of key persons who approach him in equipment and understanding. Through them is filtered into another stratum not too far removed the meaning of the situation.[12] The leader leads not because he is entirely different from the others, but because he is much like the others and may symbolize and fuse their aspirations and desires.

In the earlier stages of leadership, force is conspicuous, as in subhuman groups and among primitives of some types, force accompanied by what is roughly called "animal cunning"—a technique of combat. Prestige may continue this superiority and supplement it, may serve as a protection for a time against a challenge and a combat, and in some groups the actually efficient combatants may gather round the outworn prestige holder to protect him.

But in the elders is seen the rise of craftiness, in a form of group guidance, into the making of which personal physical ability may enter very little. The leader wins for the group through brain as well as through physical combat, and the fading of one may be made up by the importance to the group of the other. Thus the wise old man becomes a great asset for the tribe as in later stages for the nation. On a later scale this rivalry is seen in the relative positions of the "frock" and the "uniform," often competing forms of lead-

[12] See Wilhelm Vleugels, *Die Masse;* Theodor Geiger, *Die Masse und ihre Aktion;* P. Tillich, *Masse und Geist;* Leonard Nelson, "Demokratie und Füherthum" and "Erziehung zum Führerthum" in *Sammlung öffentliches Leben,* Heft 13–14 and 15–16, Leipzig, 1920; Edmund Stieler, *Person und Masse;* H. de Man, *Massen und Führer;* H. Heller, "Genie und Functionär in der Politik," *Die Neue Rundschau,* vol. 41[1], pp. 720–731; Kurt Baschwitz, *Der Massenwahn, seine Wirkung und seine Beherrschung;* José Ortega y Gasset, *The Revolt of the Masses.*

ership, alternating with social tensions demanding one or the other—reminiscent of the remoter days when the young warrior was impatient of the elder sage and demanded more battle and less counsel.

In intergroup situations, demanding the exercise of the technique called adjudication from within and diplomacy from without, the finesse of the leader becomes increasingly important to the group. Otherwise what has been won in the heat of battle may be lost in the long drawn out parleys of the peace treaty. More than one group has sat down to negotiate in victory, only to rise in equality of defeat with the foe.

More modern leadership exhibits strikingly the importance of two factors, the command of symbolism and facility in organization. Neither of these is entirely new in the history of political relations, but both are highly developed in modern times. Primitive symbolism was indeed highly important and broadly proliferated through the early tribal life.[13] It was directed toward smaller groups, however, and was far less mobile in its forms than that of our times. It was in the nature of a social heritage rather than invention adapted to a newly developing situation. The symbolisms of the Soviets, of the Fascists, of the Nazis, are brilliant examples of the newest forms of symbolic interpretation of mass desires or potentialities in varying forms. The modern rivals must struggle with each other in desperate efforts to surpass in the creation of competing types of symbolism which shall most broadly include the currents of contemporary life. By this they may stand or fall in the rough struggles in which they engage.

Symbolism is not a club, but a magnet, which draws men into the central focus of the leader group, and fuses them with the others there. It rests upon an understanding or appreciation of or sympathy with the potential responses of masses of men and women, adult and youth, measured in terms of slogans and signs with life and color and appeal. Symbolic content is susceptible of infinite variation, and even

[13] On this point see Chap. 10.

inner contradiction is not a weakness but a gain, if there develops an assemblage of appeals. Self-interest, sacrifice, struggle, ease, may all be intermingled in what may seem from one angle an incongruous and inconsistent pattern, but from another angle indicate a type of solidarity from which victory may arise.[14]

While earlier leaders wielded the ax, or invoked the immemorial mumbo jumbo of the clan, or smoked the pipe of peace in conference with their foes, the more modern type must busy himself to a greater extent with the manufacture of symbols of current value in a swiftly changing world, weighing interests, ideologies, personalities with a view to developing them into useful tools of social combat. Even if force is the final stroke, the way must be prepared by attitudes favorable to its exercise, by hates and adorations, by promises and predictions, by diabolical fixations of responsibility upon unworthy holders of power, by appeals to the emotional-intellectual life of great masses of individuals.

Organization as well as interpretation is a key to the use of symbolism upon a mass scale. It is not enough to dream or devise a catching symbol, for the techniques of modern mass action, of advertising, of assembly must be invoked, so that the symbol is impressed upon millions. In organized form this is sometimes called propaganda, popular education in special appeals. But the propagandist does not sow the seed to the four winds of heaven. He systematically surveys the field and spreads the seed mechanically in spots where it may most quickly or most deeply take root. The propaganda center of a modern power group is not like the cell of the hermit or the abode of the prophet, but has more likeness to the factory, with its huge plant, its subdivision of labor, its whir and clatter, its systematic efficiency. Education and advertising, mass production; these are its background. But this mechanical technique, however impressive, is subordinated to the ulterior purpose of affecting human behavior favorably

[14] The inner core of symbolism has been but little studied, but is of profound importance in human relations. Cf. A. N. Whitehead, *Symbolism, Its Meaning and Effect;* also the brilliant study by Jacob Wackernagel, *Der Wert des Staates,* 1934.

in the direction of a specific goal or program or person or all of these.

Large scale organization does not, however, find its limits in the massing of symbolism and propaganda, but finds its way into almost every avenue of the modern power attaining group. The prophet organizes his prophecy, not leaving his eternal truth to be discovered by succeeding ages. His followers are not an unorganized but enthusiastic mob, but a well-officered, drilled, and disciplined army—a private army of a type forbidden to fight, but ready for the modern fray of words, epithets, and most of all for systematic mass demonstrations and efforts of every description, as may be commanded from on high.

Parties are highly organized in parliamentary countries, and where the party has become in effect obsolete, as in Russia, Italy, and Germany, the new groups, the Communists and the Fascists, are equally well or better organized and active.[15] Army organization, it is true, has been historically one of the important objects of interest for leaders, and indeed still remains so, although now eclipsed by commercial organization and school organization and rivaled by civil and party organization.

It would be an error to assume, however, that a leader must himself possess the special qualities for large-scale organization of men, for this may be the task of an adjutant; or indeed the adjutant may in fact be the more powerful, with the nominal leader as his mouthpiece and instrument. But somewhere in the group of aspiring leaders there must be found the skill in mass organization which has become so indispensable a part of modern social and political control whether with Gandhi, Lenin, Mussolini, or Hitler. The cooperative enterprise presupposes a series of skills at the disposal of the power set, and their distribution varies from time to time with the exigencies of the case.

Granting that the mastery of symbolism and skill in organization are emergent in the modern leadership situation, are there further and more specific dispositions and skills

[15] See descriptions by S. N. Harper, *Civic Education in Soviet Russia,* and H. W. Schneider, *Making the Fascist State.*

which may be found in prospective holders or bidders for power? Broadly speaking, these aptitudes vary so widely in different situations that generalization is filled with many dangers, but various attempts have been made in this direction by such students as Michels, Conway, Giese, and others.[16]

All these must be regarded as tentative and provisional, however, awaiting much fuller knowledge of the inner content of the material dealt with by the commentators. In my own studies I have set up as a sort of temporary scaffolding the following series of aptitudes commonly found in a variety of modern leaders. I do not attach any great value to these distinctions, but they are perhaps useful as a basis of discussion and a point of departure in more elaborate and later inquiries.

1. Many political leaders seem to have a high degree of social sensitivity, sensing what goes on around them in the field of political and social power. It was once said of President McKinley, an adroit reader of public opinion, that he had both ears to the ground all the time; and of Hitler that he said, "I may not possess your governing ability, but I can at least tell you how to make up the public mind." The leader is likely to feel the weather and know the tides that come and go in human affairs, and to be able to measure the effect of special pleas directed toward representing or influencing these movements and potentialities.

2. The leader is likely to possess a high degree of facility in personal contacts with a wide variety of persons, enabling him to meet them without effort and with conspicuous success in case after case. When the cause is lost, perhaps the personality himself may save the day in many instances. It is one of the interesting phenomena of politics that individuals are often strongly attached to leaders with whom they disagree on every major issue—attached for personal reasons, as the phrase goes. A bold, aggressive, or sympathetic idealistic type of man may gather around him a

[16] See my *American Party System* for bibliography; H. D. Lasswell, *Psychopathology and Politics;* also my *Four American Party Leaders.*

following concerned not with alleged goals but with his own form of public activity, or perhaps one seeing in him a reaching out toward a goal to which they themselves would go if only the way were shown.

3. The leader is further likely to have great facility in group contacts, ability to know and reckon and deal with a considerable number of interest groups whose aims conflict but toward whom there must be a sympathetic attitude. This group diplomacy is of the very essence of high politics and the practitioner in this field is well equipped for that reorganization of perplexing situations which is the very task of politics on so many dark occasions. The various races, the religions, the classes, the regions, the innumerable culture groups which everywhere abound—these the skillful leader understands how to conciliate or to unite in victorious combinations, if all cannot be drawn in. Thus Laurier, a Frenchman in Canada, Sonino, an Egyptian-born Scotch-Jew in Italy, Hitler, an Austrian in Germany, Lloyd George, a Welshman in England—these illustrate the possibilities of group reconciliation, even under somewhat unpromising initial conditions. For some purposes the outsider, or the one a little to the side, may be a better conciliator, than the insider to the manner born, just because he is somewhat apart from the vested and larger interests at war.

4. From the foregoing it is clear that the leadership group must possess the facility of dramatic expression. This may take the form of the voice of the orator, or the pen of the author, or the dramatization of the behavior seen in large and swift adventurous movements, signalizing the individual as an unusual personality in his experience if nothing more. Roosevelt, Mussolini, Hitler, Bismarck, Clemenceau rank as masters in this field. And for this reason it not infrequently happens that persons without any other special qualifications than the drama of their lives are precipitated into important political positions, as in the case of Paderewski, in generals of many lands, great men so-called, especially great in some form of celebrity, it matters not what. The dramatic situation comes with special power to the average man, who reads into his leader's life the unfulfilled aspira-

tions and dreams of his own more drab existence. In the dramatic leader he follows in a way the beckoning of his own revery life. The instinct or aptitude for dramatics fits well into the modern demand for slogans and devices lifting the individual above his daily tasks.

5. In view of the conciliatory nature of many power situations, it is important that leaders possess some facility in invention, whether of formulas, policies, ideologies, which may satisfy the requirements of difficult situations into which the groups have come, and from which it seeks a way out. It is quite possible that the nominal leader may not be the actual inventor of the new law, or the new treaty, or the new plan, or the new slogan, but it will be imputed to him, even though it has been whispered in his ear by some subtler and more cleverly reorganizing mind; and in any case, he is entitled to the credit of recognizing a good suggestion and accepting and incorporating it in his political system. Perhaps Napoleon was not the author of the code that bears his name, but at any rate he listened to the suggestions and approved and acted. Certainly Jefferson disclaimed originality for his Declaration. Recent research shows that some of the most interesting speeches of Mirabeau were prepared by none other than Jeremy Bentham, but not every statesman had the wit to find or use a Bentham. Naturally the inventiveness, real or imputed, of the leader must not go too far along the path of originality, or he might lose the "common touch," and become incapable of those broad and sweeping symbolisms which reach the "heart" of the masses and upon which his power may rest. He must "edge in" as a motorist cuts into traffic. He must be inventive within the framework of the power interests for whom he functions, whether as reactionary, radical, or revolutionary. If nothing is to be done in the given situation, he must invent plausible reasons for doing nothing; and if something must be done, he must suggest the something. The unpardonable sin is to propose nothing, when action is imperative.

6. The group leader ordinarily possessess an unusually high degree of courage. This is contrary to the common impression that politicians are timid and even cowardly in con-

duct. It is often their *raison d'être* to be conciliatory and compromising, since the knots they seek to unravel are not so easy to loose. But a closer view of the lives of leaders shows that from time to time they must throw down the gage of battle and risk their all in uncertain combat. Just as a financier does not become rich by loaning money on perfect security at a low rate of interest, so the political leader can never enjoy security and quiet, except at the price of inferior position, compensation, and authority. Within and without the party and within and without the state, there are hostile groups seeking to destroy him; and while conciliation and patience may avail on many occasions there are times when these fail, and the appeal to arms, politically speaking, is the only alternative. In fact, the reputation for willingness to do battle may itself save many a struggle. It is doubtless true that the conciliator may so long pursue the processes of conciliation that he may neither recognize another situation nor be prepared to have a heart and will for it; but, if not, his life and tenure are in peril, and the adventuresome spirit of someone who has nothing to lose and all to gain may drive him back from the lines of power.

The force of prestige is supplemented by the living qualities of *empressement,* tact, humor, which tend to blend into a combination of qualities useful for the power group in the exercise of their functions. With initial impetus of prestige the reenforcement of manner transforms an original investment into a growing business.

What is expected appears in the flesh, and the anticipation is agreeably translated into realization. The great man, the great orator, the great figure in whatever order, with the manner of greatness is impressive, if he carries himself with the appropriate pose. Or he may appear in an entirely different order, as in the case of Lenin and Gandhi, who did not correspond to the traditional figures of power but whose unique quality made them impressive and whose manner continued the impression of the unusual, the profound, the great.

The *empressement* is by no means purely physical; it connotes a symbolic type with reflections in the lives of others; it connotes a form of what has sometimes seemed radiation or magnetism of a sort which is undefinable but felt in some fashion by those in contact with the personality. In the traditional ruling classes this quality takes the form of a gracious and pleasing paternalism, with arrogance and *hauteur* in reserve if need be; in democratic systems the form of a commonness and pervading sympathy with others. To act as a lord and a commoner are varying patterns of behavior adapted to different phases of human social organization.

In military groups harshness and external authoritarianism survive, as evidences of the belated character of the organization of control in a system which proceeds upon the assumption that fear and brute force are the controlling impulses in mankind—yet not without a touch of paternalism in the case of the genuine leaders of men whether high or low, but always with careful preservation of the externalia of prestige and dignity of demeanor. In modern systems of cinema representation these personal qualities may now be exhibited to thousands somewhat more intimately than in earlier times when they were limited to the relatively few.

Allied with this division is the faculty which goes under the name of tact. In this the quality of personal and social sensitivity is combined with that of related conduct based upon the perceptions and feelings without confusion or misunderstanding of the essential relations. It is a type of chart upon which are plotted the dangerous reefs and shoals; and likewise the clear channels of navigation. Touch is an elusive quality which puzzles observers in more than one field of action; the *tactus eruditus* of the physician may determine the difference between success and failure. The touch of the artist differentiates him from the crowd of those who fall short at just this point. The touch of the economic bargainer may mark the difference between the successful accumulator and the one doomed to toil without special benefit of the bargaining faculty. In somewhat similar manner the touch of the political leader or manager may readily mark the line between the likeable and the disliked. An intellectual slow-movie would perhaps reveal more precisely the exact nature of these differences in action and attitude patterns.

In the case of personal relations or of crowd relations as

with the orator the time factor enters in an important way and makes imperative the quick decision and action; but in the larger frame of social relationships of the family of power this may be by no means so important, for the long-run events may at times swing around slowly. Whereas the speaker confronted with a question in the presence of an excited throng must make an instant determination of a course and as instantly execute it, the diplomat may have many months in which to calculate the wisest course of national behavior or in the same way the administrator may meet alike the emergencies one way and the long-time problems in another manner.

Summary

The birth of power is found then in:

1. Types of social situations requiring balance and equilibrium among groups.
2. Types of human personalities requiring adjustment and adaptation, across group lines, perhaps.
3. The aptitudes and capacities of power hungry personalities with an urge for the organization and exercise of authority.

We may study the social composition of the power situation; we may examine the diverse traits and attributes of the mass of human personalities who make up the special group; we may examine the personality and experience of the prospective power holders; and in the relationship between these various elements we may see how and under what circumstances political power comes into the world.

It is of course legitimate to say that these are merely relationships between unanalyzed bundles of unanalyzed relations—between the social situation, the personalities, and the power aspirants, no one of which has been fully and satisfactorily analyzed and none of which we fully and adequately understand. This we need not contest, and indeed we may confidently predict that power situations will be far better comprehended when all of these elements are more fully understood, when sociology, psychology, psychophysiology have done their perfect work.

Chapter 2

The Family of Power

THERE IS MORE than one member in the family of power, and it is important to understand the interrelations of the offspring, one to the other.[1] Political power cannot even claim to be the oldest of the group even though often asserting a titular preeminence. The brothers and sisters of power are numerous and aggressive, and if at any moment they unite against the title holder, the reign of this authority is imperiled. Organization, leadership, responsibility, morale, and discipline are not peculiar to government, and if they were the operation of the political society would be difficult. It is not because government is unusual, but because it has much in common with other forms of social life, because like attitudes, interests, instruments, processes are known in other groups, that it is supported by the community and indulgence given for its real and fancied lapses from justice and capacity.

There is an organization of authority in the smallest unit of social organization; and in countless others stretching outward through the complicated web of social life. There are many men and women who assume some form of group responsibility at one time or another and many all the time in one form or another. They consult, determine, deputize, administer affairs in an unending series of associations and relations which are in many essential ways the counterpart of the government itself. The family, the church, the business group, the labor organization, the farm association, professional, artistic, athletic, social clubs; all those are conjoined

[1] A friendly critic suggested to me that the Family of Power should come before the Birth of Power, but I replied that in very many cases Power was born under the bar sinister; and that consequently the order of chapters was not subject to serious challenge.

in a vast network of societies which circle the whole range of social relations.

Who are these other wearers of crowns and wielders of scepters? They may be classified as follows:

1. Powers outside the political power in a given political society—other states equally equipped with the attributes of what is called sovereignty.

2. Powers not wholly dominated by the central power, as in federalistic states and loosely organized political types.

3. Powers within the power, within the circle but not a part of it, bands and gangs and groups, private in form but public in function, outlaws administering law beyond the law, with private armies, courts, and sanctions even to the use of the extreme penalty.

4. Competing groups, primarily nonpolitical in nature, religious, racial, economic, cultural, with competing loyalties and penalties—the wide range of social formations which govern themselves in great part, but from time to time impinge upon the circle of the state authority they nominally recognize.

Such are the members of the family of power, often a happy one, but at times unruly and full of feuds. It is important to examine them more closely, for they condition fundamentally the exercise of political authority.

1. If there were only one great state, the problem of politics would be greatly simplified at this point. But there are powers outside the power, in other nations or states or units whatever they may be from one period to another, who present the problem of international relations, a special subject of vast proportions, elucidated with wide-ranging erudition by many acute thinkers, and not a part of this special consideration of the nature of political power, except for certain purposes.

Looking at the outsiders, the custom and precedence established with much labor within the boundaries of the political community must now be reversed. The rulers are "superiors," looking inward, but perhaps equals or inferiors looking outward. The haughty and unbending head of the local Absolute may be obliged to bow before the will of the crowned heads without, with an accompanying loss of prestige in the eyes of local admirers accustomed to look upon authority as irresistible or even divine. The golden ceremonialism of international intercourse has done much to save the pride of humbled rulers, even in moments of material humiliation, but even the most elaborate etiquette can scarcely conceal some of the more distressing scenes in the sadder moments of defeated royalties. They must bend their spirits if not their bodies, and not the most refined sweets of ceremony can conceal the bitterness of the drink of defeat they must quaff at Waterloo, Sedan, Verdun.

There are also material limitations and restrictions often imposed upon the local rulers, by treaty or otherwise, so obvious and important that they cannot escape general notice, and menacing to the prestige of the responsible political group unless very painful explanation may be made by the professional apologists to the political community.

On the other hand there are material compensations for these losses in prestige. The threat of international frustration and defeat may become the defense of the local power holders. The possibility, the prospect of national humiliation or failure may be utilized as the occasion or the pretext for the expansion of the power of those who hold the scepter. Wide vistas open up at this point for the enlargement of authority in almost any direction deemed necessary for the attainment of the specific purpose of the rulers. With this as a point of departure and with the economic and social life of the community liable to regimentation and with the fear of defeat and loss of national position in the background, the power group emerges more strongly entrenched than ever. Armaments, tariffs, taxes, regulations, and restrictions may flourish in this climate as never before, and the burden may be borne not as a private purpose but *pro bono publico*. In this way international relations may become an aid to power holders, rather than a source of difficulty and degradation. The brethren in the family of power at this point may strengthen each other by threatening each other.

The hour of defeat and humiliation in international affairs may be the starting point for national solidarity, for the rise of a new enthusiasm for the group as a whole and its central purposes. Out of suffering and defeat there may rise unexpected resolution, persisting toward a distant goal of later restoration and even triumph. Waves of invasion and periods of occupation even may serve only to unite the prostrate community, strengthen its determination, increase its willingness to utilize political methods for the recovery of its former position. No student of history could say that this is always the case, for there are many examples of states that do not rise and powers that never rally.[2] But when one political power falls, the authority of another is increased and the power situation continues under another name and in another frame of reference.

Not only is this true but the world scene presents a brilliant stage upon which the power holders may play magnificently before a major audience. If the ruler cannot be the king of kings, as one of the crowned heads he enjoys prestige of the most impressive nature, adding to his local stature and renown as one of the world figures. Whether on the field of battle or in the conferences of diplomats, the power group appear in their most impressive role, assuming always that they emerge without too great personal humiliation at arms or in the toils of phrases which the diplomats spin.

True, the stark realities of international intercourse deny the equality of states which modern international law proclaims, and the greater and the lesser powers may readily be distinguished even by the amateur. But the formalities offset the realities to some extent, especially in the important field of prestige, so vital a factor in the maintenance of political power. Crowns, scepters, and thrones are all of the same material and dimensions and are worn with equal grace and impressiveness on heads of equal size politically by those with smaller bodies as well as those of more titanic frame. And in the slowly emerging forms of world juristic order, these amenities and illusions are persistently maintained. The externalia of authority are not allowed to draggle in the dirt,

[2] See Chap. 9, "The Morbidity and Mortality of Power."

although the formalities are not permitted to thwart the realities too long and too often.

On the side of political theory an adjustment has been made in the perplexing field of the doctrine of sovereignty, to the satisfaction of all the holders of authority. Whereas the idea long prevailed that sovereignty was essentially unlimited in the political domain, it is freely conceded that in international affairs sovereignty is readily divisible.[3] A state may possess full sovereignty or partial sovereignty, without losing the attribute and title itself, a doctrine which is oil upon the waters in the troubled seas of diplomacy. Or perhaps anaesthesia of the body politic would be a more appropriate word than oil in this case. To many a troubled and harassed political authority this theory has brought life and healing. The smaller powers accept it gratefully (with relief), while the larger powers with expectant appetites look upon it with a benevolent and knowing attitude.[4] The hyphens of demi- and semi- are dropped in the conduct of official relations and do not embarrass the course of the larger diplomacy, but on the contrary facilitate or lubricate it throughout.

In a jural order such as that of which the League of Nations is the present symbol, the process of international negotiation and the problem of exact status are materially simplified from the formal point of view. The majestic array of fifty-odd nations united is sufficient to "save the face" and avert serious loss of prestige on the part of any power group obliged to yield under such imposing pressure. Positions of priority and precedence in the parliamentary and administrative sense may be and are accorded to the smaller states, and help to maintain unimpaired their dignity at home as well as abroad. Indeed the very weakness of some states may make them repositories of power which does not threaten undue expansion under their auspices. As Switzerland became the site of the League, other powers equally

[3] See on this point H. E. Cohen, *Recent Theories of Sovereignty*.

[4] One of the most interesting applications of this theory is seen in the doctrine of sovereignty under the mandate system. See Quincy Wright, *Mandates under the League of Nations*.

above suspicion of aggression may be allocated positions of great importance in the organization of the system.

2. Another aspect of the family of power is seen in the relations between concurrent authorities set up in a larger frame, as in federalism or some like organization made up of many claimants for power yet recognizing one common authority at the central point or points. South Carolina in the American Federal Union, Bavaria in the German Reich, Ireland, Canada, Australia in the British Commonwealth, such situations present complicated problems for power holders.[5] Here in a sense the power is held jointly and severally by the brothers, who together uphold the sovereign standard. There are not many crowns, perhaps, but one greater crown, which all together wear, or authorize someone to wear on occasion.[6]

The core of this problem is the nicety of division of power among the joint possessors, these prerogatives here and the others there, and the maintenance of a going concern through all the strife that may arise over the distribution. Happy are the groups when the contest over jurisdiction becomes itself a justiciable question and a tribunal is found with juristic competence and practical judgment equal to the difficulty of the time. For otherwise the appeal may be and has been to the arbitrament of arms. Historically there have been innumerable variations of these power types, representing different forms of transition in power situations and accommodating numerous perhaps otherwise insoluble equations of unperfected authority.[7] The feudal organization, notably, was complicated by the intricate interrelation of the lord and the vassal in such a manner that the same person might be both lord of another and at the same time his vassal, each in a different jurisdiction. Complex as these situations may seem to be, they are not unworkable, provided always there is

[5] Sidney Webb, "Soviet Russia as a Federal State," *Political Quarterly*, 4: 182–200.

[6] For the large literature on this much contested subject see H. E. Cohen, *Recent Theories of Sovereignty*, chapters entitled "Sovereignty as Autolimitation" and "Sovereignty in the British Empire."

[7] See G. Jellinek, *Staatsfragmente*.

a sufficient body of general understandings as to procedure and limitations to make the scheme acceptable without too great interruption of common practice by deadlock, rebellion, war.

Inevitably the rival bearers of power will fail to agree upon many questions and may come to words or even blows, not without the possibility of civil war when the slight jural bond is snapped by stronger considerations of economic and social life. But on the other hand there may be long periods of relative calm in which the tangled relations of the family continue at once sufficiently strong and at the same time elastic enough to meet the demands of the special situation.

The recurring danger here as elsewhere in political relations is that the formal power situation survives its functional value, substitutes surviving prestige for current social utility, devotes the common force to the defense of an outworn community pattern, employs the instrument of the common weal against itself.

The politico-juristic theorists have come to the aid of the competing jurisdictions with many ingenious distinctions and happy phrases. In the United States the several states might be sovereign within their spheres, but not outside. In Germany the states might be nonsovereign, but none the less states. The jurisdiction over jurisdiction (*Kompetenz-Kompetenz*) may lie in the group as a whole, while the individual state remains dominant within its special range, subject to this higher interpretation of what the range actually is. In the British Commonwealth, Ireland and Canada are well-nigh independent yet may join in the oath of allegiance to the common Crown.

While at times it may appear that the essence of the power situation is clearness and precision of arrangement and understanding, it is not infrequently found that political relations flow on most smoothly when juristic exactness hibernates, when the question as to the ultimate of authority is not too sharply raised, when the crown remains so to speak a fiction, never actually used or exhibited. And why should not political twilight be recognized as a useful reality as well as the sharper rays of high noon? The logician may readily discover flaws in the consistency of a political system, but this may only show that he does not understand the logic of politics, if such it may be called, in which consistency may be inconsistent with reality. The power brokers sometimes understand this better than the logical choppers.

These half forms, then, these bastard types, these transition states, assert their own reality and improvise their own juristic defences. Amusing or perplexing as their bizarre forms may be to the others in the family circle having more symmetrical and conventional patterns of clothing, they take their places and play their parts, proud or apologetic as the case may be. They may even find in their eccentricity the proof of their inventiveness, the evidence of the superior political talent of a gifted people. There are many curious fish in the great sea, and the proof of piscine quality is not a special uniformity of shape or scaliness, but ability to swim, or crawl, or both perhaps, and survive, indifferent to the measurements made by the juristic ichthyologists.

3. There are the powers within the power, the gangs and groups parasitic upon the system, exercising authority in a manner similar to that of the regular political power holders. Notable examples are the American gangs, the private armies in Germany, the outlaw groups which function from time to time in widely ranging parts of the world. These are more particularly described in the following chapter, and are mentioned here only for the purpose of directing attention to the variety of types in the political group.

4. Competing social groups, with quasi-political functions. The bearers of political power are mediators in many ways between other social groups of various forms. Among these are the religious groups, the economic classes, the ethnic groups, so called, the regional groups, and a variety of cultural groups of widely ranging power and importance. The similarity between these groups and formal government is much more marked in reality than is perhaps generally perceived, for in common parlance and thought the government is often set apart as a thing by itself, as different from other organizations as the state of peace is from that of war. In point of fact these groups in great measure govern them-

selves, maintain a like system of organization, discipline, morale within their own ranks, with like problems of leadership, sub- and super- and co-ordination, social service and dictate to or resist the bearers of political authority.

Two of these organizations have sat at the table of power for many centuries, namely, the Family[8] and the Church, constant companions of the political brokers. Even more than this, both of these groups have over long periods of time been able to assume the major part or a material share of the functions often performed by governments, so called. The family still continues to be in many parts of the world, as in Chinese communities, the center of authority, with the state in only dubious ascendancy, or the family is so closely interwoven with the political group as to be almost indistinguishable in personnel and powers.[9] The power of the father, or the mother, has been the focal point in the life organization of millions of human beings, especially in more primitive surroundings. It was the great agency of power transmission by heredity and remains even in the present time an important element in the formulation and application of social rules. The family is on the whole an element of diminishing strength, but nevertheless remains down to this day an important member of the circle of social power. It yet remains as the channel of property transmission in great numbers of instances, as a school of social training often more important than the formal school system itself, as a unit of consumption, as a center of human affection.

The paternal-maternal government is by now, however, enmeshed in a mass of rules and regulations which reduce much of its former authority to a narrower range of exercise. Even this domain has never been adequately studied technically as a type of rule, comparable with that of the regular political authority, but rather as a special branch of reproduction, of moral training or of private law. In the family may be observed some of the happiest illustrations of the

[8] See in this connection Freud's book, *Das Unbehagen in der Kultur,* for a theory as to the origin of the family.

[9] See on this point L. S. Hsu, *Political Philosophy of Confucianism,* 1932.

projections of physical prestige through the growth of practical sagacity and acumen, and on the other hand some of the saddest examples of survival, through senescence and senility, of faded ability ornamented with colors borrowed from other times.[10]

In this connection it may be pertinent to inquire what is the relation of sex to the tenure of political power? The later law books are full of the civil and political rights of women in political communities; and there is no occasion for reviewing this rich material. The actual position of women in the family of power is, however, another type of question which must be considered as a part of the larger problem of the shaping and exercise of authority. The social education of children has been in large part and still is, although in less degree than before, in the hands of the mother; through the mother-father complexes emerges the conception of authority, of command, obedience, discipline, cooperation, and sub- and super-ordination which plays so large a role in the associated life.

Types of personalities are shaped in these familial relations which remain fixed throughout life and are fundamental in shaping the behavior of those who have been so influenced.[11] The rebel and the authoritarian may appear as a result of these situations; in forms that never change through life or are modified very slowly with age, social experience, and training. The suppressions, the sublimations, the aggressiveness, the fears and feelings of guilt, the insecurities that accompany these years leave their deep traces on the lives of rulers and ruled, and are a great part of the stuff from which political association is actually made. These patterns endure even through changing forms of class, caste, and government, for they are deeper than all these and sur-

[10] Aristotle pointed out centuries ago some interesting analogies between family and other forms of power. Studies in the law of the family may be found in great profusion, but from the juristic point of view rather than the governmental and chiefly with reference to property and personal rights.

[11] See H. D. Lasswell, *Psychopathology and Politics.*

vive the most revolutionary changes either in political or in social organization.

The part played by sex antagonisms and affinities in the formation of the opinions of men and women is of vast importance in the field of social and political control, and, while recognized in the tomes of government, is fully appreciated in the manuals of practical earthy power, possessed by all those who survive the rude storms of political life. This influence may appear in the domain of the family, or in extrafamilial relations recognized or unrecognized by the law: Helen of Troy; the Queen of Sheba; Madame Pompadour; Deborah and Barak; Cleopatra and Antony; Beatrice and Titus. Many important decisions have been made in or because of boudoirs, some of which but not all have given up their secrets.

It is commonly assumed that the monopoly of political power has been enjoyed by one sex to the exclusion of the other; but this is based upon a fundamental misapprehension of the nature of political authority. In point of fact vast power has been wielded by women without regard to laws or constitutions.

That the earliest tendencies evident may not be those of the more mature period of direct participation in political activities is evident *à l'outrance;* and indeed it might well be questioned whether the special influence of sex might not be expected to suffer a marked decline in the newer periods of history. The situation becomes all the more confusing, nor is it simpler, when we consider the mixed quality of sex characteristics as portrayed by the more recent students of psychology, showing that relatively few types are either masculine or feminine exclusively, but that each shares the characteristics of the other in some degree and that some approach an equilibrium. Dominant female types and docile male types are common products of our society, and play their role in the determination of the selective process.

With the decline of the family and the socialization of many earlier familial functions such as education, food supply, clothing, etc., with the rise of industrialism and the decline of militarism, it may well be that the distinctively male and female contributions to political patterns may differ far less widely than in historic times.

However this may be, the continuance of the role of sex in the formation of social types will continue, and the patterns of sub- and super-ordination as well as of coordination will constitute an important element in the organization of the political patterns of attitude and action. In the development of the understanding of human personality which we anticipate and in the relation of this knowledge of personality to the concurrent question of symbolism as a method of social control, there lie large possibilities scarcely yet noted on the map of the political scientist, and for a long time likely to lie unexplored and uncharted.

In the study of the emerging patterns of authority, these problems will loom much larger than at the present moment, and the precise influence of the sex relationship which plays so large a part in the conscious and the unconscious life of human beings will be much more fully understood, and doubtless enter more largely into the formation of types of social and political control.

How much of social and political disaffection may be due to sexual maladjustment? How far may political morale be the outcome of sex morale? How far must civic education reckon with these basic factors in human organization, and in what manner? And how shall they penetrate the realms of economic determinism, *Gewalt,* idealism, as integrated into the structure of modern thought and purpose?

Straight across the loyalties of nation, race, religion, region, class, run the lines of sex attraction and counter allegiance, playing havoc on many occasions with the integrity of the groups with which they collide.[12] And in the field of interpersonal relations, who knows what deflections may be determined by considerations other than those commonly classified as political?

Another important member of the family of power is the ecclesiastical, in its many varying forms, and in relations including union with, subservience under, and domination

[12] Guy de Maupassant, *Boule de Suif.*

over the bearers of political authority. In the church is found a formidable association with many members, much property, elaborate rules and regulations, personnel skilled in the politics and administration of religious affairs, conceded jurisdiction over great ranges of human behavior, and a voice in other ranges. The church has not hesitated to rebuke the rulers or to assist in their deposition, or to aid in the spiritual and mental preparation necessary for revolution as well as conformity. In any case it provides a moral basis for government in general and the particular governors in charge of the political association.

The church may have its own law, and the canon law has been the analogue of the civil for generations in Western Europe. The church organizes its councils and conferences, lays down its rule, provides the penalties appropriate, sets up its administration on a magnificent scale, and provides for adjudication of disputed cases through the agency of ecclesiastical courts. And all this has been fully described and discussed in countless tomes, which need no comment here. At different times this ecclesiastical government has been democratic, aristocratic, autocratic, or theocratic.

Not only does the church lay down the rules of life for its own citizens, but it may also suggest or even dictate to the political group the enforcement or aid in the enforcement of these regulations, in so far as they may be deemed essential for the preservation of the morality of men. It is precisely at this point that the church governors may develop an attitude almost indistinguishable from that of power hunger; in short the church may become what for lack of a better word we may call "politically minded"; and here may begin bitter struggles between the church and state for the right to determine the metes and bounds of human conduct.[13]

Modern nationalism raised up centers of power against the church far stronger than the Holy Roman Empire, and

[13] See my *Making of Citizens;* A. N. Holcombe, *The Foundations of the Modern Commonwealth,* with special comment on the church in leading modern states, with reference also to the attitudes of the Catholic, the Jewish, and the Protestant denominations.

the separation of church and state in some jurisdictions followed, as in the United States. The Soviet Union undertook the "liquidation" of the church. But these developments were not decisive, for in recent times the church reappeared in the democratic field as a political party itself and a part of the law-making authority. The clerical parties may thus become parts of the government in a direct and responsible sense, as well as in the more indirect advocacy of special forms of moral measures. These parties in Italy and Germany, however, seemed unable to hold their own in the political arena.

It is in no sense the purpose of this treatise to discuss the complicated relations between church and state in times present or historical, except as they illustrate the relationship of the family of power, and help to illuminate the underlying principles of the process of government. But it happens that nowhere in the great mass of political-social phenomena is there richer material to illustrate the inner quality of the political than in the interrelations between these two types of social organizations. The parallel organizations of these two groups, the competing loyalties which they present often in tragic and dramatic fashion, the jagged border line between them; all these serve to illustrate the nature of power in social relations and the intimacy of its interdependence.

And this is equally marked whether we look at the institutional side of their parallel development or fix our attention upon the aspects of it evidenced in the life of a personality. For the struggles of the rival institutions are equaled by the deadly battles within the inner penetralia of the human personality which may find itself torn by the competition of vital loyalties that split the very soul.

None can predict what the future or form of religion may become, and how it may be related to the political power group on the one side or the medico-constitutional group on the other, nor again what position it may occupy in a unified jural order, such as is envisaged by the League of Nations or other jural order. In all these developments there are interesting possibilities, which we cannot forecast. But in viewing the power problem as it actually is, the ecclesiastical group plays a role of very great importance, whether in antagonizing or in reenforcing the position of the state.

It might be supposed that the mystical element in religion would prevent conflict with the realism of the politicists. But mysticism may lead in more than one direction. It may lead toward retirement, seclusion, hermitage; or it may, quite the contrary, assume an acute attitude of earnest responsibility for the direction of human conduct, a proprietary attitude in the name of an ultra and unquestionably high purpose.[14] In order to save the souls of men or to ensure their moral welfare, in whatever terms couched, it may become indispensable to regiment and direct the lines of human conduct, directly or through the political agencies. The validity of this ultimate (moral) purpose will not be submitted by religion to the determination of any other group in society, but must be established by the technicians of morality themselves. The ways and means of establishing the implications of these principles in actual behavior will also be asserted by the ecclesiastical experts, but may be challenged by the laymen in government or elsewhere, when the aid or the tolerance of the other groups is required for the execution of a policy. And the allegation of a spiritual and therefore unreviewable purpose, or the appeal to the agencies of ritualism and ceremonialism, will not be sufficient to prevent a check on these ecclesiastical positions and pronouncements by the other groups, including the political.

If the church holds heresy as defined by the ecclesiasts to be a sin, or the taking of interest on money to be a sin, or the drinking of alcoholic beverages to be a sin, these types of bans will be reviewed by the respective groups most directly interested in the application of the principle declared; and the outcome may be dubious—dependent on a wide variety of factors, as is richly illustrated by history.

The bitterness of conflict between ecclesiastical and political authority may be attributed chiefly to two elements in the controversies, namely the silent struggle for priority in

[14] For a simple but eloquent exposition and defense of this less usual outcome, see Father J. Elliot Ross, *Sanctity and Social Service.*

command of human affairs, and the rivalry of the principle of sovereignty with that of the sacrosanct and unappealable divinity (infallibility) of purpose on the other hand. In both instances not only is prestige at stake, but a large body of personnel and of property is involved in the outcome of the recurring struggles.

In ultimate analysis both church and state appeal, though this is not so commonly recognized, to the ultimate sense of "right," which is deeper than the "legality" of one or the "morality" of other, and which is not expressed fully in the institutionalization of either. Is the church or the state "right" is a question which cannot be answered either by the authentic interpretation of divinity on the one side, or by the supreme interpretation of the law on the other. Both proceed with outward dogmatism corresponding to an inner uncertainty as to what the judgment of layman, political and religious, may be. The outcome may well be determined by the comparative proficiency of the parties in the art of propaganda and promotion; or in the last resort by anathema and excommunication, confiscation, exile, fire, and sword.

If we look in the depths of the human personality for light upon this troubled question of the priority of the religious and the political demands we find the disturbing and varying factor is the different facets upon which these lights are playing. The feelings of guilt and inferiority which so often prove the prison walls from which the tortured human soul would escape may be neither primarily religious in nature nor moral, but constitutional or experiential. They are integrated in the constitution and experience of men and find various outlets. At times one may find satisfaction and release in the beautiful symbolism of the church,[15] constantly thrust upon him by the ecclesiastical propaganda of the faith, or in the thrilling community exaltations provided by the politicists, in war, or in participation in great events and identification with great leaders and companions. In one mood the confessional may meet his need; in another the *jubel* of the vast political throng of which he is a part, or

[15] Henri Hubert and Marcel Mauss, "Le Sacrifice," in *Mélanges d'histoire des religions.*

in the leadership of the great man who reflects a thousand reveries written large in great days and great deeds. In the dark hours of suffering and sorrow we may become pious or patriotic or proletarian; and if piety and nationalism and the proletariat do not agree, then there is distress until decision cuts the cord. It is in such inquiries as these, as well as in the citation of the historic narratives of the struggle between church and state, that a more intimate understanding of the conflict between these two power hungry groups may be found in great measure.

Nor can we ignore the paradoxical fact that these groups may interchange their functions and their moods. The ecclesiasts may take over the ordinary functions of the state, and the state may in turn assume the more common tasks of the religious brethren. The church may become more politically minded in the worst sense of the term than the state itself, *i.e.*, power hungry, corrupt even. On the other hand, the officials of the competing organization flying the banner of the state may represent in certain moments the idealism, the sacrifice, the altruism, the religious aspiration of mankind in a particular group and in special moments. Were these factors constant, the difficulty would be less acute; for then priests would not bless wars, and kings would not battle for the gods.

The family and the church have been historically the most important members of the family of power, but they do not exhaust the long list of those later born but increasingly important. Conspicuous among these are the economic classes, as they are loosely termed. The agrarians, the oldest of them all, business or the bourgeois, the labor group, assuming that only laborers labor; these groups are themselves made up of many different and discordant elements and contain many types of personalities, often with more in common across the group lines than within them. Each of these groups possesses an organization of its own, a form of inner government of its own, and a disposition to dictate to the elder brother of politics, or at least to obtain his good offices in the promotion of special claims. From time to time the line between the special group organization and the holders of political authority may become a most precarious one, if one assumes that in the tangled skein of social control these factors must be kept rigorously apart.

The oldest of these groups, since the days of the nomads, is the agrarian. Land, patrimony, and political power have been woven into a close fabric of control for long periods of time. The ownership of the land carried with it the control of the people on the land and attached to the soil. The great lords were the landlords. They were not merely related in some manner to the government, they were the government, or the governors, perhaps more accurately speaking. By common consent the political community accepted them as the rightful rulers and their rules as the natural course of life, and accepted also the transmission of their authority through a biological line of succession. It was even difficult to distinguish between private law and public law; between the rights of the individual as a landowner and the rights inhering in the community itself. Likewise the landlords were warriors and the occupants of the land owed them service on the field of battle as well as on the field of agriculture.

How did these men regard themselves, as landowners or governors? Both, for they were the fathers, the trustees of the community, not to be sure under law, except the customary law, but under God or some other divinity to whom alone they were accountable. Their judgment was as good in politics as in economics, and their responsibilities were to themselves.[16]

In later times the smaller farmers occupied a different status, but were for a long time still the dominant factor in the determination of political tendencies and personnel; and still later the organization of farmers became a powerful agency in the affairs of the modern state. Their independence and isolation have made perfect organization difficult to achieve, but not impossible. Frequently their most effective line of influence has been exerted through political parties in which their numbers may be very important. In the more

[16] Methods of resistance to irresponsible and other forms of power are discussed in Chap. 6, "The Poverty of Power."

recent stages of political development, however, the farmer has found a way to action through occupational associations, of the type of the Farm Bureau in the United States, and like organizations elsewhere, even to the "Green International."

These groups are frequently able to accomplish the defeat of hostile measures in parliamentary or other bodies, to carry through their special sets of measures, and to obtain wide recognition at many points through effective lobbying and other political pressure. The tariff on food or on machinery, or the tax on land, or the support of agricultural research, the organization of farm credits or the subsidy of farm economics, or even the redistribution of population and the decentralization of industry; these are affected by such organized agencies of social and political pressure.

The urban-industrial movement in all western lands has, of course, greatly weakened the earlier authority of the agricultural group but by no means destroyed it, and the farmer therefore sits at the round table of power, with the other forces already described. His prestige may be diminished, and the trend may lead still farther in this direction, but the substantial weight still remains; and the family of power must still recognize the very great strategic importance of the agrarian element in the process of social and political control.

With the rise of industry and the development of the system which has come to be known, loosely, as capitalism, the group of business came to hold an important place in the power situation, in many ways comparable to that of the agrarian group in earlier times. The traders, however, did not desire to become the actual and personal government of the land. They remained in great part outside of the formal government. Business might dictate to the government, without becoming the personal proprietor of political management. At the outset industry wished to be freed from the exactions and control of government, and was satisfied in the main with a policy of laissez faire. From within business began to be ruthlessly competitive, without any marked development of common rules and regulations within its own borders, but later integrated its force in large and often monopolistic units.

In the highly industrialized countries, the business group, although loosely organized, was intimately related to the political management group, which was regarded as in great measure, corrupt, tardy, or incompetent from the point of view of swiftly changing industrial enterprise. The governmental group, on the other hand, derived in large measure from the landed gentry, affected to look down upon trade and industry, and were well content that trade should not molest their monopoly of officialdom. Trade regulation, banking and currency, and foreign policy began to fall, however, into the hands of the industrial group, and their will was likely to find its way into governmental action, except at points where they encountered the resistance of the older agrarians or the protest of the mass. Their concentrated economic power began to make them influential in the new techniques of political campaigning and in the control of the political press, as well as in the cruder forms of outright personal corruption of the official staff.

With this development there went a negative theory of the value of state activity, the danger of excessive "interference" with industrial enterprise, especially in social legislation and in laws directed at the central control of industry, or ventures in the direction of collectivization (competition with business). This was marked in England, where it did not affect the prestige of government materially, and more pronounced in the United States, where the antigovernmental propaganda reached the form of what amounted to a "boycott of government," a social dislike of the governmental type of activity and its personnel in general. At this point, business became not only a fellow member of the family of power, but dictatorial and often contemptuous of its more impecunious *fratres*.

In the course of time, business became still more highly concentrated, and began to develop more fully its own internal government. Corporations, trusts, holding companies, powerful trade associations developed, both special and general, and built up smaller governments and administrations of their own, as in the case of the United States Chamber of

Commerce,[17] or on a larger scale, the International Chamber of Commerce. In cities, states, provinces, smaller units of like associations sprang up, reaching higher up into the large areas, national and international.

A wide range of activities fell within the compass of these newly forming groups, including production control, fixing of prices, trade practices, attitudes toward labor, foreign relations, taxation, and finance. The paternal aspects of industry were also reflected in the benevolent organization of government within the confines of a single enterprise, where various forms of politicization sprang up at widely different points.[18] Company unions, organizations of shop government, works councils in many different experimental forms became the commonplace of industrial life, and in these undertakings were seen many of the characteristics of ordinary political government.

Indeed, as the units of industrial enterprise became larger and larger, with a scale of operations involving now many thousands of men, large revenues and properties, broad plans for further development, the whole business enterprise took more and more the characteristics of the state itself. Railways, coal, steel, oil, sugar, liquor, became kingdoms in themselves. To make the situation still more complex, these units extended beyond the boundaries of particular states, and became international in many of their activities and institutions.[19]

But these new industrial empires with their kings and czars and grand dukes find the state on the one side and labor on the other, and are obliged to conduct their affairs within the limits set by these two counter organizations, likewise equipped with men and money and some knowledge of the technique of social welfare. The church and the family

[17] See H. L. Childs, *Labor and Capital in National Politics,* a special study of the United States Chamber of Commerce and the American Federation of Labor as quasi-governmental agencies.

[18] See James Myers, *Representative Government in Industry;* H. Dennison, *Industrial Engineering.*

[19] F. Delaisi, *Economic Myths and Political Realities.*

are likewise a part of the play which now becomes more complex.

It is now important to examine the latest member of the family of power, under the name of labor. This newest comer obtained a position only as the result of a long struggle for recognition as other than a bastard child of society, at first placed under the bar sinister, and only slowly admitted into the fellowship of his elder brothers at the table. Slavery to serfdom, serfdom to status, status to organization and recognition, recognition to control, is the progress of the organized labor movement into which so many millions of the human kind have been drawn and to which they now acknowledge an allegiance second only, if at all, to that of the loyalty to the nation and the church.

Here also is a form of internal government, with personnel, program, social tactics, disposition either to command the government or to dictate terms to it, and with many notable successes in its archives. The number of trade-union members in the world is difficult to measure exactly but may roughly be placed at 44,000,000. Furthermore, this group of organizations is rounded out in the international organization of workingmen, two internationals, in fact, the communist and the other, sometimes characterized as the red and the yellow. The trade-union groups constitute a formidable world of quasi-political management in themselves and tend to become centers of authority of the most important nature, with economic, political, social, cultural implications of vital significance. Whereas the business group may employ the agencies of corruption, social influence, or the army, the labor groups may make use of the strike, of various forms of sabotage, of political action through political parties, of riot and revolution. They enter the halls of state in person, take an active part in the affairs of the government, obtain in this manner not only personal social prestige, but important results for their movement as well.

Important differences must be observed at this point, however. The labor movement cultivates an inter- or supernational basis, in that all workers are included in the fraternity of the proletariat, and the economic class becomes theoretically the basis of the new order of things. Furthermore, in the communist branch of the labor movement, the greatest emphasis is laid on the importance of social revolution as an indispensable feature of the inauguration of the new regime. As the ecclesiasts once argued that without the shedding of blood there is no remission of sins, it is maintained that without violent revolution the desired social transformation cannot be achieved. The parliamentary action in which communists participate is not designed as genuine participation, but as an exceptional opportunity for propaganda on a dramatic scale. In practice, however, the parliamentary way once acquired may not be so easily cast off and vested interests in political positions may become an item to reckon with in the further determination of a party policy. Only in Soviet Russia has the proletarian group assumed the actual political direction of the community and "liquidated," to employ their own term, other and competing members of the family of power, including particularly the church and business. But while the proletarian group has taken possession of the reins of power in Russia, the political government has not disappeared, but on the contrary has been endowed with far greater powers than ever before under a régime of collectivism. Thus the apotheosis of the group of toil climaxes in the activity of the state, for while the three factors of (1) the party, (2) the trades unions and (3) the all-Soviet parliament each possesses great power, the dominant figure is that of the political party, itself a political agency, set up over the parliamentary authority in fact if not in name.

In all the great industrial countries of the world, the labor group has acquired a seat in the family of power, and, however unwelcome a guest from the point of view of the older brethren, is widely influential in determining the course of the state, in addition to the ordering of a great variety of activities local to its own organizations. It sits now alongside the family, the church, the agrarians, and business.

But the question may properly be raised at this point, are not these new organizations of labor and business tending toward the elimination of the political and the substitution of the purely economic directive factors in human society, toward depoliticization, *Entpolitisierung*, as the Germans say?[20] Is not the economic influence and organization tending to replace the political in the conduct of human affairs, and is not the state likely to go the way of the family and the church as directive agencies in the field of human behavior?[21]

From one point of view the substitution of the economic council for the political might signify nothing more than the employment of one name for another, an exercise in logomachy of little importance to the hard realities of power. What does it matter whether the government is called an economic organization or something else?

From another point of view, however, the implications of the proposal are more significant. It is plain that both business and labor have been in recent times somewhat hostile to the agency called government. Business has been unfriendly to the government as a regulator of industrial activity, while not unfriendly to government as an aid in the advancement of external trade or internal order in industrial disturbances. On the other hand, labor has been unfriendly to government invoked against it in strikes and other industrial tensions, but friendly when applied in the field of social insurance and social legislation generally. In the background there has been of course the Marxian theory of government as the agent of capitalism, and Mill's doctrine of laissez faire.

These two interests and ideologies have sometimes been combined in the conclusion that the specifically political organization may well be replaced by the specifically economic organization; and frequently this assumption or conclusion passes unchallenged, prophetic of the optimum condition.

But if we inquire what is meant in this connection by the term "economic," the reply is not very clear. Either economic determination is a narrow way of saying social determinism, or it emphasizes only one element, an important one, in human relations. If production, exchange, consumption of goods is the center of economics (assuming that nothing has been smuggled in under the term "goods" broad

[20] See K. Mannheim, *Ideologie und Utopie;* H. Freyer, *Soziologie als Wirklichkeitswissenschaft.*

[21] See W. K. Wallace, *Passing of Politics.*

enough to include all life satisfactions and utilities of whatever nature), it is clear that there are many other determining factors in human behavior.[22] Family, national, religious, racial, cultural patterns of many kinds cut across the path here, and present a broad range of human motivation and interaction. It is true we may decide that all of these are at bottom "economic" in character, but if so this extends "economics" to include all social relations, and makes the term quite a different one from that with which we started the discussion. We should then be saying that social forces determine social conduct. "Social control" would be substituted for "political" management, and we should begin again the advance toward division of labor, with the prospect that the name of the new division would read suspiciously like that of government again, however it might be pronounced.

But this illustrates vividly the whole pattern of the political. The church began to assume the functions of government; the national state arose and depoliticized the church within limits; business sprang up and demanded first freedom from and then domination of the state; labor resisted certain activities of government, courted others, and at times repudiated the whole doctrine of the political. In the meantime the growth of large-scale business and large-scale labor necessitated a new orientation and a new form of social cooperation and control, a new shaping of that group adjustment and adaptation which is the essence of the political power situation. If the personnel of the *Politiker* and the general understandings and formulas and the specific mechanisms are wanting, then it becomes the task of the time to reform them in such manner as may be useful to the newly emerging community. In the family of power the question what the name of this member is may be regarded as relatively unimportant as long as the function is performed and the social need is served. But in view of the historical recurrence of like situations we need not be much concerned over the disappearance of the name itself.

[22] Cf. E. Boehm von Bawerk, *Karl Marx and the Close of His System,* for a criticism of Marxian economics.

But the power family is not exhausted by the enumeration of the state, the family, the church, business, labor; for there are many more brothers and half-brothers and step-brothers to be considered. Among the most persistent of the associations which demand representation are those based upon a pattern, called "race," a term far more vague than it seems at first, partly ethnic in nature and partly a cultural pattern having little to do with racial difference.[23]

In a sense the bond of the race is blood, biological and ethnic. Yet even among the primitive types, exogamy becomes necessary in order to avoid degeneration in breeding. But in another sense race refers to a way of life transmitted to a group as a social heritage to be treasured. Language, literature, music, art, group memories and hopes, group peculiarities of behavior, around these cluster important groups of mankind.

The literature of politics is filled with the celebration of these distinctive qualities of the several groups and their preeminent position in the world. If the group is small it is qualitatively great; if it is young it is full of vitality and promise; if it is old, then it may revel in a wealth of tradition of great days. Be it black, white, red, or yellow, an array of story, song, memorials, ceremonials, greatness past, present, or millennial, weaves a pattern of loyalty which becomes one of the most closely meshed fibers in the social world. Tribalism, feudalism, urbanism, nationalism are only some of the forms in which the racial groups find political expression.

These ethnic or culture groups find seats at the round table of the family of power, and often conspicuous ones. They are not to be elbowed out or shouted down by raucous voices or stared out of countenance by a scowl. Their problems are perhaps the most difficult of all in the political situation, for prestige is of primary importance in their world, recognition, toleration, domination if possible. The pattern is persistent beyond most others. It cannot be readily or quickly modified

[23] On this point see C. J. H. Hayes, *Essays on Nationalism;* also his *Historical Development of Modern Nationalism;* and the bibliography there cited.

by economic advantage although not indifferent to such considerations; it cannot be suddenly converted to religious attitudes, for these may be reenforced by the tribal pattern itself. It is not readily suppressed by superior force, as many a conquering host has discovered. From crushing military defeat "races" may rise triumphant, dominant in culture—even when subdued in battle. Romans, Chinese, Poles, may win or lose, but still stand like a rock as a group, waiting an hour when the flag may be again unfurled.

The racial minorities and the racial majorities alike sit at the table of authority, demanding and commanding as the occasion offers, insistent and persistent perhaps beyond all other groups, with the exception of the ecclesiastical. How these beautiful and powerful groups of symbolic synthesis come into being is one of the most fascinating studies in human relations, and one to which much more objective study should be given, since most of the students have been either friends or foes of a particular type the glorification or defamation of which is their goal. Of particular interest would be a study centering around an analysis of the demands of the racial groups for political recognition or participation, ascertaining under what pressures these demands rise and fall. Under what conditions does political recognition become an indispensable part of the "race" urge, and on the other hand what are the conditions under which this fades away, merged in another unity of emotional or interest appeal?

The history and tactics of racial minorities and majorities are close to the problem of political power, and the racial composition of the political community is of vital importance in the interpretation of its inner meaning.[24] These groups are culture bearers, and under their banner come also economic claims and religious interests and other social demands which may be appropriate. Along with language come the gods and

[24] See studies in my series on civic education, especially those of R. C. Brooks, *Civic Training in Switzerland,* and Oscar Jászi, *The Dissolution of the Habsburg Monarchy,* for brilliant illustrations of the problems of multiracial governments.

gold as well; and the combinations often test to the extreme the elasticity of the political community, as well as the toughness of the "racial" group.

The racial sets do not develop uniformly an inner government of their own, but hope for a flag proper and a political order of the usual sort. When all else fails they may prefer their Ghettos or their courts, or their own special tribunals. But their association is not commonly a highly organized, disciplined government such as one may see in the church or in industry or labor. Behind the singing society or the *Verein* or the school, there may be, it is true, some form of government, but ordinarily this is more loosely developed than in some of the other types of the family we consider. The penalties of racial insubordination, however, are no less fearful and its rewards no less alluring than those of the other groups or the political. The race may confer immortality and fame on those it favors, and enshrine them in song, sculpture, memorial days and observances, confer the degree of hero on those who have served the race and whom it chooses thus to honor. No special mechanism need exist for this purpose, but out of the folkways of the group there may shine this special form of exceptional distinction. The racial group may on the other hand inflict the severest penalties upon those who deceive or betray it. The hell of the church and the prison of the state and the poverty of the economic group may be surpassed perhaps by the bitterness of the scorn and exile to which the renegade may be condemned by his cultural colleagues. No group may more thoroughly punish offenders than the apparently powerless culture center.

The cultural groups are not wholly without organization and government, however. There are racial societies in all lands, both in their political milieu and outside. All nations are full of associations for the promotion of the special form of culture of the particular group, French, German, American, British; and their auxiliaries are found stretched around the globe in many cases of larger or more mobile groups. Poles, Hungarians, Irish, Greeks may seek refuge under another flag where their own has fallen and wait a favorable moment for revival of their political prestige. Thus modern

Czechoslovakia was made by a treaty between Czechs and Slovaks negotiated in Pittsburgh, Pennsylvania, in 1918. True, the sun may not always rise again, but hope does not die, and in the darkest hour the racial enthusiast remains firm in expectancy of a better day.

These patterns may fade, but their colors are fairly fast. In the long run they may be caught up in another scheme of life; England, Scotland, may furl their local flags, the regions of France come together under a larger banner, and the older flags adorn the museums. Genoa and Venice and Rome, Bavaria and Saxony and Prussia cease to war upon each other and assemble under a common symbol of larger unity, in which all the older cultures find their niche.

At any given moment of political association these racial ethnic-cultural groups constitute one of the major problems of statecraft, and elicit the most refined tactics of the diplomat, where blood and iron do not become the final tribunal.

But these associations do not exhaust the membership in the family of power. There are many interesting and important forms of association of a territorial or regional or neighborhood character, which have their chief bond of interest in the common and familiar contact which is so magnetic a factor in human relations. The soil itself may become an object of adoration, the soil which one perhaps has helped to make, and with which one has worked through the long seasons of toil to the harvests; the familiar places woven through and through with emotional tensions of many moving forms, dark and bright; the friends with whom one comes in contact from time to time; or the friends and the scenes together; the sense of locality, the neighborhood, may well become a powerful bond of interest, which will defy even the more elegant figures of the more nationalized and decorative world.[25]

And the outcome of these is the ever recurring nostalgia which is so important a factor in human relations on the humbler scales of life it seems, but perhaps far reaching in

[25] Jacob Wackernagel, *Der Wert des Staates,* Teil II, §5, "Das Staatsgebiet."

meaning, if we fully understood the role of the familiar in the symbolism of life. The mobility of the human race may be readily overestimated—there are millions who never budge from their countryside; and there are thousands more who ache with longing to return to the old familiar spots in which experience and emotion are so intimately centered. The locality thus becomes a circumference of opposition to the centralizing tendencies of authority. Not only is the foreigner an enemy, but the remote friend is less worthy of trust than the visible and tangible one.

Local groups no longer celebrate their local gods on their local altars, but there are still local genii of the place; and there are still great powers of cohesion in the locality, as every political agency soon discovers. There is a massive power of resistance in the local area which may defy and even thwart the invincible magnitude of the central power. In many political orders the local trial by jury is a veto upon the wider area of the law, not a final veto, it may be conceded, but a suspensive veto. Even in a highly centralized administration such as that of France, the local *maires* may make themselves felt against a power that becomes too insistent in its intrusion upon their localism. Furthermore, the local area may become the ally of any other aspirant for political recognition and authority. The religious, the racial, the economic interest, find a powerful friend in the local and the parochial; and their united efforts gain immensely in effectiveness when they clasp hands. In a situation like that of Ireland where the local, the religious, the racial, the economic, all point in the same direction the trend is strong. The combination develops a tenacity capable of the utmost defiance in attitude. Regionalism thus becomes an important factor in the social composition of power, whether regionalism in the very narrowest sense or regionalism in the larger frame of an extended localism. In the world economy and order, nationalism itself becomes a form of regionalism.[26] The home territory may not be organized as a form of gov-

[26] On the relation of localism to the recent mobility and facility in intercommunication, see the final chapter.

ernment like that of church or business, but ordinarily is included in the governmental ordering. But it possesses an *esprit* of its own, a facility in demand and resistance that makes it necessary in all political calculations.

Around the table of power another brother often sits, or stands perhaps, since he is not always offered a seat; the intellectuals, the intelligentsia, science; masters of the techniques important to social organization and engineering. At one period these custodians of science are represented through the church; at other times whisper in the ear of power as advisers and consultants. In more modern times, with the vast growth of science and the immense projection of the school and of research, it may be said that science is accorded a seat at the table of power, almost, although not quite perhaps, recognized as one of the family. These groups cut across the lines of the church, of economic classes, of racial and cultural cohesions, and are indeed occupied in the service of all of the members of the family of power to such an extent that no separate representation may be required. They are busy weaving the cultural heritage of the race into the new discoveries and inventions of the day, and projecting them on into the morrow. And science may be and is integrated into the government itself, as well as magic and force.

Science is not ambitious for autonomous government or group independence as are many of the other members of the family, and in that sense does not threaten the position of the political power. Theories of the rule of the philosophers may be evolved from time to time, as in Plato's "guardians" or the modern picture of the technocrat's state, but on the whole these do not seem a serious menace to the sovereign state. In recent times, it must be observed, however, that science occupies a far more important position than in other periods of history. The immense proliferation of the school, the universality of education, its range of years, the growth of adult education; further, the vast expansion of natural science, of machine technology, the rise of social science and engineering; these have contributed to the growth of science as a factor in the power process not only in the state but in all the other integrations of social power.[27] Indeed the very fact that all the members of the family claim to represent science makes a separate seat seem unnecessary, or inexpedient.

In individual states, however, the representation of scientific knowledge is increasingly important, and various forms of technicians become increasingly significant in the affairs of society. Further, in the larger field of international relations the scientific groups tend to stretch across other boundary lines, and in the Committee on Intellectual Cooperation of the League of Nations find a rudimentary form of organization, less powerful at the moment, however, than the international organizations of many scientific societies more specialized in nature.

The other members of the family of power look a little askance at science. They rejoice in its powerful aid in propaganda, in war, in industry, in its support of the various claims advanced by different groups from time to time. But, on the other hand, they look with fear upon its fundamental disregard for established authority in any field, even its own. They can never be sure that the basis of their command may not have disappeared even as the order is issued; and they cannot reckon on the assured support of their position. Thus there arises a feeling of rivalry between the power groups, built upon what has been, made into a control pattern of today, and science which looks forward as well as back and may dispel the illusion upon which authority rests.

Neither business, nor agriculture, nor labor, nor racial groups, nor the church, nor the state itself feels entirely at ease with the restless curiosity of science and its constant logical and experimental challenges and tests of their comfortable power assumptions. But notwithstanding this they will not attack it from the front, but endeavor to utilize its forces where they may.

The swing of modern life toward new forms of group organization and pressure has raised many important figures,

[27] See my *New Aspects of Politics;* E. A. Mowrer, *Sinon, or the Future of Politics.*

which tend to rival the political government, as well as to rule themselves in many particulars. The study of pressure groups and propaganda reveals the fact that these agencies already outstrip the political parties in some systems of order, and even the government itself at times. The most important of these have already been mentioned in the consideration of the church and the racial and economic groupings, but there are many others not to be omitted in a careful inquiry. These groups enroll large numbers in their membership, develop the arts of propaganda, and are able to exert extraordinary pressure upon governments, to such an extent that they are entitled to seats in the family of authority, along with more highly formalized associations. They may on special occasions be able to dictate to the government on special points, in which for the moment they are invincible. They cut across the lines of other groups already considered, religious, racial, etc., and develop a position of their own, which may be for the moment more powerful than that of the longer established centers.

Innumerable other forms of association present the parallel phenomenon of elaborate inner government and strongly presented political demands. There are professional associations, cultural societies without reference to racial relations and cutting across them all; there are associations of consumers as well as of producers; there are innumerable groups bound together by a long series of common experiences and symbols, arising in innumerable ways of life.

Guilds of many sorts have gathered to themselves politico-economic powers of wide variety and importance; trading companies have been invested with hybrid forms of authority that defy the analysis of the jurist at times; and trading associations and quasi-public quasi-private concerns of all sorts have from time to time wielded great authority midway between politics and business or agriculture, or slavery and peonage.

It is with this chain of groupings that the political association must constantly deal, and its rise or fall is measured to a great extent by the skill with which the relationships are handled. Government is not a thing entirely by itself, but one of a series of control systems, each with its own internal mechanism and system, and each endeavoring as occasion requires to influence the course of the formal political government.

The politics, the administration, the leadership, the formal and customary rules, the processes of adjudication, run along like those of the state, although not always precisely parallel. In their totality these sets of governments might seem a hopeless maze through which the individual might wander helplessly, but in practice the system does not encumber as much as it facilitates social action.

Not only is this true, but the special groups often take over the interchangeable functions of social control and service, as situations arise in which this seems most useful to the society. Thus the church may be found behaving like a state, or a chamber of commerce may seem to be a government, or a labor union. For juristic purposes we may distinguish sharply between a public and a private corporation, but for social purposes the lines are not so plain. There may be trading companies with quasi-industrial and quasi-governmental authority; there may be ecclesiastical authorities with courts and penalties and jurisdiction over chattels and goods, material as well as spiritual. There may be guilds with politico-industrial authority covering a great part of life. There are families which combine not only political, but economic and even religious authorities in one corporate or personal type. Bizarre forms of political organization are almost as common as social organization itself. The feudal life was filled with interconnections much more complex and intricate, and with legal orders and ranks in great profusion, with one law for one and another for another, with high, low, and middle justice. The establishment of one law, of the due process for all, of the central national state, greatly simplified this process, to so great an extent indeed that the complexity of social government has been somewhat obscured in recent times.

In later years as the growth of groupism became more evident there have appeared political theories known as pluralism, developing the position of individual groups, and even placing them on the same juristic level with the states[28]; and various doctrines of guild socialism and syndicalism have exalted the position of sundry groups to a rank much like that of the political association, or even equivalent. With this controversy I shall not for the moment concern myself, citing these ideologies here as an illustration of the more recent recognition of the complications of the family of political power which we undertook to examine. Nor shall I deal here with the emerging forms of political authority coming out of the more modern tendencies, looking in the direction of future types of political life, reserving this topic for the concluding chapter.

[28] C. E. Merriam and H. E. Barnes, *A History of Political Theories, Recent Times,* Chap. III; F. W. Coker, *Recent Political Theory.*

Chapter 3

Law among the Outlaws

THERE ARE OFTEN found irregular members of the family of power within the framework of a regularly constituted political society. Although not recognized by the law, and indeed pursuing unlawful purposes, they maintain associations resembling government itself in many ways. Organizations of pirates, thugs, thieves, swindlers of various descriptions, the Mafia, the "Chauffeurs," the Vehm, the Underworld of certain cities and countrysides, the Upperworld of conspirators.

A rich variety of political organization and experience is to be found also in cultural associations, racial, religious, and otherwise, living within the shadow of the law, yet building up their own system and order beyond the law. In these bodies there may be observed the recognition of the necessity of organization, a body of general understandings regarding the purpose and methods of the group, elaborate forms of organization, types of civic education, maintenance of morale, laws of discipline, sanctions.

It was none other than Immanuel Kant who once declared that it is possible to have an orderly government among a kingdom of devils, considering their external behavior as order, their motives as morality. This was, however, an inadequate analysis, for devils also have a moral code as well as a form of law.

Law among outlaws is one of the most striking of all political phenomena, for it illustrates the survival of the political power situation when it has been formally repudiated. The rejection, however, is not complete renunciation, but only the rejection of certain phases of the legal order. All the forms of law and order are never outlawed. It is impossible to find a perfectly lawless group, however antisocial it may wish or seem to be.

No tyrant can be wholly tyrannical and willful, however much he may desire to become so. Perfect despotism and perfect anarchism are both caught in their own logic, and trapped there. No one becomes entirely unlawful however much he professes to be so, or however fervently he desires to emancipate himself from all the conventions of legality. Insistent reminders of the governmental order creep in at the back if they are thrust out at the front. And not infrequently those who sought to defy and escape order find themselves enmeshed in a system of discipline far more rigid and relentless than that from which they fled.

The means by which these groups obtain their immunity from destruction by the regularly constituted authorities are as varied as the special background of the particular political association. Some of these situations are deep rooted in human nature, as in the case of thieves and robbers, defying generally accepted conventions of behavior; others in some tension of the political order which leaves an opening for the entry of an inner system.

The immunity obtained may be secured by corruption of officials, by fear less frequently, by processes of adroit evasion, by tolerance on the part of officialdom and populace or large sections of it. Even in the case of the more commonly recognized outlaw types, such as bandits, a form of protection is obtained through the creation of the hero type which may endear itself to great numbers of the population.

The gangs in some American cities had as their basis in their most palmy days a widespread opposition to the enforcement of the Eighteenth Amendment and the social necessity of organizing a system by which the alcohol the community desired might be provided to quench its thirst. Here a power appetite and an illegal thirst made common cause. The gang basis had already been laid in the condition of widespread police corruption, levying upon gambling, prostitution, liquor, and to some extent upon criminality;[1] and with this as a base it was possible to develop and organize a more comprehensive gang organization. This reached its climax

[1] See Herbert Asbury, *The Gangs of New York;* John Landesco, "Organized Crime in Chicago," in Illinois Association for Criminal Justice, *Illinois Crime Survey;* my report on Chicago crime conditions, *Report of the Chicago City Council Committee on Crime,* 1915.

under the nominal leadership of Al Capone, who at one time employed a private army of 2,000 men and managed an annual budget of many millions. Here was a kingdom in itself with revenues and resources, government and law, all its own, with fixers, distributors, collectors, killers, educators, with strict discipline, with both public and private police on its civil list. But the justification, socially, was stated by Capone. "I gave the people what they wanted. Why all this fuss?"

A still further development is seen in the form of racketeering groups, operating on a considerable scale in some cities, and covering a considerable range of industries. The maintenance of these organizations requires the cooperation of several elements in the power situation, labor unions, business men, politicians, with an administrative force recruited from "strong arm men" and "killers" of various sorts. Such groups, if not adequately checked by vigorous measures, may for considerable periods of time terrorize the community and impose their will on great sections of its activities, while operating in the shadow of the law.

The organized gangs of the Upperworld are less picturesque and more "respectable" than those of the lower depths, but in principle their *modus operandi* is much the same, and their codes are not dissimilar, although their moral position is less criticised, as becomes the pillars of society. In defiance of the law, they will also justify their nonconformity on the ground of the unfairness and folly of the rule and proceed to find the way to nullify it within or without the law, preferably within.

In the United States, industrial combinations and adventurers in violation of the law have been widespread for a long period of time. Gentlemen's agreements regarding price fixing, evasion of the prohibitions of combination, contributions to the corruption of legislators and other officials; these have often been the staple of political industrial life.[2]

[2] A recital of these exploits is given in *They Told Barron* and *More They Told Barron*, edited by Arthur Pound and S. T. Moore; cf. also J. T. Flynn, *Graft in Business*. At this point consult *The Techniques of Graft*, by V. O. Key; *Robber Barons*, by M. Josephson.

Laws have been brushed aside by methods as criminal in fact and in form as those of the gangs which we officially hound and destroy. But the grip of the greater gang upon the machinery of the law is too powerful to make it easy to bring them to justice; and in many instances it is true that the defense was the unreasonableness of the law, and even its special character of blackmail and extortion, particularly in the case of proposed legislation.

The analysis of gang organization and procedure, while varying widely in different situations, throws important light upon the nature of orthodox political power itself; and it is accordingly useful to examine some of these principles of outlawry, of the law within the law and against the law.

Elements in the legal situation which the criminal groups commonly repudiate are the "unfairness" of the law and the "inequality" of its administration. Thus the law may be said to protect property which is unjustly acquired (Robin Hood theory). Its penalties are said to fall unequally upon offenders. Some escape altogether and others receive widely different punishments for the identical offense, ten years' imprisonment for one and nothing for another equally guilty. Some escape by bribery, it is said, or by the ability to retain exceptionally effective counsel. These rationalizations are tributes to the legal theory and unconsciously recognize the basis of government and the *raison d'être* of the whole power situation. Read in the mirror, these inverted words are the most impressive eulogy of government, for their assumption is that if the law were just or justly applied, then it should be obeyed.[3]

At the basis of gang organization there may be found in many instances the idea of contract among members as the basis of the system of order or disorder. Some of these agreements read like old-time social contracts of the type found in the formation of newly organized political communities. The following instances illustrate this form of arrangement,

[3] An interesting illustration of the governmental process is seen in the Constitutional Convention held by the inmates of Sing Sing penitentiary, where a set of rules and regulations was adopted by the prisoners.

which is carried over into the world of organized crime—piracy in this instance.

> *June the 30th day,* 1683. Articles of Agreement between us aboard of the Camillion, Nich. Clough Commander, that we are to dispose of all the goods that are aboard amongst us, every man are to have his full due and right share only the Commander is to have two shares and a half a share for the ship and whome the Captain please to take for the Master under him is to have a share and a half. Now Gentlemen these are to satisfy you, as for the Doctor a share and half, and these are our Articles that we do all stand to as well as on [one] and all.
>
> These are to satisfy you that our intent is to trade with the Spaniards, medling nore make no resistances with no nation that we do fall with all upon the sea. Now Gentlemen these are to give you notice that if any one do make any resistances against us one any factory [on any pretext] hereafter shall bee severely punish according to the fact that hee hath committed and as you are all here at present you have taken your corporall oath upon the holy Evangelists to stand one by the other as long as life shall last.[4]

The summary of *La Coutume des Frères de la Coste* indicates some of the things which that code institutionalized:

1. An oath of fidelity by the sign of the cross.
2. A free discussion and vote on every important question.
3. An equal distribution of food.
4. No women on the boats.
5. No thievery.
   (It made the first offense punishable by cutting off ears and nose; the second, by marooning.)
6. No private quarrels on board ship.
   (Private quarrels were settled by combat before the assembled groups; first wound ended the combat.)

[4] Daniel Defoe, *Romances and Narratives.*

7. Each expedition had a definite charter-agreement, signed by all:

   a. Distributing, in advance, all possible spoils.
   b. Insuring members compensation for accidents in the line of duty.

On another ship, when it was captured, was found the following draft, or agreement, of articles or orders, for the direction of the men, whether on shore or on board.

I. That every man shall obey his commander in all respects, as if the ship was his own, and we under monthly pay.

II. That no man shall give or dispose of the ship's provisions, whereby may be given reason of suspicion that every one hath not an equal share.

III. That no man shall or declare to any persons or person what we are, or what design we are upon; the offender shall be punished with death upon the spot.

IV. That no man shall go on shore till the ship is off the ground and in readiness to put to sea.

V. That every man shall keep his watch night and day, and precisely at the hour of eight leave off gaming and drinking every one repair to their respective stations.

VI. Whoever offends shall be punished with death, or otherwise, as we shall find proper for our interest.[5]

Forms of what we call civic education are also found among outlaw groups. Courses of training may be arranged for those entering the profession. While formal degrees are not granted, an equivalent distinction is conferred upon the candidate who passes his tests in the picking of pockets or service as a lookout, or in the execution of those found guilty and sentenced to death.

A captain of thieves is a sort of absolute lord over all those who put themselves in subjection to him. He has the

[5] Daniel Defoe, *Romances and Narratives* edited by G. A. Aitken (London, 1895), vol. XVI, p. 336.

privilege to examine all novices that are just entered, put them to trials of their skill, ask them questions related to their calling, and finally to assign them such provinces in the commonwealth of thieves as he thinks most suitable to their genius, to which they are obliged to keep, upon forfeiture of their honour. He has always a reserve of the most experienced and active fellows, whom he sends upon any sudden and difficult enterprises, and who are always to be near his person. No man in the fraternity must forget his point of duty, or exceed the bounds of his commission, by meddling with another man's charge, or attempting things which he has been told are above his capacity. The usual time of probation is about three months, during which the young initiate is as constantly at his exercise before the captain as a trooper's horse that is not broke is at the riding-school; he must scale a wall, snatch off a periwig, steal a watch and do a hundred things of that kind.[6]

Or in the Mafia:

Within the society the strictest and most truculent discipline was maintained; no one was admitted until he had passed through an arduous probation, having proved that he was brave and could keep a secret. To show the first, he was required to wound and kill anyone designated by the chiefs; if victims failed, the probationers were set to fight each other with knives; sometimes the candidate was called upon to take up a piece of money from the table while the members stabbed at it with daggers. The noviciate lasted two, three, sometimes eight years. The *picciotto,* or probationer, spent his time in the service of a full member, who employed him in various perilous enterprises, watching the execution closely and judging his conduct in the act. When at last he was deemed qualified, he was sworn to fidelity on crossed knives; the terms of the oath required him to be the enemy of all authority, to have no relations whatever with the police, never to betray thieves or other criminals, but, on the contrary, to show them warm sym-

[6] *The Complete Newgate Calendar,* vol. II, pp. 319–320.

pathy and support. After this he came in for his share of the general fund, which was distributed every Sunday in one of three proportions: the *camorra,* which was a full allowance, the *barattalo,* a half allowance, and the *sala,* the small slice.[7]

Various essential qualities in the legal order survive in the illegal groups. Among them are loyalty to the group in the face of immediate disadvantage to the individual, who now finds his satisfaction in conformity to the code of the gang; careful determination of policy; energetic and skillful execution; the validity of agreements regarding duties and rewards; the indispensability of courage and the vileness of the "yellow"; hatred of the "squealer," the "rat," the betrayer, the "double-crosser"—the traitor, in effect. These are survivals among criminals of the criteria of more lawful backgrounds. There is also evident the importance of looking after the unfortunate member of the gang, the caritative function of the society; the qualities of honor, truthfulness, within the group, not outside; hatred of hypocrisy.[8] In times of war, indeed, criminals frequently became patriots, enter the military service, and come out with excellent records. Notable among recent examples of such service are the Foreign Legion of France and the Arditi in Italy.

In these codes then, which exist not merely on paper but find their way into actual practice, there is an implicit recognition of many of the basic characteristics of governmental order of the very sort it is sought to overthrow, thwart, or supersede. Thus out of illegality comes a form of law, and out of immorality emerges a type of morality. Is something wrong here, either in law or in morality? No, for the outlaw's challenge is not that of the foundations of the legal and political order as such, even when it seems to be, but of the application of the order in some special situation. The narrow or unintelligent view taken by the criminal may make him antagonize the law, but has not changed his fundamental recognition of its value. He finds it necessary to institutionalize his

[7] A. Griffiths, *Mysteries of Police and Crime,* vol. II, p. 423.
[8] Jane Addams, *Democracy and Social Ethics.*

behavior and come into symmetry with himself. Criminality is anticonventionality, but conventionality is always subject to exceptions; otherwise it need not even be discussed. Many conventions are illustrations of the fact that there is or has been disagreement on fundamentals. Automatic behavior is not conventionalized, for it does not require this form of support.[9]

The power balance of the gang is not widely different from that of the community itself, as is evident from the codes of action, showing their kinship with the forms of the political, the juristic, the moral. On every level when the political association fails to function, loyalty to the state begins to slide down the gauge, but new forms of loyalty thrust themselves up through the débris of the old.

From another point of view, we may observe from time to time racial, religious, class, regional groups, organized inside the jurisdiction of an established political order, but organized for resistance to some specific rule or preparing for the overthrow of the existing order and substitution of another. History reveals a long series of such inner governments which may rise to power or to joint power or perhaps gradually disintegrate and disappear. Some of these groups may be organized and ruled by exiles from without, as in the case of Masaryk and the Czechs.[10]

The émigrés may or may not return, but in the meantime there may develop within a particular state this incipient form of political rule setting aside—for its members—to greater or less extent the established forms of government and law.

Such organizations, and history is full of examples, cannot be described as parasitic but as revolutionary in character,

[9] "What the law calls crime is merely conduct which is declared to be socially harmful by the group or groups in a state which are powerful enough to influence legislation. The concepts of crime and of antisocial conduct may vary greatly in a feudal society, where these groups are small, and in states where social life is highly organized and differentiated, such as in modern industrial democracies, that crime ceases to be an index of antisocial conduct." Thorsten Sellin, "Crime," in *Social Science Encyclopedia.*

[10] T. G. Masaryk, *The Making of the State.*

awaiting the assumption of governmental responsibility. However, they illustrate vividly the characteristics of some of the members of the family of power.

The racial or other revolutionary leaders who carry on warfare without war and within the boundaries of an established governmental order are heroes to those whose standard they bear. In the histories of the race or group they appear as martyrs, and are enshrined in the affectionate memory of their people. Exile, imprisonment, or death are to them the honorary decorations of the group, the distinctions of which no government can deprive them. They become the nobility in their social world.

An interesting contemporary illustration of this inner organization is seen in Germany, where the Hitler army was composed of enrolled volunteers at one time reaching the estimated figure of 400,000. These men were regularly organized in military form, disciplined and officered, paid by the organization, provided with brown uniform with insignia and banners, held their drills, parades, and demonstrations, and were known as the Shock Troops. They were in many instances housed by the party and held available for all types of demonstrations, mostly peaceful but at times involved in violence. The marching to and fro of these organized and uniformed and officered armies of course marked the organization of an *imperium in imperio,* especially in a country with the size of the regular army limited to 100,000.

In periods of sharp social tension, religious, economic, racial, or like phenomena are evident, and in each instance illustrate an important aspect of political power.

Many interesting but little-explored types of political associations are found in such places as military prison camps, vigilante organizations of various sorts, unemployed camps, secret societies, and other forms of what might be called "irregular" governments, retaining many of the characteristics of "regular" government. The activities of these associations illustrate the process of control developing inside the law or on the border of the law.[11]

But why stop here, one may say. Great prophets have been

[11] Paul Cohen-Portheim, *Time Stood Still.*

great prisoners, have they not? Socrates, Jesus, Huss, Savonarola, Gandhi; and the great exiles as well. The world is full of their wanderings. Were these men criminals? Yes, by the terms of the law. And crime is defined by the words of the law. Criminals may teach morality, truth, patriotism; and have done so in many of the most important moments of human experience. And there is nothing to make sure they will not do so again in other moments, when the crust of the law becomes too stiff to move with the changes of social movements deeper down.[12]

Criminalistics and juristics are not so remote in their relations as sometimes seems, particularly in the tension moments of social growth, when new patterns of conduct are developing or old ones are in mortal conflict. The outlaw groups are not so far out, taking the world as a whole, as one might think. They have with them the wisdom of the recurring periods when individuals recognize themselves as rebels, and groups prepare to circumvent the law, within or without the charmed circle of regularity of behavior. To those who look closely at the relations of the family of power, it is plain that the rationale of law involves something else than the rigidity of logic. Aristotle spoke of the golden mean in government as a principle of action, and the British philosopher Bagehot of "illogical moderation" as a leading principle of politics. The stronger systems of power allow for the drives in human nature, for the competition of aggressive groups, and do not demand too insistently the letter of the law in all instances, realizing that if this is overdone, inner rival groups will arise within their juristic structure. The completeness of power is not the perfection of meticulous enforcement of law, but the achievement of functional balance for which the political community and order exist. The majesty of the law is not the end at which society aims, for law is an instrument in the facilitation of human relations.

If then there are gangs within the law, the difficulty is not wholly with the wickedness of perverse persons, but with the failure of the functional system in which the law is set, and

12 M. Nomad, *Renegades and Rebels.* Cf. Sellin, *Social Science Encyclopedia,* "Crime," especially p. 568.

from which it derives its justification in the social sense of the term. The adjustment will be made not merely by the more vigorous enforcement of the law, but in the reorientation of the law to conditions in process of readjustment. If the rule meets the social needs of the group as a whole, there will be little room left for competing loyalties in the form of inner centers of quasi-governmental association. Master criminals and bandit kings and queens will doubtless always be found, relying upon their ability to elude the law, but their tenure will be short and the confines of their kingdom narrow.

Undoubtedly the constitution of the criminal and his social experience have much to do with his status, although how much has not yet been established as clearly as some suppose.[13] On the whole, the line between the criminal and the noncriminal, especially in an age of swiftly changing mores, is more sharply drawn than actuality warrants. The juristic analysis of legal is adequate within its limits, but it does not go the whole way. Indeed one might suspect from the savagery with which the boundaries of law are fixed that the community might doubt them somewhat and desire to drown its own doubt in exaggerated distinctions. In a sense everyone is likely to be guilty of some social deviations, sometime, and find his scapegoat in excoriation of crime in some other form. But this is also a social factor in the development of the criminal gang within the law, and here we approach the inner meaning of the political situation again.

In the coming period there may be many criminals, because there will be more rapid change in the basic features of our society and more rapid shifts in the mores, and more efforts to reenforce mores with regulations sanctioned by the state, in the field of social hygiene, education, industrial regulation. What possibilities there are in the rules and regulations of medicine and constitutionalism, psycho-physical; what possibilities of graft in the type of collectivist state, or industrial regulation under some other form; what wide range of possibilities in a mechanized community where a minor interference with technology, for example, may be a major and

[13] Franz Alexander, *Der Verbrecher und Seine Richter;* J. Galsworthy, *Justice.*

disastrous offense against society! Medical, industrial, morale crimes! *Quel avenir!* It may be well to recognize the change long ago forecast by Butler in his *Erewhon*, when the criminal is the sick, and the ill person is the criminal!

Already the special "constitutional" techniques are assuming part of the functions of the court and the formally organized judicial administration, with respect to mental and moral responsibility, with respect to degree and type of treatment. Civic education may be supplemented by the study of the physical and mental constitution of the pupil, and many twisted experiences and constitutions untangled before their possessors become criminal charges upon the community or fall into that discontent and malaise which render them a permanent source of danger to the balance of the political community. At the risk of seeming somewhat chimerical, it is nevertheless of basic importance in considering outlaws to direct attention to the possibilities of this new form of social and political control emerging quietly and spreading out over the community as a conservative, preventive measure.

Along with this or between this and the educational system go the new devices and skills of the technical social worker, mediating between the home, the school, the hospital, and the government, and endeavoring to develop a social environment adapted to the needs of individuals otherwise swallowed up in the stream of economic and social bewilderment. All this may profoundly affect the nature of crime and the origin and status of the outlaw.

But are there no lawless growths in other members of the family of power as well as the political? They may, indeed, be found in all orders of association as well as the governmental. In the church the great crime is heresy or immorality; in business, disregard of the profits code of the time; in labor, disloyalty to the group of toil; and in all these associations there are outlaw groups organized against the organization. The heretic, the fraud, the scab, are all found guilty by the rules of the particular association in which they are found and appropriate penalties devised. But what is a heretic, and what is fraud, and what constitutes a traitor to the labor cause? Heresy and fraud take on different forms from time to time, and occasion the most violent disputes on the part of the best intentioned. And in both cases the government is often called upon to intervene and add the terrors of the law to the opprobrium of the special group offended. But in these other groups there is often greater freedom of entry and departure than in the political series. The dissenter may leave the church and found another, at least in modern times although this has not been historically true; the business man is welcome to form his own group and carry on his enterprise if he can, but often he cannot, and again appeals to the state for some way out. In cultural associations, the same principle usually applies, and there is consequently not quite the same occasion for the inside formation of special gangs who operate in the manner of the political.

Interest, profit, monopoly, the corporation, the union have been developed from time to time against the code of the day. The organization of labor itself appeared only in the face of determined opposition and denunciation, and even now the industrial union is obliged to make progress against heavy odds. In the ecclesiastical groups heresy after heresy has swept in and been borne down or remained to conquer. In all these instances, the disaffected have organized their interests and developed an *imperium in imperio*, an outlaw law.

In conclusion, then, the phenomenon of the inner group within the scheme of power is not merely a picturesque example of political association alone, but affords an insight into the nature of the political. Looked at from the point of view of the orthodox antiquities of criminalistics, these deviations may seem like unpardonable sins, monstrous in their organized iniquity. But in the light of the power association, they are unmistakable *indicia* of the failure of the political group to function fully in the given situation, and the social composition of the specific case will reveal the torsion point. It is not the inborn viciousness of man, but the inadequacies of a social plan that will be revealed by the diagnosis in such a case.

It will be seen that the inner rival group may be a maladjusted member of the power family, a race, a class, a religion, a region, in which the will to power has not been recognized or satisfied and in which the urge drives the group forward to demand other forms of authority, even if furtive and covered over by the screen of legality. And these groups may become the foundations of new régimes or the material from which patriotic history is written.

And finally in the group there are found the survivals of the scheme of government and law from which they would be free. For plainly within the outlaw power is written the other power, as applied to a different set of conditions it is true, but essentially the same in its inner composition. No new law has been invented but the old has been transplanted and taken over, as if it were now the property of the outlaw, and even his own creation. Organization, division of labor, discipline, loyalty, education, responsibility, courage, technical skill, emerge as the basic qualities of an extra-legal organization, enforced sometimes with a swiftness and certainty of justice not surpassed in the world of regular law itself.

Chapter 4

The Credenda and Miranda of Power

IT IS THE WAY of power to surround itself with an array of things to be believed and admired, credenda and miranda. No power could stand if it relied upon violence alone, for force is not strong enough to maintain itself against the accidents of rivalry and discontent. The might that makes right must be a different might from that of the right arm. It must be a might deep rooted in emotion, embedded in feelings and aspirations, in morality, in sage maxims, in forms of rationalization among the higher levels of cultural groups. The eye, the ear, the aesthetic sense, must be attracted and enlisted also, if whole-souled admiration and loyalty are to be maintained.

Miranda

And first of all, are there really any special things to be admired in power? Is not power on the whole forbidding and unfriendly? Is power a pleasant companion one might choose to live with? Figures representing power are often lions, bulls, eagles; and its monuments are massive and stern.

In the beginning, however, power was not made so unattractive in mien. Powers were fathers or perhaps gods, or sons or grandsons of gods, who had come down to earth, relaxing with members of the human race in earthy ways comprehended by earthlings. Mars was perhaps a trifle grim, but Justice was said to be blind, and blindness is never terrifying. And Jove was not in every aspect forbidding; the adjective "jovial" has preserved for us this connotation. Fathers are perhaps terrible but not without feeling, not without their blind human sides from which the adroit may approach them, and surely not without affection for their offspring. And there were also mothers who held the reins in some of the human orders called matriarchal.

From the beginning the power situations have been woven

about with garlands to cover the sadder aspects of the incidence of authority. Many of the most attractive symbolisms designed by human creative and artistic skill have had for their object figures of the political world, around which they have draped their decorations. No other relationship has supplied more moving imagery for mankind than these political personalities and situations.

Beginning with fatherhood and kingship, political symbolism was wrought with infinite variety, and often with great beauty as well as force. Freud himself has not been able to improve upon the technique of deriving authority from the father principle, by protest or projection,[1] and its validity as a transition for the further growth of another and perhaps rival allegiance. It was with personalities that power was concerned and around which it centered, personalities who were fathers or gods, attractive individuals who led their people, their families, or those of their own blood or imputed to be. Thus the important element of leadership was thoroughly recognized *à l'outrance* in setting up the primitive symbolism upon which the rulers might rely in times of stress,[2] and it cannot be denied that personal leadership is a continuing factor in political and social cohesion, of the very first importance in all systems of organization, political or otherwise. With this hereditary-father-king-patrimonial system, a whole series of miranda were developed in a period extending over hundreds of years, and continuing indeed down to our own time. The system of admiration was readily extended to the group of families taken together as a ruling aristocracy of the better folk, whose superior blood and breeding fitted them for governmental position. The doings of the royal family and of the blooded people were thus made an easy center of daily and unending admiration, unshaken by the occasional breaks in the line or the personal lapses of the superior. In our own day, the absoluteness of authority has been abandoned, but the importance of ceremonialism re-

[1] *Totem and Taboo; Group Psychology and the Analysis of the Ego,* 1922.

[2] See Elizabeth Weber for illustrations of tribal initiations into citizenship in *The Duk-duks.*

mains little diminished. Modern states still retain symbolism as the center of their political system.

But the creation of attractive qualities in the personnel of government is by no means restricted to royalty and aristocracy. There are conquering generals and admirals, great statesmen with magnificent achievements, competent administrators of numerous types, judges with Solomon-like intuition, and lesser personalities, both dead and living, scattered all along the way. The list is by no means limited to the older aristocracy, for as the democratic movement developed other leader figures came to the fore and added to the meaning of governmental miranda—the Lincolns, the Gladstones, the Mazzinis, the Briands, the Stresemanns, the Lenins, the Gandhis, the Roosevelts, and a long line of others enhanced the prestige of the government. In any given moment indeed government may be said to lie in the confidence reposed in living persons who interpret it to the members of their political associations. These bearers of power are many and may be found, must be found, in humbler as well as in higher walks of life. They form the living guard of prestige, in every land. When government ceases to recruit them, or only the poorer sort, its strength begins to decline.

The symbolism of government, which in more recent times has been developed on a large and impressive scale by such new groups as the communists and the fascists, has been utilized in all times in a less systematic manner and with less conscious purpose. Without attempting a complete catalogue of the types of symbolism, attention may be directed to some of the more important forms of them. They include:

Memorial days and periods
Public places and monumental apparatus
Music and songs
Artistic designs, in flags, decorations, statuary, uniforms
Story and history
Ceremonials of an elaborate nature
Mass demonstrations, with parades, oratory, music.[3]

[3] See description and discussion of the modern forms of these symbolisms in my *Making of Citizens*, and in the other volumes of the same series in greater detail.

The political group has appropriated more days of the calendar than any other except the ecclesiastical. It has taken over perhaps the largest proportion of territorial space for public uses and has endowed streets, ways, places with power group names, and has generously equipped them with monumental advertisements of power. Public buildings are more impressive than those of any other group with the exception again of the church, and in modern days the factory and the skyscraper. Music and song have contributed to the glorification of the power association in some of the most striking rhythms ever devised, rivaled again, however, by those of the church, and by other types of music. What should we do without the "Marseillaise," "Deutschland über Alles," the "Internationale," "Giovanezza," "America," "God Save the King"?

Many early dances were often centered around a political object, notably the war dance, while others mingled sex, state, agriculture, and religion[4] in effective blend, as indeed did much of the earlier symbolism. And the rhythmic march of the parade in later times has been full of impressiveness for participant and beholder alike.

In the earlier stages of human association magic played a prominent role in political as well as in other social affairs.[5] Magic, medicine, religion, government were often closely interrelated, reenforcing each other for purposes of social morale and control. The miranda and the credenda were indeed blended in such fashion as to be indistinguishable; and functionally they were often marvelously integrated in patterns of behavior. Good magic and bad magic, black art and white art were indeed differentiated as time went on.

But magic still lingers in modern times, and still functions as an important factor in many social and political relations. It still is reflected in the forms of ceremonialism and ritualism of our day, and still may be observed in many of the types of mass appeal on the emotional level. Diabolism on the one

[4] E. S. Ames, *Psychology of Religion.*

[5] Lynn Thorndike, *The Place of Magic in the Intellectual History of Europe;* W. E. H. Lecky, *History of Rationalism.*

side and divinity on the other still survive as basic factors in the process of political control.

Artistic design has contributed much to the miranda of politics. Color, form, motion, have been summoned to weave a halo around authority and give it beauty as well as force. The fleur-de-lis, the lily, the rose, the whole garden of flowers has been appropriated to political decoration. The ceremonials of political life are likewise impressive and often beautiful and attractive and effective in their symbolism, and they range over a wide way of life. In the case of hereditary groups indeed they omit no phase of existence from the cradle to the grave. Each step of the road is invested with a wealth of ceremonial adorning it. But much the same symbolic effect may be built up around a democratic or communistic régime, substituting the people or the class, their heroes living or dead for those of the aristocratic group. The most striking examples of this are seen perhaps in France where, since the Revolution, the symbolic life of the nation has in no sense suffered from lack of artistic representation and expression.

The nature of the grand ceremonial is such that it stresses the element of adoration in the psychology of power. The elaborate series of ritualistic steps, under no circumstances to be varied, imposes the idea of conformity and obedience without question. It is obviously difficult to argue about rituals, however absurd they may be from a rational point of view. Whether one should bow right or left, or bend the head, or the knee, or the whole body, or advance or retreat, or speak or be silent, or what words should be said in accordance with custom, is a matter to be learned and followed but not to be disputed. No one can argue with a ritual in process. Even the absurdity of the ritual may endear it to the hearts of those who have long followed it, and render it immune to criticism by the new recruits. Only the ritualisms of other power groups appear ridiculous, never the rites of the one to which allegiance is owed.

But while the ritual is approached with a spirit of conformity, there may be a sense of satisfaction in its performance, as we swing along in its rhythm and beauty, if, as the phrase goes, we "enter into the spirit of it." Thus in the most subtle fashion the power purpose and the aesthetic sense are blended, and the power process is identified, not with blood and cruelty but with harmony and beauty.

The political group, to be sure, has no monopoly of ritualism and is rivaled by the church and by endless cultural groupings running through all social organization. How the old ceremonies ever lose their apparently impregnable position is another story with which we may deal in considering the disintegration of authority.

Story and history are other means of producing admiration for the personnel of the power group and for the power situation itself, story in the early stages and history in the later. The well-nigh magical influence of stories upon children and adults as well opens an important avenue to the celebration of power, either directly or, perhaps more effectively, in indirect fashion. They listen even when they do not fully understand. For in this mood of relative approachability, lulled by the voice of the professional narrator in the early times, and in the later thrown off guard by the scientific mask of the historian, the subject may readily be indoctrinated with whatever the situation demands. The qualities and the achievements of the heroes may be imparted and inculcated to the very greatest advantage and without much possibility of resistance. For if the story is really good, what matter whether it be really true. If it does not embody the literal truth, it may express the ambitions of the group and its dream picture of itself in its best moments. And this logic may lead us on until criticism of the story becomes an evidence not of intelligence but of unpatriotic attitude. The textbooks and histories of every nation furnish irrefutable evidence of the latitude allowed the group historian.[6] One of the first tasks of a new régime is that of producing another set of histories, or indeed they may precede the overthrow of the old, providing another interpretation. Communist history is not the same as that of the fascist, or fascist the same as that of the democrat. It is true that there are limits to which story and history may be

[6] Cf. J. Prudhommeaux, *Enquête sur les livres scolaires d'après guerre.*

modified to serve the group purposes, but for the moment we are dealing with the miranda of the state, and it is patent that in any case the historical is the material out of which adoration may be and frequently is shaped.

Among the methods of creating group worship, the mass demonstration is one of the most impressive and effective, if one may undertake to differentiate between the various devices. Here again the double effect is produced (1) of power impression on the individual, and (2) of personal satisfaction in participation. Even the hardiest spirit enmeshed in a large hostile demonstration[7] is enormously impressed with its power feeling—the sheer weight of numbers, the volume of sound that beats upon the ear, the solidarity of the mass, the unity of purpose; all these together make a large crowd seem like all the world. The individual encompassed cannot fight against the crowd; he cannot be heard above them; he is psychologically beaten down by them. No matter how right he may be or feel he is, the roar of the crowd renders judgment against him, and there seems for the moment little left but submission or, if possible, escape, but there is no escape. There is perhaps no deeper sense of isolation and abandonment than that of the individual caught in an unfriendly demonstration.

But, further, the participation in the mass movement brings a sense of satisfaction to those who are a part of it in spirit, for in a manner common enough but not well understood fundamentally the individual is lifted up and exalted by the sense of the mass movement. Perhaps this is the "shared experience" of which Dewey speaks, or perhaps the identification with the larger dream person floating in one's reverie moments, perhaps it is a throw back to the days when sex, war, religion, and agriculture were intermingled in the savage dances. In any case it has a compelling power, and effects the release of not unpleasant capacities for enjoyment, enlisting the eye, the ear, the emotions of pride and exultation which may spring up, "within the breast," the phrase is. What this may mean in terms of measurable psychophysical reactions

[7] Theodor Geiger, *Die Masse und ihre Aktion,* is much to the point in explaining this psychology; also G. Le Bon, *The Crowd.*

we do not begin to know. But the shining and uplifted faces of the crowd are the external evidence of the inner situation, and subsequent behavior offers further testimony. Participation in one great demonstration may change the current of a life, and transform the indifferent into an undying zealot or a crusader. And every modern group organizes these mass movements with full realization of what is involved in them.

Here we come upon the pleasure side of power, one of the satisfactions derived from its exercise, to offset the darker side of the power phenomenon. Music and the voice of the orator may add to the enthusiasm of the crowd, one through rhythm and the other through a combination of rhythm and appeal to emotions and in some measure to reason, combined with the appeal of a personality which in turn may be rooted still more deeply in well-established prestige. All this may once more tend to revolve the scene around the leadership principle which lies so close to the center of political authority; and once more aesthetics and authority are found in combination.

The technique of the great platform orator has been much admired but thus far astonishingly little studied in any scientific sense, and both the external technique of the orator and the inner manipulation of the symbolic appeals through which he operates still remain an art but little comprehended objectively even by those who are familiar with power situations. Just what happens in the speaker-crowd situations still remains to be closely studied, and in this relation will be found one of the chief elements in political authority, although not the only one.

For many persons, we do not know how many, statistically, and for all of us at times, life is heavy with fatigue. Or if not weariness then boredom bears down heavily upon us. "I do not know what to do with myself," is the cry not only of the child, but also of the adult on many occasions, when time hangs heavily. Impulse, suggestion, imagination at this moment may find an easy road forward. Whatever will lighten and brighten the hours is welcomed. And this may be as true of leisure as of toil, for in one the anticipation or the recollection and in the other the present demand some lifting up of the spirit to dispel the tedium that may otherwise descend like a fog. It is for moments and moods like this that the glitter and allure of showmanship is adapted, and it may attach itself around a political, religious, or racial interest, if not that of the aesthetic or the avowedly recreational.

It is then in situations such as have just been considered that the miranda of the political are developed with infinite variety in widely different areas and peoples, under many diverse sets of circumstances, under many different régimes, but with some inner unity of technique and purpose. The club is not forgotten through all this intricate process, but it is for the moment laid aside, hidden under flowers and decorations. The king-father-local-god combination of factors effective in the earlier days has been gradually but never wholly replaced even to this day. It was succeeded by other forms of attractive symbolism resting on another basis. But the ruler may still be the little father of the people, as in Soviet Russia today. The ruler, if not kingly, may be a genuine "leader," in whom the older qualities of the royal may be contained. Mass psychology is perhaps better understood than in any previous period of history, and its practices are of far-reaching importance in the social construction of political power. The political group has been hard pressed in recent times by the counter symbolism of the competing social groups, notably of labor, but has shown itself capable of invention of a high order.

It may be pointed out that the political power group may also bring tributes of admiration for other reasons than those discussed in the preceding pages. It may bring to many persons substantial advantages of a material nature, economic, educational, medical, social in the broadest sense of the term. A long series of institutions might be enumerated which have for their purpose the satisfaction of a wide variety of needs in the social group. These are examined, however, under the head of social interests as a part of the basic power situation, and may be differentiated, not too sharply to be sure, from the types of miranda which have just been developed here.

The question may be asked, Is it better to bind a people together by more material interest bonds than by mass psychology? Or which is the firmer tie, if a choice must be made between them? The ideal situation is to unite them in a common enterprise, with both substantial benefit and the broader attachment for an apparently nonsubstantial motive; and to this end the power holders constantly strive. The relative strength of the two elements we have no scales to weigh or rod to measure. The hungry may forget their hunger in a patriotic demonstration, and patriotism may not be proof against unpatriotic prosperity, at least not for long. Which has the strongest nerves, the stomach, the eye, the ear? How shall we measure dreams against food; wounds against aesthetics? Here we approach the penetralia of power which no one has yet mapped out, and few have even attempted to explore.

In the endless shifts of power there is abundant material for study of subtle nuances of authority, and it may be presumed that in the not distant future important inquiries and discoveries will be made in this *terra incognita*. In the twilight zone of transition loyalties may be discovered and many of the hidden springs of power. What is it that determines in cases of doubt the wavering loyalty torn between competing attractions of authority, between inner yearnings reaching blindly now this way and now that?

Credenda

The credenda of power are not wholly unlike the miranda, but may be found upon a different level, on a platform of rationalization. They contain the reasons which oblige the intellect to give assent to the continuance of authority. And this assent may be due to government in general, or to particular holders of the power, or to the special system of authority in vogue at any given moment in a particular unit of power. The club and the mass movement are not enough in the later stages of human development, and systematic explanations of authority have been devised for more than 2,000 years, as a means of reenforcing the other aids of the power group.

Traditionally the most common reason for obedience is no reason at all—not to raise the awkward question: to assume obedience, as the parent, associating obedience with affection and protection, superiority, and perhaps a little pressure of force.[8] So the fatherhood of power was simple; and the rule of the elders almost as simple. Magic and the club were at hand to quicken the sluggish imagination or silence the querulous tongue, raised like that of Thersites. But in time the ideologies of power appeared, and began their century-long struggle for survival.

It is not my purpose to write another history of political ideas, but it may not be amiss to recall again the chief types of credenda. Broadly speaking, the principal forms of belief have been as follows, with due apologies to the numerous variations and overlapping forms:

1. Political power is ordained of God or the gods.
2. Political power is the highest expression of expert leadership.
3. Political power is the will of the many or the majority, expressed through some form of consent.

1. The divinity of power is related to the paternal character of power, and also to the historic character and the traditional nature of authority. Saint Thomas gave a deadly blow to this doctrine nearly a thousand years ago when he distinguished between the nature of government in general, which might be, he thought, attributed to the Divine Will, and the special form or holder of power in a given system and at a given time. The old theory lived on, however, and was even stronger than ever in the days when the altar and the throne united in an effort to pool their shaking fortunes and completely seal the way of escape for the dissentient. Magnificent rhetoric and sharp-tongued logic were at the service of powerful courts and of pompous though often stupid kings. Whatever else they may have lacked, they were never wanting in *empressement* of courtly elegance and finely polished cultural background. King James himself produced an elegant plea for himself and his fellow kings. But the great weakness of the *jure divino* school, looking back upon it from a safe distance, was the willingness to argue at all about the ultimate nature of authority. The divinity of the crown was strongest when it was least a subject of contention. The dialectics of the divinity were open to question and paved an easy way for rational

[8] Cf. Felix Adler, *The Punishment of Children.*

dissent. When magic must be argued it ceases to be magic, and royal divinity can maintain itself best by the avoidance of argument, unless it is prepared to produce the proof of the miraculous.

The king was most powerful and his fellow claimants with him, when he was surrounded by the aura of the miranda, in the midst of ceremonies and rituals which could not be disputed, which gave a sense of power, a feeling of admiration, but no disposition to dispute regarding the great center of the royal solar system. Their royal majesties in their royal make-up on the royal stage were like players in a great show, interesting and engaging enough without attempting a logical argument to prove their reality. The play was the thing, not the logic of the eminent jurists. What royalty could best use was playwrights and scene shifters, not logic choppers and precedent citers.[9] The divinity of the king might be plausibly contested, but if he acted like a king, that could not be controverted, for here kingship could be proved by kings. The modern kings understand power better and are fully conscious of the value of the show itself, without reference to historical or logical basis or origins. They realize that many who care little for kings as legal creations are interested in great shows that center around important appearing and majestic persons, with the externalia of power rather than its juristic content.[10]

2. The second great ideology of power centers around the superior ability of special leaders, aristocracy, experts, élite, however selected.[11] The masses are ignorant and incompetent, it is said, or in any event not specialists in the field of

[9] Michael MacDonagh, *The English King;* James A. Farrer, *The Monarchy in Politics.* Compare, however, Bernard Shaw, *The Apple Cart,* at this point.

[10] See John Merriman Gaus, *Great Britain, A Study of Civic Loyalty,* Chap. III, "The Personification of State," pp. 36 ff.

[11] Modern expressions may be found in E. Faguet, *The Cult of Incompetence;* Henry L. Mencken, *Notes on Democracy* and other writings; Benito Mussolini's speeches; Adolf Hitler, *Mein Kampf;* V. Pareto, *Sociologie;* R. Michels, *Political Parties;* Oswald Spengler, *Decline of the West;* José Ortega y Gasset, *Revolt of the Masses;* Gaetano Mosca, *Elementi di scienza politica.*

governmental affairs, and their interests are best served by the talents of superior persons gifted with the ability which the masses lack. This is the central theme that echoes through Plato's *Republic*, the endless forms of aristocracy, the modern élite in Italy, the German demand for *Fuehrerschaft;* and it contains a powerful theoretical appeal to those who reason about affairs political.

One of the oldest forms of superiority is indicated by age and the precedence of seniority. This was coupled with paternity in some cases. But in the main, historically, this aristocratic group laid its foundation on the same basis as the crown, namely, in the assertion of special hereditary transmission of power as the ultimate basis of power. Blood and breeding were held to be the chief factors in the title of the aristocratic group. Divine right, paternity, possession of the land, these were the elements in the claim to obedience on the part of the masses. The nobility were perhaps better able than the kings to give a good account of themselves, for while the royal line might produce an ass for a lion, this was not likely to be true of the whole noble group, some of whom would always be outstanding in their services to the community. The conditions of inbreeding were less severe, and many a conspicuous person of talent might be ennobled without being born again. They were able to bring to their aid the miranda of power in much the same pattern as royalty itself, if on a somewhat humbler scale. The pomp and ceremony of courts and kings were theirs, if in lesser degree still in the same general style. In the antechamber of the king, if not indeed in the king's bedchamber, was usually found indeed the actual government, resting somewhere in the hands of some royal favorite or some clique or set, who for the moment had the ear and the confidence of the nominal ruler. Wise was the all highest ruler who chose from among the scattered talent of his group those with keenest brain and strongest hand to swing the sword of power in his behalf, claiming success as his own, and shifting responsibility for failure to his chancellor, by whatever title known.

The most perplexing rivals of the hereditary legal aristocracy in many periods, and especially in the more recent, were the ecclesiastical leaders, coming often from another and socially less highly rated class, and challenging the superior position of the political group. Bishops and cardinals had their position to protect and their own interests to serve as well as the grand dukes, and they were not hesitant to press them forward in many cases. Church leadership was in no sense hereditary; its leaders were recruited from generation to generation out of the mass of the community, and they felt none of the pride of caste so evident among the other aristocracy. They were masters of a symbolism and an organization able to meet that of the aristocracy, and in addition they might count on logical facility in presenting their case and on the prestige of divine sanction in a more direct and unimpeachable manner than the state representatives. It was the weakening of this ecclesiastical group at the moment of the rise of nationalism and absolutism that afforded the legal aristocracy its greatest opportunity for unrestricted development of their position, for the brief time before the upward swing of democracy and the opening of careers in business comparable to the earlier lines of advance in the church.

The latest style of credenda in this field is the doctrine of the élite, the necessary and natural leaders in every community, who are entitled to the control of government and affairs by reason of their natural superiority.[12] These leaders are not selected by the process of heredity, but in other ways, not necessarily legal in nature. The method of choice is not limited at all to legality, for the true élite make their own legality as they go. If they are eligible under the given system, they enter into power; but even if not, they enter into power positions and contruct the appropriate edifice of legality. Neither the indicia of competence as shown by administrative or other service or by some series of tests; nor, on the other hand, the proof of biological descent is the decisive criterion of éliteness.

The modern group, in short, has taken a leaf from the book of the church and from that of business enterprise and

[12] V. Pareto, *Sociologie* sec. 2031, 2032, 2056; Adolf Hitler, *Mein Kampf;* J. Goebbels, *Die Zweite Revolution;* Diana Spearman, "The Psychological Background of Dictatorship," *The Sociological Review*, vol. 26, p. 158.

avoided the implications of biological dicta, while at the same time keeping discreetly away from too strict an examination of what constitutes eligibility to the new group. The circulation of the "élite" is the newer term under which the movement of the ruling class is characterized, and there is constant shift in the strata of power.

This doctrine may be applied to the position of an individual and outstanding leader, who may take a wide area of power in hand and become a dictator under one title or another. Cromwell and Napoleon pointed the way, breaking aside from the hereditary group and making new paths of their own toward large authority. Lenins and Mussolinis in our own day have made the same political play, while minor "leaders" all along the way have seized such power as they were able to grasp.

The credenda of the élite are ones that are readily imposed upon mankind. But they also raise perplexing questions which may shake implicit confidence in the validity of the credenda. How can we be sure of the genuineness of the true élite as against the impostor? How can we secure their responsibility or trusteeship for the community? How can we establish a reasonably continuous line of leaders in the community, without too great breaks in the political operations? What if there are competing élites?

In the ecclesiastical and in the professional worlds the identification of the "leaders" may be established by a series of tests which roughly at any rate measure the putative ability of the candidate, and these are administered in accordance with established institutional arrangements. In business the test of the leader under modern conditions may be established in terms of production, salesmanship, profits, in pursuance of a system of accounting well-enough understood. Civil service likewise provides for elimination and selection under a rigid system of choices. The test of the "real" leaders, the élite, the *Fuehrer*, must be made in some other category, perhaps of results measured in some statistical or other evident manner, or of general satisfaction, or morale; or indeed by the logic of the leaders themselves if some other rival group is able to dispossess them. And if there is doubt, the decision may be given by force.

The responsibility of the "leaders," under the ancient régime, was secured through responsibility to the God or gods of the particular group, in the absence of constitutional or legal measures. The divine responsibility might be given effect at times through the ecclesiastical representatives of the Almighty, although such a result was not sought or welcomed by the élite; and it might also be supplemented by the *leges imperii* of which Bodin and others wrote, the basic laws of the land which the ruling group must not violate, except at great moral and sometimes physical risk. In last resort again responsibility might be secured through sabotage, low morale, and even by revolution in extreme cases. Or in modern times vague forms of electoral responsibility may be set up under such control as to render them harmless gestures, the irony of which must not of course be too evident.

The continuity of leadership under the rule of the élite may be obtained through some form of institutional contrivance, avoiding the necessity of popular appeal through the electoral process, and if this fails through the fresh force of the rising élite who now take on the authority. In any long series of situations it is likely that the former, the institutional contrivance, emerges as the bridge from one leader to another, with the strong probability that the élite will select themselves in a process of cooperation, and even that the individual *Duce* will project his leadership on through his personal choice of a successor. And it may reasonably be assumed on the basis of observation that the rigidity of the institutional contrivance will constantly tend to antagonize the newly rising élite springing from some other groups or social levels, or the will to power of some unrecognized personality who claims to be what the system denies. For the forcible circulation of the élite is more interesting to rulers as a theory for acquiring power than for transmitting it. The rule of the élite rests then upon the theory of the importance and necessity of leadership and the organization of the supporting *empressement*, with a dash of force in the background.

3. Political power is the will of the majority expressed through some institutional form of consent. This is the great

credendum of democracy around which the institutions of universal suffrage, of representation, and of legal responsibility have been constructed and operated during the last three hundred years especially. This conception rests partly upon the distrust of the responsibility of so-called ruling trustee groups, partly on a belief in the wide distribution of ability among mankind at levels often unrecognized, partly upon an appreciation of the meaning of fellowship, fraternity, in human relations, and partly upon an institutionalization of schemes of civil rights on the one hand and parlimentary-electoral mechanisms on the other, with a reservation however of the morality of illegality in case of emergency. These credenda, it is important to observe, have obtained wide support from time to time in the ecclesiastical organization and in the industrial working class movement; and still further in the folkways of great numbers of the human society as education, leisure, industry, and government have opened continually broader opportunities to the mass of mankind. The democratic principle in the ecclesiastical selection of personnel, the career opened to talent in the Napoleonic days, the opportunities in the business world and in labor leadership, the purchase and sale of titles even: all such social circumstances have tended to emphasize the importance of the mass in the reconstruction of social organization.

From the mass point of view this type of theory strikes deep into the center of the social group, for it (1) recognizes the dignity, value, and potentiality of every man, (2) provides institutional devices for the protection of his individual position, and (3) prescribes the responsibility of those for the moment entrusted with political leadership. The whole doctrine is so set up as to favor the recognition of the personality, in a manner not provided in any other system of credenda; and it adapts itself to the mass organization of symbolism on a great scale, as symbolism and participation become of very great importance. It is even possible to transfer the doctrine of divine right to the mass and make the voice of the people the voice of God. This form of credenda underlies the movement called democracy, and also socialism and communism, reluctant as the latter group may be to concede it.

As against the greater landlords who held both property and political authority in hereditary tenure, the democratic credenda made great progress and was further rooted in the position of the individual small land-holding peasant. And as against the medieval restrictions upon trade, the democratic idea also made progress and found favor with the new industrialists who saw in it a weapon against the landowners and their power combination against the tradesmen. In more recent times, however, the democratic credenda encountered more serious opposition, especially in industrial situations, where it was charged that the democratic formula was in effect a protection for plutocracy and made easier the subjugation of the many through the very forms of their deliverance.

The Marxian ideology repudiated not only the credenda of democracy, but even the organization of government itself, in a frantic desire to escape from the implications of the industrial oligarchy known as the bourgeoisie, and a furious battle was begun in many quarters against the assumptions and conclusions of the mass doctrine. In spite of the fury and at times the bitterness of the controversy between the Marxians and the democrats, an intimate examination of the structure of the socialist and communist state (or whatever the appropriate name may be for what is commonly termed the state) leads to an unavoidable conclusion that they are fundamentally democratic in basic assumptions, already enumerated, namely, the belief in the wide distribution of ability among mankind, the appreciation of fraternity among mankind, the emphasis on mass sentiment as the ultimate point of departure and control as against an élite in whatever form. These propositions are inherent in the socialistic and communistic systems, although the institutionalization of a system of responsibility on the part of the rulers to the ruled is obscured by the dictatorship so-called of the proletariat.

In the writings of John Dewey the doctrine of modern democracy is most clearly stated, and in form more truly fraternal perhaps than the socialistic form.[13] The doctrine of

[13] *Democracy and Education; Human Nature and Conduct; The New Individualism.*

"shared experience" is in a sense more social than that of the socialists, since it not only places the ground of sympathy upon an economic basis, but extends fraternity to the whole range of human experience.

That a special form of industrial organization has made use of the democratic mechanism may be no more of a warrant for its repudiation than the fact that the government has been likewise employed. In the French Revolution there was an energetic and determined effort to get rid even of French dialects and literature which had been employed by the ancient régime.[14] There are many illustrations of inability to distinguish between the means and the purpose for which the means are employed in social relations. The anarchists, or one wing, have from time to time proposed not only to destroy the state, religion, and capitalism, but also to extend the work of devastation to the prevailing system of culture as a tool of tyranny.

These, then, are the more important systems of competing credenda. They are all related to the miranda of authority which have already been described. One may say very broadly and with oversimplification that the first two systems have proved strongest in the symbolism centering around personalia, while the latter, the democratic, contained deeper elements of appeal to the mass sentiment underlying political action. If power is personal leadership, the king and the king's court are the figures upon which the robes of authority may be most gracefully hung, but if power lies in fraternity, in the essential dignity of human nature, in the community feeling, the stronger impression may be made by the dramatization of the mass itself as the source of authority and the object of adoration and belief.

More basic principles in the common credenda of the power group are those taught in a wide variety of conflicting systems:

1. Respect for government—deferential attitudes.
2. Obedience.
3. Sacrifice.
4. Monopoly of legality.

[14] A. Mathiez, *Les Origines des cultes révolutionnaires.*

1. Respect for government is a cardinal principle underlying all systems of government of every type. Whatever may be the difference in the derivation of authority, whether divine or human, the outcome is the same—namely, deference for the institution of government, and respect for its administrators, regardless of their personal qualifications. The family, the church, business, labor, may from time to time sneer at the state, or at some particular form or phase of it, but the basic attitude remains the same throughout, whether the government be paternal or fraternal, centralized or decentralized, of the many or the few. The degree and form of respect for government may vary widely from place to place and time to time, and through widely different types of external expressions of a presumed inner attitude, but the inner spirit remains much the same, as far as the government per se is concerned.

The widest range of variation is in attitudes toward the bearers of authority and the degree and type of submission to be displayed before them. The army has developed a standard form of external respect in the form of the salute, which is a continuous reminder of the visible presence of authority—institutionalized deference. "Attention" is likewise a pose of deference. But there are innumerable other forms of prescribed submissiveness, bowings, genuflections, risings, prostrations, bootlickings, crawlings, acclaimings, applaudings, and other external evidences of the internal approval of authority. The feebleness or cessation of these manifestations is an important index of trouble for existing power.

2. A second canon of the credenda is that of obedience to the authority established, without special regard to the method in which it was set up. Obedience indeed is the *sine qua non* of authority, and all governments are built on the presumption that conformity is accorded by the bulk of the community to most acts of authority.

It is indispensable therefore that the importance of obedience be instilled in each generation from the earliest to the latest moment of life. Every system of ideology and of symbolism contains this principle as one of its chief precepts. This idea may be inculcated as a duty, as the result of a contract, as a matter of expediency, as a pleasure even, by fear or force; but it is essential that in the end result it appear as an accompaniment of power, as a vital part of political behavior.[15]

The implications of obedience and the degree of its implicitness may vary widely with peoples and circumstances. All systems contain safety valves against too complete an obedience, under circumstances where church, or wise men, or some group or other may stand in the way of the madman who may have stepped into authority; but in the main they all arrive at the same point, the generality of obedience by the bulk of the community. The generality of this tendency to obey is the basis of military discipline and the foundation of civil order as well, and underlies the whole fighting and building power of the group.

The inevitable exceptions are only the proof of the rule. It is not that every law is always obeyed, but that generally speaking the bulk of the laws are obeyed by the bulk of the community. Some governments have indeed recognized the right of revolution in the fundamental instruments of their establishment, as in France and the United States, but these declarations have been unusual and have disappeared in the course of time.

That the government must be obeyed is then one of the important credenda of all power groups, and is usually imposed with success upon all communities.

Why do men obey? Some from theory of one sort or another. Some without thought. Some from fear. Some from expediency. Others are caught up in sense of enjoyment of the process of surrendering themselves to a higher power which thereupon assumes the responsibility of their ordering. Others are swept on with joy in the sense of following a leader who may embody on a larger scale their own aspirations and ambitions. The consciously and the unconsciously inferior may follow with a feeling of exaltation, not unlike that which is found in religion, finding peace of mind, security, in the quest for certainty and authority.

[15] James Bryce, *Studies in History and Jurisprudence*, chapter entitled "Obedience."

3. A third canon of the credenda is that of willingness to sacrifice for the general good of the group. This is perhaps implicit in obedience, but it carries obedience forward beyond mere conformity. The citizen or subject must be willing to obey even at the loss of property, liberty, life; but more than that he must be on the alert for the common good without being expressly commanded to do a specific thing. He must possess the continuing willingness to care for the good of the power group of which he is a member. The most dramatic expression of this willingness is seen in the unlimited sacrifices required by war, both for combatant and for noncombatant as well. But in times of peace the maintenance of the spirit of sacrifice is equally important as a means of bridging over otherwise intolerable and impossible situations, through "public spirit," "good will," "patriotism."[16]

On the whole, the community presumably serves the generality of interests, allowing for forms of exploitation by minorities and their failure to appraise correctly the value of their own services. The citizen is trained to believe this and that it is his duty to sacrifice himself if necessary for those who interpret and administer the common good.

Why should he do this? The political explanations of this process have been many, varicolored through many centuries of experience. But at this point all the other members of the family of power come to the aid of the political group to reenforce the claim of sacrifice. The family and the church in particular, but likewise the race, the class, the region, add their voices to the general chorus of insistence upon sacrifice as an essential of group life and advancement. The whole mores of the associated life bear down upon the citizen to compel him to give up his apparent advantage for the larger interest of the whole. They wind around him a chain from which it is well-nigh impossible to escape.

But it is a chain from which he does not wish to disentangle himself in many instances, for nature has provided the basic compensations and satisfactions which make sacrifice itself a pleasure, or if that is not perhaps the word, a fulfillment of

[16] See Chap. 8, "Abnegation and the Road to Power."

his personality. No element in the whole credenda, not even that of obedience, in itself a discomforting and barren precept, to many, has the wide vogue attained by the doctrine of the importance and necessity of sacrifice in the interest of the group. None is more beautifully and constantly interwoven in the miranda of the group than this same doctrine or more harmoniously intertwined with the whole network of social organization and allegiance.

4. Another canon of the credenda is that of the monopoly of legality.[17] It is one of the articles of belief constantly inculcated in the political community that the government enjoys the exclusive right to a type of social authority called the "political"; along with this goes the doctrine that every attempt of every other group to infringe upon the government's monopoly will be punishable by the community in such manner as may seem appropriate.

The generally conceded possession of such a prestige position is of very great value to any contending group, and in cases where the outcome is otherwise doubtful such a belief may swing thousands one way or the other. In crises it may determine the attitude of smaller numbers in strategic positions, such as the army or those in leading places. The group carrying this banner appears as the trustee of the social and political order, as the representative of the basic function of the association, as the special custodian of the greatest treasures of the political world.

The dominant group of course persistently spreads the doctrine that no other and rival group possesses similar rights, and moves vigorously against any claimants of equal authority. All others are rebels, outlaws, pretenders, Absaloms organizing their revolts in their caves of Adullam, or Lucifers plotting against the Most High. In Soviet Russia, in Italy, and in Germany at present, the official party alone has the monopoly of legality and no other association may lawfully assemble, organize, or function as a political party, except under penalty of the severest form.

In recent times this exclusive right of the political group

[17] See Introduction.

has been contested by Duguit and some of the Pluralists, who of course maintain the equal right of all other associations and deny the superior validity of the commands of the state.[18] From this point of view every association has power and right in proportion to its contribution to the social welfare or social solidarity, and no one is entitled to claim legalistic priority as over against any or all of the others. The laws of one group are as good and valid as those of any other group. Whatever may be the sounder position in political theory, in actual practice, in the mustering of power, the symbolic value of legality is of far-reaching importance and it is never neglected by any realistic dealer in political power.

But these lists do not by any means exhaust the credenda of politics. A long series of beliefs must be added to cover the special virtues of special political systems. Each political system presents a body of credenda regarding the qualities of that particular state, England, America, Germany, France, Italy, Japan, and so on through the list of the fifty-odd units of the present world. It is to be believed that each of these nations is in possession of qualities and skills that mark it out as a chosen people. These enumerations of characteristics take on the form of jingoism at times and again are somewhat careful analyses of the supposed special faculties of a people,[19] resting on a psychology or perhaps even biology of the people, and finding inevitable expression in their government. These somewhat naïve assertions of national or group priority began in fine form with the discovery of the superiority of the Greeks over the barbarians and have continued down to this day. Much of this enumeration to be sure is inclusive of cultural traits in general, but a special section is devoted to political national gifts and to the very special advantages of the governmental system in question. In any case the boundaries of the land must be approved, except where fate has unduly limited them; the form of government is approved; and, above all, the spirit in which it is administered.

18 C. E. Merriam and H. E. Barnes, *A History of Political Theories, Recent Times,* Chap. III; F. W. Coker, *Recent Political Theory.*

19 Cf. F. H. Hankins' characterization of these analyses in Merriam and Barnes, *op. cit.,* Chap. XIII.

From a world point of view, if anyone might take such a view, it may be difficult to understand why such different traits should produce such like results, but to the special national groups no such difficulties are in evidence. If the German monarchy and the British parliamentary system and the French republic all produce the optimum conditions, happiness, culture, it is an effect of the governmental institutions just the same—in the world of credenda. If the different French and German army systems each produces the best soldiers in the world, that does not interfere with the credenda regarding the local system, or the quiet borrowing of one feature from another. Touching these points the credenda have learned not to be too critical.

In modern times these credenda and miranda are developed systematically in far-reaching systems of civic education, which build from the ground up. Beginning with the early years of childhood the process of instruction extends over a long period of years, directed with great ingenuity and unflagging persistence toward the goal of producing what are called in modern parlance 100 per cent citizens of whatever nation or political group.[20] The modern system of mass education has basically altered the earlier situations in which the subjects were not educated and obtained their line of belief largely from ceremonialism and in informal ways. Now, however, the struggle for the schools is almost as significant as that for the control of the army, perhaps more important in the long run, and becomes the basis for broad campaigns of morale building effort.

In these systems the credenda and the miranda are blended, the eye and ear are trained along with the emotions and the intelligence, and the subject is pointed toward an end result—the absorption of the special beliefs and ceremonies of the state. In the newer political associations such as Soviet Russia and Italy these plans of political education are especially developed, and range over a wide area of life. The Soviet system has the triple task of replacing religion, capitalism and

[20] See detailed discussion of these systems in the series on *Comparative Civic Education,* a study of the systems of eight nations.

democracy with a new idea scheme, and of filling this with vitality and interest. The remarkable methods by which this basic plan has been carried through are well described in the analysis of Harper, which developed in detail the intricacies of this complex method of inculcating doctrinal conformity.[21] But many systems, such as the French, American, German, are not far behind the others in the completeness of the effort to reach especially the youth. In Germany the task was complicated by the division into at least three main groups with differing ideas of the ideology to be taught the oncoming generation, but the system is now unified in operation.[22] The Orientals have not omitted this important factor in the fixation of the national political pattern and have made great strides recently in the direction of comprehensive organization of the national ideology and symbolisms.

I shall not undertake here the fuller discussion of these vast systems of civic education which have become so essential a part of the power equipment of the modern nation, or consider the many problems arising in the most effective construction of these pedagogical propaganda forms, noting merely that some of the most vital of the power problems center in the processes so often only remotely associated with the grimmer realities of conventionalized authority.[23]

Credenda and miranda, we may conclude then, are corner stones of the power situation. Power seeks to project itself into prestige, and prestige to transform itself back again into power. Ideology, symbolism, the club, are never far apart; and they reenforce each other in many ways. The raucous voice of command, the bearing and gesture of authority, the fixed and piercing eye; these may go a little way, but not all the distance.

Adept authority moves in a mysterious way its wonders to perform. It may fill a man's stomach with food or his pocket with gold; or it may stretch his neck or cut his throat; or

[21] S. N. Harper, *Civic Education in Soviet Russia.*

[22] See Paul Kosok, *Modern Germany, A Study of Conflicting Loyalties.*

[23] See concluding chapters in my *Making of Citizens* on this subject.

tickle his fancy; or it may scowl him into submission; or again it may fill his eye and ear with music and beauty, his soul with fire, his mind and spirit with undying conviction. The god of power knows how to woo and win, as well as how to break and destroy. Flowers, songs, rhythm, sculpture, painting, memorials, may be the lure of power, while great mass movements may swing the individual along on an irresistible tide which he does not even care to oppose.

Thus power becomes both beauty and duty; and whether it brings death or life may matter little, in comparison with the warm and vivid reality of the splendid moment in the span of one's existence, the moments transcending the life of the individual and carrying him out on the golden sea of sacrifice, devotion, participation.

Chapter 5

The Shame of Power

THERE ARE ASPECTS of power which are not attractive but repulsive. There is a darker but none the less real side of behavior, a phase of authority hateful to many; to some indeed shamefulness appears as the typical power situation rather than the credenda and miranda.

What are these other factors in the maintenance of authority? We may look now at power from beneath, at the incidence of power from the point of view of those upon whom power is exercised. We may note:

1. Violence, cruelty, terror, arrogance.
2. Hypocrisy, deceit, intrigue.
3. Corruption and privilege.
4. Inflexibility, stubbornness.
5. Backwardness, tardy adaptation to progress.
6. Indecision, impotence.

These are qualities which have the effect of driving men away from government, or of weakening their loyalty to it—the obverse side of the credenda and miranda of authority. Wanton brutality, hypocrisy and deceit, corruption and favoritism, inflexibility, indecision at important moments, falling behind cultural advancement; these are the underside of government. When political loyalty springs up it is in spite of and not because of such types. These are the qualities that have driven many fine spirits into life-long rebellion against the state, others to temporary hatred, and many more into attitudes of fear and distrust that color their whole relation to the political arrangements by which they are surrounded. Every personal injustice experienced in the political association rankles in the soul—the brutal word, the cruel blow, the lie of the government, the penetrating stench of fraud and its acrid taste, injustice, arbitrary inflexibility and arrogance, stupid, silly adherence to the ways of the past, the disgusting impotence of authority; these are what might be termed the shame of power. And who can deny that they color the views of men?

To some the greatest shame of the state is what Tagore once termed its "inquisitive stare," invading and breaking down the privacy of the individual life. The limits of publicity, or the lack of limits, may be for many the most hateful feature of Leviathan. We cannot escape its all penetrating inquiry, its unsleeping eye, its brutal pulling aside of the curtain of individuality and personal retreat. Even in the isolation of the prison, the eye and ear of the keeper are never far away, and surveillance broods over the institution. The arm of the law may strip the mind as well as the body and in its restless curiosity leave us no peace. Whichever way we turn we find its army of officials, its unending array of inexplicable rules and regulations, its hateful fines and penalties for inadvertence—all enmeshed in brutality, corruption, and hypocrisy.

It is not important to present here a complete catalogue of all governmental aversions. It is sufficient to outline the scope of the seamy side of authority, and how power may be a nightmare to many spirits who have seen or felt chiefly its slimier manifestations. It is these qualities that have inspired the long series of challenges of the state, ranging from the repudiation by the anarchists to the milder protests of the libertarians of countless shades in many periods of human experience. All the fellow members of the family of power have at one time or another raised their voices in vigorous denunciation of the action and spirit of the state, and their books are full of antigovernmental literature, inspired by invasion of the sphere of the family, the church, business, labor. For what field is there untouched by the foot of the official?

Violence

And first of all is the worship of force and the love of its exercise. "The State," said Treitschke, "is no Academy of Arts; when it abandons power in favor of ideal strivings of mankind, it denies its own essential being and goes down."

The sadistic quality in human organization is expressed in the exercise of brutal, raw force, in the name of the law. It would be useless to undertake an analysis of the force, cruelty, and terror administered by governments in the course of their functioning.[1] The darker pages of historical inquiry are filled with the description of instruments and occasions of torture and punishment, inflicted from time to time upon the objects of the state activity.[2] Nothing but a limited knowledge of the physiological possibilities of suffering has checked the brutality of governors, broadly speaking. Restraint, the lash, torture in many forms, mutilation, humiliation, isolation, exile, and finally death, are items in the thick catalogue of force. The rack, the boot, branding, the dungeon, the "hell hole," boiling water and molten metal, crucifixion, burnings, sawings, and pullings asunder. These are only a few of the devices from time to time employed in the service of the state. The "third degree" is a modern form of combined physical and mental torture.[3]

Of all these implements perhaps the prison and the gallows

[1] H. E. Barnes, *The Story of Punishment, A Record of Man's Inhumanity to Man,* and bibliography cited there.

[2] For philosophies defending torture, see Joseph Kohler, *Das Wesen der Strafe.*

[3] "Suffering in every shape and form promotes integration, arrests differentiation. Therefore, every pain, in extinguishing part of the individuality, extinguishes part of the guilt of individual existence, and death balances the account of individualization, by annihilating individual existence.

"The significance of expiation lies in purification, in catharsis. It is a purification, not of the individual alone, but of humanity as a whole. Mankind which sighs aloud on account of the misdeed, is delivered therefrom, and the poison poured into mankind by the misdeed is consumed, is neutralized by its antidote. Mankind groans aloud over the enormous misdeed; it revives when the guilty head has fallen. To regard purification and catharsis as limited in its effects to the individual, is to overlook the organic unity of mankind, is to forget the terrible ravages which disease of a single cell works in the whole body. . . . Expiation by pain, then, is a purification, a catharsis, not restricted in its action to the individual member, but saving, by its health giving properties, the organism as a whole."—Joseph Kohler, *Das Wesen der Strafe* quoted by H. Oppenheimer, *The Rationale of Punishment,* p. 191.

are the outstanding symbols. Down to the present hour the prison stands as the most striking evidence of the brutality of the group of power, and in a sense of its futility; for while detention may at times be inevitable and salutary, the institutionalization of restraint has been one of the greatest tragedies in social organization. Based upon a dubious psychology of the deterrent value of punishment, or at times on the notion that penitence and reconditioning of behavior arise from solitary confinement, and resting on an often unwarranted confidence in the discretion of prison-keepers, the prison process has given unusual opportunity for the cultivation of hate of government and its ways. Only too often the crime of punishment has been a term too full of meaning.[4]

It is the humane theory in many jurisdictions that only so much force may be applied as is necessary for the attainment of the immediate purpose of the law; but the institutionalization of this provision and its administration, through human and at the same time on human personnel, has proved one of the greatest problems of a going government. The third degree of the police and the sadism of the keepers may thwart the most benevolent intentions of the makers of the law, as innumerable inquiries have shown beyond any question.[5]

Toward the outside one of the instrumentalities of the state is force. In simplest and most urgent form the type may be a purely and genuinely defensive action against determined groups who would destroy or enslave the inner group; but beyond this there may be other wars of dubious defensive quality, wars for the expansion of the group and the diffusion of its special culture and trade through other less favored states. In war force is employed primarily against the foe, although incidentally the organization of discipline may involve the forcible treatment of the members of the army or the citizenry with whom it may come in conflict. At the same time the belief in the psychology of force may make it expedient to cultivate respect for this quality in civil situations.

[4] M. Wilson, *The Crime of Punishment.*

[5] See *Reports* of National Commission on Law Observance and Enforcement.

War itself is a vast organization of force, bringing pressure upon the will of the enemy group, the traditional incarnation of the final physical impact. In more recent times, however, the psychological elements in the war situation have been increasingly important, and once led General Ludendorff to exclaim of the enemy at that time, "His pen is mightier than his sword," referring to the propaganda methods of the Allied powers.[6]

The celebration of war has called forth many eloquent defenses, ranging from sad necessity to essential morality; but, on the other hand, the religious groups have from time to time denounced war, although again condoning and blessing it. The jurists have been engaged for more than three hundred years in the effort to abate the horrors of war, or to prevent it altogether through processes of conciliation, negotiation, arbitration; and the struggle still goes on.

Mussolini once said:

> And three cheers also for war in general. It is cursed in word and deed by a herd of bastards and fools and infinitely blind and ignorant multitudes, nevertheless, the adorable facts will not change their form and their onward march. War, a physical and spiritual fact combined, cannot fail to exist in a world in which everything from the act of thought to that of undertaking and accomplishing the slightest deed of free action, is a struggle and war against something or somebody.
>
> The instinct of war is in human nature, together with all the other instincts that make up man's specific personality and that determines his every choice, which reason, the most subtle instinct, but sanctions, as everyone knows. And to this fact which might justify war only as a fatality must be added another, which makes us love it, that war is also one of the most fruitful mystic manifestations. Like a storm that relieves and refreshes nature when it is charged with electricity and full of bad vapors, war comes and stirs up in society and in man the putrid sediment of hatreds

[6] See H. D. Lasswell, *Propaganda Technique in the World War.*

accumulated by the competitions, the base calculations and the gross and beastly habits of the world. It arouses in the soft and sleepy individual mind those flying energies which without war only the privileged person knows who lives the life of thought and dreams. It is creative of new values, a sower of seeds. War that brings grief to hearts otherwise closed, that leads to risks and abysses, that puts death before all our eyes, is the great revealer of the most jealously hidden truths. For only at the sight of death does the soul of man go deep and awake in its simplest essence; it is exalted in heroism or it is spent in the ignominy for which it is made and where none without the irresistible event would have cast it. War is justice, nobility, and brotherly pity, . . .[7]

It is clear then that both within and externally the power group is characterized by the employment of raw forms of violence, of which it has been accorded by common consent the monopoly, but that in both instances there is seen a continual advance toward the limitation of the cruder forms of pressure. The prison tends toward the hospital, and war moves slowly toward arbitration through the organization of a jural order in which the theoretical outlawing of war becomes a fact.

Violence has followed slowly the lines of intelligence in the ways and means of attaining social ends. If the criminal, the insane, and the poor were thrown together it was because no one knew better, and when wiser ways were found, corresponding alterations in policy were made. The brand of Cain is recorded in the Bible, and the punishments of state show the same trend toward personal disfigurement. When the enlightened ones discover a way to obviate the clash of war, its application will not be far away. This is only saying that the sadism and crudity of government are a reflection of the social life in which it moves. The only special liability of government lies in its possession of the nominal monopoly of

[7] Quoted by H. W. Schneider, *Making the Fascist State,* pp. 259–260.

violence, by common consent, and the consequent special responsibility for its wise employment.

It would be an error to conclude, however, and common experience instructs us otherwise, that brutality is confined wholly to the circles of political power. There is still violence in the family over wife (or husband) and children, in industrial relations, and in numerous private acts of personal chastisement, skirting the edges of the law. It is also true that the shame of the power group must be shared with the other members of the family of power. The family, the church, the racial and cultural groups, trade and labor, and landlords have pressed the government into the forcible protection or advancement of their claims. Religion, race, trade have demanded that the state take up the sword or build the fire or set up the gallows in their behalf; and often they have not stipulated any limitation of methods in the pursuance of their purpose. The church has not stopped at torture, business and labor at the sacrifice of thousands of lives, the racial groups have written their lives in letters of blood; and the dissenters in all groups have been repressed at the behest of the special interests requiring the bloody services of the power brokers.

Deceit and Hypocrisy

The exercise of political power is often associated with the employment of deceit, intrigue, hypocrisy; and this has been a means of arousing indignation or creating lack of confidence in governmental declarations and in its behavior. Is the state to be trusted? Or is the word of the church or of business better? Where may we most confidently look forward to straight and open dealing?

In war, of course, the obligation to abstain from deceit is entirely waived, and espionage, lying, and hypocrisy are the order of the day. Even here there is a field within which truth prevails. There must somewhere be found faith in agreement, let us say for the flag of truce or *kamerad,* or armistice, or parole.

The world is full of broken promises, but are there more in the world of politics than elsewhere, or are they more serious in their implications? Shall we say that "diplomat" and "demagogue" are the most effective words in the vocabulary for double-dealing? Or are there underlying circumstances conditioning and in a sense interpreting the quality of political deceit? Whatever the precise explanation of the case, it is at least clear that the miranda of politics, as commonly understood, do not include diplomacy and demagogy. In appraising the power group, the general inclination is to rate on a low level the qualities of behavior in these special fields; and the prestige value of government suffers accordingly. The diplomat has been defined as one who finds in words the best means of concealing thought; and the demagogue, where he is insincere, as the symbol of loathsome public deception. Even the system of justice has suffered at this point through the practice of allowing the lawyer to defend in court a defendant whom he knows to be guilty, and to plead for complete release. The legal basis of this is well understood by the profession, but it is by no means so impressive from the point of view of the layman.

Whether in reality unusual employment of the technique of deceit may be charged to the power group may of course be questioned, and comparison set up with the standards and practices of other groups. It is sufficient for the moment to concede that hypocrisy and deceit are among the qualities which have helped traditionally to throw government into disrepute, in the absence of other counterbalancing considerations.

It is important to look at the fundamental conditions affecting the validity of this judgment.

(1) The political position is often subject to more pitiless publicity than that of other groups whose daily statements and doings are not so closely recorded and do not offer the same possibilities in the way of proven inconsistency. If the professions and promises of many an individual were carefully set down and attentively studied from day to day or from time to time, it might be found that consistency was not uniformly evident. Ready and facile explanations might be promptly forthcoming. If the same type of personal records as Joyce's *Ulysses* were widely available, we might con-

clude that the policy of the government is singularly consistent and straightforward. The oscillations of statesmen, however, are all recorded and publicly discussed, or some of them. The curve is projected in a direction from which it must be recalled, and sinuosity may be taken for insincerity.

(2) The political power situation in its very nature involves compromise and conciliation between conflicting appetites of groups and individuals. A balance must be struck between these various elements in terms of some common understanding and interest. But this situation lends itself to a degree of ambiguity, a type of flexibility, through which the different elements may find some way of escape, some "saving of face," ultimate if not for the moment. A very successful arbitrator of disputes once laid down the following principle of action. "When I give the decision to one side, I give the arguments to the other; and in this way both receive a degree of satisfaction, one for the moment and the other in anticipation."

The elusive "formula" so frequently a way out of a perplexing situation must be elastic and even ambiguous in its terms in order that it may survive the scrutiny of very widely different elements. The same is true of the party platform, at least under a two-party system, where a broad basis of agreement must be found, and elements of straddle and compromise may enter.

(3) Since power is at the highest point in legality there is a tendency to emancipate the apex of the political from the bonds of the moral, on the high ground of the greater expediency, *raison d'état,* reasons of state, or other phrase covering the same general meaning. Whether nations or rulers are bound by their promises in the same sense as individuals has been a subject of animated discussion for many generations. And here in point of fact a double standard of morality has developed. From within the government may be justified, or even applauded, for trickery or deceit necessary for the promotion of the national advantage, as interpreted by the state itself. From the point of view of the family of nations the repudiation of agreements is immoral and is fol-

lowed by various forms of punishment in many cases, or in general by the loss of international good will. But the temptation is for the sovereign in either internal or international affairs to set a different standard of morality from that which applies in private relations, and to find a functional justification for this position.

These then are the basic situations underlying the duplicity of state, and it is in the light of them that the power group must be viewed; publicity and countercheck on consistency, the problem of group adjustment of competing claims, the tendency to assert the *grande morale* as against the *petite morale* as a justification for unusual behavior on the part of the sovereign at home or abroad.

It must also be observed that in the juristic field the element of fairness and consistency reaches its highest point in political relations. Here uniformity and adherence to agreements and contracts, according to established rules, possess a high value, and are enforceable by the prevailing customs. Indeed, to such an extent does this attitude prevail, that the adherence to the older agreement may in fact constitute the social injustice of the present day; and this especially in rapidly changing social situations.

The interesting question may be raised, What is the essential nature of intrigue? Is it a general term used for the purpose of characterizing somewhat offensively such tactics as one does not approve; or does it really refer to a special form of technique in the domain of social or political relations? If the latter, what are the component parts of the process and the problem, if they are capable of description or interpretation?

Included in the repertoire of intrigue are such weapons as cultivation of the discontented; misrepresentation of motivation on the part of rivals; fomentation of jealousies and rivalries; circulation of slander or gossip detrimental to the rival; circuitous weaving of a way toward a desired object, as against more open attack such as military, parliamentary, polemic, propaganda of more open type. In every political association errors will be made, which may always be emphasized and misconstrued by the rival, even if he would have pursued precisely the same course himself under identical circumstances.[8]

The intrigue is circuitous, zigzag, tortuous, indirect, concealed in its objectives and methods, camouflaged under other colors, doomed to failure if its path is fully revealed at any time, even though its general existence may be known. And its operations may be more dangerous than open attack for which authority may be prepared.

But again intrigue is by no means peculiar to the world of the political; for it may be found in others of the members of the family of power, and indeed in the behavior of the individual apart from any special form of organization. Indirection and deceit are in no sense monopolized by the power seekers and brokers, for this is a quality they share with many other members of the human family, both male and female. Openness and frankness are characteristic of many phases of human life and of many personalities in a high degree, but they are equally lacking in others. The devious way of the life course of most individuals or of many of them finds its analogue in the indirection of the political aspirant. Although, when written large upon the scale of political action, these characteristics are subjected to universal denunciation and disapproval, except as special political groups may themselves become the beneficiaries of the indirection, in which case deception reappears as adroitness and even as statesmanship.

Corruption and Privilege

A further element in the shame of power is the frequent corruption of the government, corruption designed to advance the interest of particular persons or groups in contravention of the common understanding, expressed in formal law or usual practice. This may be a characteristic of immature governments, it is sometimes said, but it may also characterize those on the decline. Justice, law, and administration have been from time to time in different political situations

[8] Cf. *Memoirs of C. M. Talleyrand-Périgord.*

and even now are subject to barter and sale, but furtively and not according to any public understanding. If privilege is institutionalized, it ceases to be special and becomes a part of general custom, as was the "squeeze" in China, or various forms of tribute still found in remote parts of the world, and some not so remote. If the government becomes a public prostitute, the situation would be clearer than one in which virtue is publicly professed and meretricious relations established privately.

There is here, however, as at other points, a close relationship between power and the other members of the family. The venality of government is seldom a thing apart, although government may often be made the scapegoat for the sins of the others. Business morality may be suspected if it is found that government is the tool of trade or branches of it. And the query must always be put in corrupt situations where government is bought, who is the buyer, the government or the privilege seekers? It is quite true of course that government may be the chief offender and in effect an institutionalized extortionist, as was seen in the Mafia, where only strangers were plundered.

Nor has corruption been unknown in the circles of religion from time to time, in special types of situations especially exposed to it. It may be true that, with modern egalitarianism, the dislike of special favor or privilege has been intensified to a degree not observed before in relatively undemocratic situations, and that we may now resent graft as a characteristic of government more than in other periods.

In a broader sense corruption is not too widely removed from the pressure of all types of groups upon government, where power has large and substantial favors to bestow upon its favorites. Taxes and tariffs and bonuses to great and small of one sort and another are the staple of governmental activity not infrequently, but at times it becomes difficult to draw the line between the favor purchased by campaign contribution and that bestowed in pursuance of some special gift, acquired in some less regular manner.[9]

[9] James T. Shotwell, "Democracy and Political Morality," in *Political Science Quarterly*, 36: 1.

Inflexibility

The converse of favoritism is the quality of inflexibility. To many persons the greatest weakness of government is its failure to differentiate its rules in individual cases, even when injustice is obviously done in the particular instance. The world echoes the indignation of thousands of outraged persons who have suffered because of the inability of the law to meet their special case, without fault of the victim of the incidence of authority. There is perhaps no reader who does not carry in his memory the recollection of some sad moment when the general rule "did him (or her) wrong." He was a day late in his payment, or he forgot to fill in the blank (or perhaps even to sign his name), or some official failed to do his duty and the next official could not exercise any discretion.

In very many of these instances, the victim is really suffering unavoidably from the operation of a sound general rule operating upon a person without comprehension of an administrative situation. He complains against the inevitable and unavoidable. But in many other cases the bureaucrat seems unnecessarily inflexible and even stupid in his immobility; or worse, he is indifferent, and fails to conceal his inner attitude; or is inept in explanation. Listening to the run of questions asked of an official in daily contact with many persons, it is easy to see how this official indifference and boredom develop, but from the point of view of the citizen each new incidence of authority has a fresh sting.

This is a situation that arises in school, church, business, and is in a sense an incident of institutionalization. But the very force back of the state may make the resentment of the subject all the greater. He may have a greater feeling of helplessness, and rage all the more wildly. If corruption or favoritism is present or suspected, or if it is felt that the official is piecing out his subordinate position with "a little brief authority," the exercise of which placates him somewhat, the pressure of indignation will rise still higher.

To many persons, then, government calls up the picture of an unending procession of tired officials, bored in manner, or arrogantly inflexible in position, lording it over the helpless humans who fall into their hands for the moment.

Thus the majesty of power may be lost in pomposity; its solidity in petty inflexibility; its broad view of social relations in blindness to personal realities; its human side in the impersonalism of officialdom.

Who has not cursed M. le Bureau under such conditions?

Backwardness

Government may suffer from the gap between social change and the policies and methods of the governors, and from being unprogressive or too slowly progressive. In periods of intellectual freedom, the government progressed perhaps *pari passu* with the other social advances of the day as in classic Greece and Rome, where magnificent public works and undertakings were characteristic of the time. Government rested heavily for long periods of time upon tradition, and during these times it compared not unfavorably with other institutions likewise constructed from the material of tradition and likewise bound by it. The church was also traditional, and so also was agriculture, while industry in the modern sense of the term had not come over the horizon.

The modern growth of science and technology imposed a severe test upon all social institutions and demanded rapid change and adaptation to keep even pace with the great discoveries of the age. Inventions of all kinds, in the field primarily of natural science but also in the domain of social reorganization, made it imperative that government should move with expedition to meet the new world into which it had suddenly come. This period however coincided with the advent of the theory of laissez faire in many states, and in others the older standards of feudalism survived and made adjustment difficult. Only in Prussia was there made of the feudal state something approaching a modern scientific organization through the union of elements, administrative, industrial, scientific, under auspices somewhat patrimonial in nature.

The lag between government and science was made all the

more evident in many Western states by reason of the fact that industry, while retaining a free hand for itself, demanded the restriction of government. Natural science was itself irresponsible for the moment in relation to social affairs, and the rise of social science made slow progress against traditionalism and personal preoccupation with industrialism and private profit.

The wider the gap between governmental enterprise and business enterprise, the stronger the demand for the further restriction of government, the less the confidence in its capacity, and the weaker its personnel recruiting power in a world of competition. And so on around the circle. When toward the close of the recent period the demand for social regulation arose, fear of strong government as a regulator became more marked. Furthermore, in international affairs the difficulty of keeping pace with the times became greater as the unit of human intercourse in trade and elsewhere became larger and tended to approach the world range. The pangs of scientific adjustment were intensified by the still sharper development of nationalistic arrangements and nationalistic jealousies, which inhibited the impartial, objective, to say nothing of scientific treatment of the larger problems precipitated by the new era of intercourse. Intercommunication and its realities were challenged by nationalism and its realities of emotion and antagonism. The collapse of the jural order in the world war was the catastrophic climax in this inability to keep pace with the advance of the cultural and scientific movement of the time—that is, in governmental arrangements recognizing and embracing the new developments.

Indecision and Impotence

A further factor in the unpopularity of power groups is found in the indecision or impotence of authority in moments when action is imminent and urgent. Inaction has been the capital crime of more than one ruler or government. Whether this may reasonably be attributed to the personal incompetence of the particular holders of authority, or to the complexity of the conditions in which they find themselves, makes little difference from the point of view of general prestige. Rough judgments are ready for use, even in impatience and unreason.

And the very function of political power makes it frequently impossible to proceed without long delay. Compromises, adjustments, understandings must be reached, before the way is clear for advance; and these may not be readily forthcoming in a given case. The Polish nobles exercised the *liberum* veto upon each other until the hour of dissolution arrived. The Frankfort National Assembly of 1848 disputed over the bill of rights until the opposition rallied and reestablished the old régime. Adjustment, conference, deliberation are among the essentials of the political, but all may make for indecision and postponement when the need of the group is action. Out of such material dictators and despots of various forms have arisen again and again and held sway until some other day brought back the more diversified distribution of power. But dictators and despots in turn may become indecisive and incompetent. The very jealousy with which the liberty of the people may be guarded by division of governmental authorities through a series of agencies may defeat its own purpose by paralyzing the political group and leading the way back to the despotism it sought to avoid.

But, it may be asked, is this inaction more characteristic of the political group than of any others? The answer would be, no, only to the extent that governments may assume a wider view of their own responsibility than other groups sometimes do. If only one interest is to be consulted, the problem is relatively easy, but if many are concerned and the emerging policy is to be an adjustment of these interests, then the solution is more difficult to discover and apply. Any group undertaking to make a settlement of a series of interests in the given society will experience difficulty in arriving at an outcome promptly in many classes of circumstances where the way out seems blocked. And this is true whether decisions are rendered by many or by a few. One man may be as much befuddled as a hundred, and may find the King of Indecision dominating him as truly as a larger group of individuals. The great indecisions of history may be found in the camp of the one, as well as of the few or the many. The problem lies rather in the complexity of the situation than in the plurality of the persons making the decision.

In contemporary times the indecisions of government have in some measure been imputed to it by business and labor groups dissatisfied with governmental policy and demanding that more be achieved in their particular interest. In such cases the residual responsibility of government, the common understanding that what no one else can accomplish, the ruler must care for, falls with especial weight on those who hold the power positions, and who may be blocked by those who charge them with inaction.

But the underside of power is not without its own power factors. There are those who in a way enjoy coercion and passively accept violence from the stronger, if they are convinced of superior strength. The aggressive impulse of the strong may be matched by the surrender impulse of the weak. Some who are tricked admire the cleverness of the trickster, and concede their own stupidity without compunction. The grafter and his control, and they are many, are not displeased with a situation from which they emerge with some additional utilities. The weakness of government is not displeasing to those who might be disturbed by a strong hand and a powerful will; and the slowness of government is not unacceptable to those who prefer what is and has been to something different. The traditionally minded find a friend in a traditional government which may fit them and their interests like an old shoe. The more rapidly everything else changes, the more some may wish to cling to an unchanging government, as well as an immovable religion. Thus it appears that some of the weaknesses of power have their own strength, and are not so ill adapted to the great mass of mankind as it might seem. The overrationalization of the power process may lead us to overlook some of the basic drives toward which the power group direct their manipulations. The power equation, or net result, is satisfied by whatever means may be at hand, and in each of the above enumerated elements there is a form of response, not perhaps rational, but real none the less, and an important part of the material of the political. If men either fear force from physical shrinking or find pleasure in it, or if deceit fits in their own mental pattern, or if corruption only excites their envy, or if traditionalism seems more comfortable, then these are basic facts to be incorporated in a working political system, and not discarded because they do not conform to other standards or types of behavior that a particular observer may prefer.

Finally the question may be raised again, how far are the types of difficulties just discussed peculiar to the power group and how far are they the general characteristics of all institutionalizations? Are we dealing with a special class of phenomena or with a more general situation? Are there like manifestations in the organization of the church, of business, of labor, of various cultural organizations? It must be observed that there are many more points of likeness than might at first be recognized. The power group, it is true, possesses a monopoly of violence and restraint of persons, but other groups have a brutality all their own. The church may cost man his peace of mind in this world and perhaps in the next; the business group may deprive him of his living and employ hunger and need as physical impulses to conformity.

Violence is by no means unknown in the circles of labor organizations. Deceit is in a sense perennial; adjustments and arrangements must be made, with alleged reasons that do not always fit the facts in a given case, whether in church, union, university, or factory. The eye of the administrator, ranging over a wide series of cases and having in mind the good of the order, may perjure himself a little in the greater cause he serves. Are there not sophists in religion, and is there not the phrase *caveat emptor* in industry? One may deceive to save a soul, and one may conceal some of the facts or distort others in order to make a sale. Proudhon once defined commerce as buying for one centime what is worth five and selling for five what is worth one. The mental reservations of the diplomat have their counterpart in other organizations as well, for is there not diplomacy in all institutions?

Corruption and favoritism are not unknown as power devices in social organizations. Particularly in industry there has been a wide ranging sweep of this practice, frowned upon by law and by commercial codes of ethics, but incorporated in practice in a greater degree than in government. At some points the business system is a triumph of honor, but at others falls far short of this ideal; and especially in a period of rapid change becomes almost terrifying in its sweep and consequences. There are Kruegers and Insulls to consider in weighing relative types of corruption. The fact is that commercial fraud has been making disquieting progress in recent years and the ways and means of checking it are not yet fully in hand.

Inflexibility, sluggishness, and impotence are ills to which any group may from time to time succumb and are not characteristic of the power group exclusively. The higher and greater publicity that surrounds the governmental processes may illuminate the delinquency of the political association, but there are like moments in the life span of all institutions, moments when indecision and faltering bring the function of the group to failure and shame. The church is split into many competing factions, whose lack of cooperation tends to bring the efforts of the separate sects to naught. Industry is torn in two by the tragic failure to reconcile in some generous formula or association the interests of the owners and the workers. The labor group itself is divided into warring camps of communists and socialists, and competing craft and industrial unions, in a factionalism which may defeat the very function of the group itself.

Backwardness is not alone characteristic of the state, but may be discovered in other groups, which likewise do not utilize the opportunities afforded them by the application of the latest knowledge brought by science from its inquiries. Scientific societies themselves may become the leaders of laggards if such a term is appropriate. Universities become fossilized and scientific societies reject with scorn the ideas of the revolutionaries who upset the work of vested scientific interests. Government, religion, like business and agriculture, face the problem of adjustment to a flood of inventions and discoveries such as men were never before obliged to utilize in so short a space of time.

The aversion to political power must, we may conclude,

be examined alongside those of other institutionalized orders and viewed as a phenomenon not of the power group alone, but of associated life in general. There are special features of the power situation which are characteristic or unusually developed, as in the case of violence and public hypocrisy, if there be such a term, but many of the weaknesses of political power are found in parallel columns in the ranks of social power.

Here once more it may not be inappropriate to emphasize the interrelationships of social groupings and the fundamental likeness of any of their foundation lines. The education and cultural conditioning found in one is, in a measure, transferred to another. The helpless citizen who flees from the state may take refuge in another group, but here again he may encounter practices that once more grind his troubled soul. He flees perhaps from one circle to another, but cannot escape the limiting circumference of group authority; or the continuing disillusionment of group maladministration and what seems betrayal or contradiction of an ideal purpose. Even an anarchist finds himself encysted in society and bound by its inevitable laws of behavior. He may become a communist but would not be encouraged by the story of Emma Goldman in Russia; or he may find refuge in a monastery, but there will also be regulations to obey and discipline to observe. Even in heaven and hell there seem to be established orders, if Lucifer and the seven circles are fact and not merely fiction. But, if the latter, then they merely depict the imagination trammeled even in its dreams.

If shame is a common characteristic of the functioning of all social groupings as well as of the state, perhaps shame has a mission, and we should not be so much ashamed of shame; or at least may place it in a frame of reference where it may be understood.

The shame of power as here discussed must be placed over against the miranda and credenda of authority to obtain a clear view of the diverse factors in the formation of political allegiance. In the balance and offset of these negative and positive elements we may be able to discover at a given time the social composition of civil power.

There are divergent currents of which some draw the individual in and others propel him out from the central political loyalty. But to these tropisms there must also be added the credenda of the political association, and the solid social interests or functions served at any given time. The groups and the individuals in them are traders in a sense and are making their bargain with the government as best they can, commanding, compromising, sullenly retreating. The solidity and permanence of authority are the outcome of these various tendencies in the group and in the individual member of it.

Is outward power the mirror of the life within, so that we may find the picture of the state in the struggle of the individual constitution the conflicts of which have been a little unveiled by the eye of the psychoanalysts; or is the life within the mirror of the power without so that we may say "My mind to me a kingdom is"; or is the secret perhaps in their interaction?

We do not know all that is necessary to answer this and related questions; but upon the approximation to such knowledge the guidance of great states and the welfare of mankind in no small measure depend.

Chapter 6

The Poverty of Power

IT IS THE purpose of the following pages to study the incidence of political power from the point of view of those upon whom power is exercised rather than from that of the authoritarians themselves, from below rather than from above. There are innumerable and admirable treatises and manuals describing and explaining how government reaches down, but the special purpose of these paragraphs is to consider how power is received from below; how the under group by whom the incidence of power is felt may defend itself against the pressure from above. What are the ways and means, the attitudes and devices by which those upon whom power is exercised protect themselves against its excesses?

There is a wide gap between the apparent omnipotence of authority and the actual operation of power, between the iron fist of force and its incidence upon human flesh and feeling. And, notwithstanding the recurring illustrations of this in period after period of history, there is nothing more surprising to the holders of power, or perhaps to its subjects, than the frailty of their commands in certain types of crises. The throne and the crown and the scepter are there; the army is there, with its disciplined ranks and its deadly weapons of death; the prisons are there, tightly locked, with the malcontents safely behind the bars. There are no imposing centers of resistance. Yet, when the order is given, obedience is reluctant, partial; resistance widens; and as penalties are made heavier, opposition becomes stronger. The law seems dead; it is dead.

The checks upon authority are as numerous as its prerogatives and more inevitable in their recurrence. It is not the present purpose, however, to deal with all of the kinds of formal limitation upon political authorities. Nor is it the intention to consider the elaborate network of restrictions which have been woven in a period of constitutionalism, the systems of civil liberties and rights which have been characteristic of the last three centuries, and particularly of the last century. Many notable procedures and processes have been wrought in all Western states, and their operation has done much to prevent the arbitrary action of government from rudely impinging upon the life of the individual. The growth of constitutional government, of the *Rechtstaat* in place of the *Machtstaat,* is the expression of the determination to protect the (ruled) community against the abuse of the very function which brings community into being. Progress in this direction has been one of the most signal advances in respect for the dignity of human personality. The civil and criminal procedures which have been set up in the systems of the Western races are the visible protest against the autocracy and irresponsibility of earlier authority.

These guaranties have been further reenforced and validated by the organization of representative and responsible government through which protest may be made against arbitrary conduct and by means of which authority may be peacefully terminated and other agencies substituted. The further organization of political parties and the security of the right of free association, with freedom of speech and press, have made possible defenses against the incidence of authority, unwarranted or undesired. Notwithstanding the undoubted fact that these procedures have been twisted into defenses of privilege on various occasions, especially in the heat of the industrial struggle, and in other instances as well, there is no shadow of doubt that they have served their intrinsic purpose of legalizing resistance to the nominal authority in the political association and making possible the complete overthrow of the sovereign through an orderly process.

It is contended that the whole apparatus of parliamentarianism, civil rights, electoralism is, under a capitalistic system, void of meaning, and in fact deceptive in that the mass are unable to exercise effectively their nominal authority. But communism itself, as evidenced in organization of the Soviet Union, has recognized the principles of responsibility and set up a type of representation, with tasks similar to those of the libertarian group, although administered for a different end. Likewise fascism, as exemplified in Italy and Germany as well, has set up a mechanism in which responsibility may be nominally enforced through a representative agency. In both cases there is a suspension of the operation of these institutions in their entirety, on the plea of temporary emergency.

Dictatorships can at best be but temporary devices suspending the action of the checks upon the power of the nominal government. No dictator rules without the aid of some group alleged to represent the community, as a check on his otherwise irresponsibility. He may expect to postpone such a check indefinitely, and he may weaken and camouflage his irresponsibility for a time, but in the long run the brake becomes evident; and perhaps more evident than the nominal dictator in the end.[1]

It is the special purpose of this chapter, however, to deal with those forms of the defense of individuals through other than the institutionalized agencies set up for that purpose and fully formalized in the life of the political community. There are many other procedures and instrumentalities of great weight in a political society which may be utilized whether there are constitutional rights set up or not, and to these attention is now directed.

The methods of resisting the powers that be are numerous and varied as the types of aggression, and their classification is very difficult, owing to the wide range of situations under which resistance may be made. There is organized and unorganized resistance, violent, nonviolent, and (if there is such a term) quasi-violent resistance, to special acts or laws or to entire systems and orders of things—racial, religious, economic, political. The techniques of resistance run through a series of acts, aimed at the whole category of credenda and miranda, emphasizing all of the factors in the possible

[1] F. Cambo, *Les Dictatures;* Otto Forst de Battaglia, *Dictatorship on Trial;* Diana Spearman, "The Psychological Background of Dictatorship," *Sociological Review,* 25: 158.

shame of power, limited only by the imagination, ingenuity, and persistence of the dissenters and protestants.

For present purposes we may tentatively classify them as follows: (1) Relatively unorganized murmuring and grumbling, obvious disrespect and dissent—a sort of low-level functioning of the deference and submission which are required by the credenda of politics. (2) Organized and active resistance, accompanied by incidental or intended violence. (3) Organized resistance without the use of violence, as seen in Tolstoy's system and in the civil disobedience of Gandhi.

These categories overlap to some extent, and I offer this scheme only as a temporary rack upon which to hang certain facts. Undoubtedly further inquiry and thought will develop much more adequate and defensible forms of classification than this, when this relatively unexplored region is surveyed and mapped adequately.

It may be noted that there are two interesting techniques of power little discussed in the books: (*a*) That of the antiauthoritarians who devise ways and means of opposing the government without resorting to war or to too much violence. (*b*) That of the authoritarians who devise ways and means of repressing the antiauthoritarian technicians without too much violence. Each considers a type and style of action which will operate without too great disturbance to the public or without forfeiture of the good will of the mass. While there is a wide range of opportunity on each side of this line, there are also limits which may readily be encountered by those who carry their tactics too far in the given mood of the public. The stake of the game is the crown of control. On the whole, this constitutes one of the interesting and valuable fields of research in the technique of political science, instead of belonging in the archives of the secret police or the underground hiding places of the rebels.

1. The mildest and yet one of the most effective methods by which the underdog protects himself is that of grumbling, with obvious gestures and expressions of dissent, halting short of disrespect that would call for discipline or short of

making the community so uncomfortable as to arouse its rage.

The most telling protest may, indeed, be made by doing nothing at all. Silence may greet the king, the prince, the president, and nothing more—no cheers resound, no loud huzzas, no reverent faces lifted up from humility to meet the smile of the most high; only silence or scowls or averted faces. If the king may send his subjects to prison or the gallows, they may send him to Coventry with equal assurance and perhaps more effect. The vocal boo or the hiss or the angry gesture is an additional but scarcely necessary touch to this demonstration of lack of confidence. Silence may leave the ruler legally as sovereign as he was before, but rob him of what makes his power agreeable. Smiles and sneers are a type of unconstitutional limitation upon authority.

Nor can anything well restrain the pen of the cartoonist or the satire of the writer or, least of all, the tongue of the gossip. There is always the effigy and its possible burning, with all the implications of the scene. The ingenious underdogs may carry on an interesting attack, without the violation of a single letter of the law. What statute can compel smiles or applause or the externalia of deference? What law is effective enough to compel and enforce cheerful association against the will of those associated.[2]

What shall the hard hand of power do when little children march behind and mimic the goosestep of soldiers; when women spit in the faces of the conquerors? What shall authority do when a newspaper appears with every page blank, and marked *Censura* as in the case of *L'Avanti* during the World War? What shall be done when the common course of social amenity is stopped, and silence and scorn take the place of friendly greeting and conversation? What if those who enter and come out of prison are hailed as heroes or martyrs? These difficulties may be overcome, to be sure, but

[2] When the City Council of Berlin wished to reach the Empress in 1900, they omitted the usual resolution of felicitation on the occasion of her birthday.

not through armed violence, not by the prison and the sword.

Murmuring is evidence of low morale which will readily express itself in specific forms of a very definite nature. The output of labor will be less, the soldiers will fight less bravely, the task of administration will be greatly increased, and the skies will darken generally. The effect is not merely the saddening of the spirit of the ruler, but his very serious weakening at important points in his program of power. Good will is as important an element in government as in any other walk of life, and no ruler can carry on indefinitely without it.

Is ill will, then, a political power? I do not remember seeing it in any constitution, national or local. But it is a substantial obstacle in the way of power; it is a factor with which government must reckon in the elaboration of its plans. It is for our immediate purposes a weapon in the hands of the weaponless, a weapon of which the most complete disarmament may not deprive the individual or the group. Even in prisons the inmates may bring their will to bear upon the keepers by simple devices of disapproval, accompanied by no violence whatever.[3] And in the larger economy of states, this ill will may be the decisive factor in the execution of any large policy in peace or war.

In particular holders of power the murmurs of disaffection may arouse another emotion, that of fear of the rival who may capitalize the disaffection of the people or the group, and convert it into strength of his own, which may overwhelm that of the government in power. Absalom was not the first or the last to sit at the gates and sympathize with the grievances of those who came and went, as a preparation for an uprising.

In the modern power situations where votes are still counted as tokens in the political process, the disaffected member of the party effectively shows his displeasure again by doing nothing. He does not vote against his party, but he does not shout for it, and the outcome may mean defeat for those who did not reckon accurately with his disquiet.

[3] Research would reveal many impressive illustrations of the power of mute resistance, of ill will.

In military situations, when victory may hang on the last desperate effort of the soldiers, poor morale is the preliminary to defeat, and no commander, dealing with the spirits of youth, would for a moment forget the far-reaching importance of the fighting spirit and good will of his men. Here again the remedy in the hands of the underdog is as simple as that of doing little or nothing. He does not desert; he fights, but with relative feebleness, not giving the last extreme effort that might spell victory. He advances more slowly and he retreats more quickly.

A more generalized term for this behavior pattern in later years is found in sabotage, the special home of which, however, is industrial rather than political relations; "ca' canny," restriction of output, literal obedience of erroneous orders recognized as such, and in some instances deliberate steps toward the destruction of material; or, more commonly, the slowing down of the productive process upon which the owner's profits depend. In the church the faithful begin to fall away, perhaps without a word or sign. Not heresy but indifferentism spreads quietly through the ranks. In other competing groups the same phenomena are equally evident and the same folding up of the support upon which reliance had been placed. The competing loyalties of which social life is made up afford the individual wide opportunity for transferring the seat of his interest and affection, and in many instances he will do so, to the discomfiture of the group that confidently counted on his allegiance. Even as the formal efficiency of the organization increases, the good will upon which it rests may weaken, and the form becomes empty of life and spirit, dead or dying.

Malaise is, then, a factor in government, the possibilities and actualities of which have never been thoroughly explored by scientists; nor are they fully understood by the masses who are able to use them if they would. In any group, unconscious of it though they may be, there is a road toward the obstruction of their rulers and their rulers' plans—by doing nothing or expressing even in artistic fashion their disapproval and dissent. I am not speaking here of illegality or of revolution. The reasons why this is not done more frequently are chiefly the innocence of the group regarding the power they really possess, the drawing off of their leaders as they rise to consciousness of ability, and the counter measures of attraction taken by those in authority to offset the dangerous tendencies of ill will and indifference. The science of good will has not been neglected by those dealing with masses of men, and many devices have been developed by astute governors.

2. There are cases in which there is organized and systematic opposition, with incidental or intended violence. The disaffection in such cases may apply to a particular law or rule, or to the entire system of economic or political organization. A law may adversely affect a religion, or a particular race, or a class, or a region, and the resistance may be generalized to include a considerable group of persons, organized now and systematizing their efforts.

What if the law forbids one's religion; or the use of one's native tongue, at least in schools; or forbids free speech and assembly; or imposes an intolerable tax or other economic servitude? The coercion of considerable minorities in such cases is extremely difficult, if they are disposed to resist with any degree of firmness. Their passive resistance may be very difficult to break down, and the ensuing mood of irritation and perhaps savagery against the stubbornness of the recalcitrant may readily lead to the acts of violence which are characterized as atrocities. These in turn become the basis for wider and more enthusiastic and determined opposition, now directed against the atrocity as well as the original offense. The history of racial and religious relations is full of shocking instances of this type, which if prolonged may finally be transformed into feudistic situations of crystallized hate, as in the British-Irish situation, where centuries of antagonism have sown the seed of a bitter harvest.

In such a struggle it soon becomes evident that the processes of the criminal law and the capacity of the prisons are calculated on a basis of intimidation rather than of wide-ranging punishment. If any considerable group persistently holds out, where shall we confine them? How many shall we fine, beat, imprison, execute? The limit is soon reached, and may be found either in the weakening of the will of the underdog for the moment or in the reconsideration of the plan by the political superior. Where there is a jury of the vicinity, how shall anyone be convicted? Furthermore, there are serious complications for the law, since the law-breakers if respectable and numerous tend to make all law-breaking tolerable and to break down the common disapproval of violation of law. In the United States the enforcement of the Fugitive Slave Law and later of the Eighteenth Amendment presented serious problems of this nature, and shook the foundations of the government.

Laws against poaching, smuggling, and providing for various forms of unpopular taxes are constantly violated, on principle as well as for personal reasons. In these instances, however, the group opposition is usually not so coherent, and the problem is that of a somewhat widely diffused but unorganized opposition to the rule of the law. The price of peace may be an illogical moderation in the enforcement of the law, with sporadic and warning examples from time to time, but with no systematic and continued effort to make the regulations effective.

Religious, racial, and economic struggles have had even more profound and far-reaching effects, with wars and unending feuds as the outcome, with century-old grievances becoming the center of modern social political problems. Unquestionably resistance may be broken down with a forceful enough hand, but the price may be very high. The *Kulturkampf* in Germany set up the Center party; the suppression of the socialists inaugurated the parliamentary life of that group; Protestants in Czechoslovakia after the lapse of centuries clamored for the reopening of the case of John Huss and his retrial and vindication.

The minority may reveal their attitude in various organized manifestations which are within the law, but perhaps not within the spirit of the power group. Parades, meetings, demonstrations, boycotts, strikes may be within the limits of the law, and they may be employed by those who are opposed to a special type of governmental action. In demonstrations the murmuring of the many is organized within the scope of legality. Even where public assemblies are permitted, the secret gathering is extremely difficult to prevent—that is, without too close an approach to forms of espionage and acts of brutality which in turn only strengthen the will of the minority and weaken the position of those in nominal power. It is awkward to forbid a religious assembly even if in point of fact it may have a political purpose and expression; it is difficult to prevent all racial and cultural meetings and associations even though they have political implications; it is still more difficult to suppress sport associations even though it may be well understood that they have political meaning. In the end the government cannot prevent human aggregation and association, and if it does foolishly endeavor to do so, the blow recoils against the government that directs the tactics of suppression. In any event, it is impossible to control association outside the boundaries of the state, in some other land now made a basis of operations.

In special tension moments it is not difficult to proceed against demonstrations by the simple process of refusing the necessary legal permit, but over a long period this method has great difficulty in maintaining itself—and, indeed, becomes impossible except by the use of such force as may defeat the very purpose of the regulation originally. It will prove impossible permanently to prevent a considerable group from assembling in any form whatsoever, if there is a cultural pattern of any degree of fixity. There will at least be christenings, weddings, funerals; there will be social assemblies in one form or other; and the line between these innocent aggregations and the dangerously political will prove the more difficult to draw as the tension increases. Ruthless determination may go a long way in this direction, it must be conceded, and there are minorities that have been extirpated or entombed in particular regions, but the persistence of the Jewish group is a striking evidence of the futility of persecution as a means of destruction of a determined and cohesive society defiant of the power group. *Déraciner* is an easy plan to project, but the roots are deep. In more than one case by some subtle process of transfusion the minority has reappeared in the center of the power group again, similingly triumphant.

Great parades, demonstrations, manifestations may then become an instrumentation of the aspirations of the minorities, who are for the moment against the rule of the nominal power group, against a specific measure of that government, determined to break its force, presumably by legal methods but no more than passively observant of deeds of violence. And this refers not merely to party protests and demands for the change of laws or the enactment of new ones, but to protests against existing and established power situations, which it is proposed to oppose with a degree of effectiveness remote from mere verbalization. As the great parade flows through the streets, the voice of the orator inspires the assembled masses, the cries of the crowd echo their determination, a transformation may take place in the power balance, unless offset by counter measures of the dominant group.

Faced by formidable opposition, authority may adopt the severest methods of repression in the hope of stifling the voice of criticism. Freedom of speech may be suppressed, freedom of the press and freedom of teaching in the schools and institutions of higher learning. But experience shows that there is no assurance of safety even in the most drastic measures of this type. The quarantine of ideas is never wholly effective; indeed, the very secrecy with which opinions and ideas must be communicated adds an element of interest and mystery otherwise lacking. All tongues cannot be muzzled; gossip and fugitive prints take the place of the press; secret meetings are held under the ban of the law; the mind of the scholar escapes the movement of the law and makes its own way in the world, even from prison walls or exile. The severity of repression itself arouses the belief that what is suppressed must be important, and emotional tension reenforces intellectual conviction. In modern times the world has grown smaller, intercommunication is more intimate; the radio and the press, the stream of travelers make the blockade of the objectionable idea increasingly difficult, and in the end impossible, except at a prohibitive price. How discouraging to violence to observe that the more intelligent the methods used to repress intelligence, the greater the probability that intelligence will emerge as joint holder of authority. Such is the way of intelligence, itself one of the members of the family of power.

These demonstrations may or may not be accompanied by physical force. Violence may be incidental, or it may be intended in some instances as the preliminary to revolution, racial or economic; but it will usually be violence of a type designed to skirt the border of the law and avert open conflict with armed authority. There will be beatings, assaults, burnings perhaps, rough handling possibly, all with a design of intimidation and provocation. In a series of incidents of this type there will be instances of the unintentional taking of life and also of deliberate infliction of death upon representatives of government. In various groups from time to time there has developed the cult of terror, with or without group sanction.

The recent struggles in Ireland and in Germany afford ample material for the detailed consideration of such situations, but the annals of all peoples are full of like instances of the contests in which authority is resisted by considerable and organized sections of the community, either as an incident to resistance against a particular law or as a protest against a whole system, and perhaps as a preliminary to revolution, racial, regional, economic, personal in nature.[4]

In the Middle Ages the ban upon the community was a special form of resistance on the part of the church, and in the case of the individual the measure of excommunication. These were drastic and effective remedies which the political power group found difficulty in resisting for a long time. And more than one ruler was figuratively speaking brought to Canossa.

The twentieth-century struggles between church and state illustrate the modern version of the same situation of resistance to government. In modern times the industrial groups

[4] See Georges Sorel, *Reflections on Violence* (published in a Collier Books edition—Ed.).

have developed their own special techniques of resistance to the majority decree. In each case the instrument is economic pressure, the strike in one case, and the threat of unemployment in the other. The strike is a weapon which may lawfully be employed in accordance with modern standards and which contains large possibilities of successful action on the part of the under group. When broadened into the general strike, the stress becomes far greater, and may even approach the line of actual revolution.[5] The individual strike, continued or intermittent, may serve as an effective protest against a special form of legal regulation, as a means of calling attention to a state of mind, as an organized gesture of protest, or a preliminary of defiance. A stoppage of labor in a key industry serves to call general attention to a grievance—a strike, for example, in the post or the telephone service, even if continued only for a short period. More commonly employed to obtain concessions for the field of wages and working conditions, the measure may be utilized for purposes of political pressure, as a protest against a particular law. The threat of a strike may be equally effective at times, as in the notable instance of the Adamson eight-hour law enacted by the United States Congress under pressure of the railway workers, or in some instances of threatened strikes in war time.

The general strike comes closer to the edge of direct political action, or even to revolution. Sorel pictured the general strike, when labor is fully organized, as the means by which the ruling group would finally be dispossessed and the proletariat take their position in the center of authority. He assumed sufficiently complete organization to make comprehensive control over vital industries possible, and the further development of solidarity of sentiment, adequacy of tactics, and confidence in leadership. And in the Sorellian theory, indeed, the whole process might even belong in the category of the myth, with value for propaganda even if never achieved.

The British general strike of 1926 afforded an interesting

[5] See W. H. Crook, *The General Strike,* and the bibliography there cited.

example of an orderly protest on a very large scale, and raised the question whether such a plan could be regarded as revolutionary or as within the framework of the regular political order.[6] A form of control arose within the labor group in which was for the moment the seat of actual power in a range of affairs, shifting the government from one member of the power family to another. In such a situation the government rallied to its assistance a series of volunteers, in effect representing the middle and propertied group.[7] It is clear that if labor were sufficiently well organized and extended its membership to a sufficiently large number of key industries, it would become increasingly difficult for any government to oppose its demands. But, on the other hand, it may be pointed out that with so formidable a membership and organization, it might be even easier to control the formal government.

As the church may excommunicate and the labor group may strike, the business group may threaten the power holders with financial panic and collapse through the control of credit and the general custody of employment and prosperity. On more than one occasion the propertied groups while in a political minority have been able to drive hard bargains with the political authorities, either through real or fancied alternatives of industrial inconvenience or ruin. Concessions, loans, privileges of one sort and another are not unknown in periods of tension, when the holders of authority are in sore need of support, directly financial or otherwise, and their will may be bent by business groups threatening calamity or even collapse.

In a wide range of instances, then, the minority defends itself against the majesty of the law and the symbolism and force of authority by an appeal to the general assent underlying government. And, powerless in certain cases, it may yet be able even in weakness to break the grip of authority and compel the retreat of the lawmaker. But the special cases where this is most effectively done are those in which the

[6] See *Parliamentary Debates, passim.*

[7] See Crook, *The General Strike,* for reference to Belgian and French strikes especially, where acute situations arose.

resistance to the law meets the support of some other member of the family of power who joins hands in the common effort to block the course of the political power group. Along this way political power has met with many a severe reverse, drawn away from the base of social prestige, and caught at awkward angles of incidence.

Other important types of resistance within the law are those developed by groups with a revolutionary purpose avowed or thinly concealed, but are not prepared for open resistance against the dominant group. Many of these are racial groups, awaiting the hour of emancipation; others are economic class groups or nationalistic groups awaiting the power moment. The Irish group is in no sense pacifistic and is frankly irreconcilable to British sovereignty. The communist and fascist groups are opposed to the existing régime and not to be classified as opposed to violence.

In all these cases provocative tactics are devised and put into operation, with only a minimum of violence but not without an element of terrorism, illegal in nature or closely on the border of it. What are the provocative tactics by which the political order may be successfully defied? They may include a wide variety of measures, ranging from boyish pranks to seriously organized disturbances. They are marked by slight infractions of property rights and violations of personal integrity short of death; street altercations and disorders without special rule for settlement or decision; disturbance or breaking up of meetings; newspaper and other publicity on the border of the censorship; insulting signs and inscriptions; and defamation of memorials especially attached to another group. The study of the credenda and miranda of the rival groups supplies the key to the special sanctities of the opposition and opens the way to most effective insult.

The organization of minority groups in a period of highly developed mustering and symbolizing of masses of individuals may result in the formation of private armies, in a way within the law. When it was proposed to grant home rule to Ireland, Lord Carson began the formation of a north-of-Ireland army, drilled and disciplined within the law, or nearly so. And within Ireland there was organized the republican army at a later time. The "Red Front" of the communists and the Hitler army in Germany are examples of organized, trained, uniformed forces existing within the state, and tolerated by it, notwithstanding the announcement of a revolutionary purpose. In the case of the Hitler army, there was the additional feature of special barracks for the armies, who were recruited chiefly but not wholly from the unemployed and paid by the party government.

3. Another method of resisting the power group is that of organized opposition without the use of any violence. The roots of this technique run far back into the history of religious attitudes and organizations, and involve a wide range of theories of government and of religion. In American experience an interesting contribution to this subject was made by Thoreau in his essay *Civil Disobedience,* and the sect appeared known as the "Come Outers," who came out from both state and church alike, undertaking a general boycott of civil and ecclesiastical organization. The history of anarchism is also full of illustrations of attempts to set up forms of social organization eliminating entirely the element of coercion.[8]

Count Tolstoy[9] advocated as a special theory of social action the most complete possible boycott of the government. This involved nonpayment of taxes, nonuse of governmental institutions, no resort to courts of law, and in general abstention from all forms of cooperation with the power group. If the individual was not able to go all the way, perhaps he would go a part of the way, until such time as he had acquired courage to make the complete distance.[10] This was, to be sure, a philosophy of anarchy, but it indicated a line of tactics which might be followed with some show of success and yet remain within the law, in accordance with the Tolstoian doctrine of nonviolence.

Gandhi, the Hindu, trained in the theories of Tolstoy, in the doctrines of Jesus and Buddha, in the English school of

[8] See "Anarchism" in *Social Science Encyclopaedia.*

[9] L. Tolstoy, *Slavery of Our Times;* and Gandhi, *Writings.*

[10] M. I. Markovitch, *Tolstoi et Gandhi.*

law, and in the hard school of practical experience in South Africa and India, evolved still more elaborate and refined methods of noncooperation. Among the more striking of the special forms of protest were: wholesale submission to arrest, as in South Africa, and the consequent flooding of the prisons; wholesale evasion of the salt tax; refusal to accept office under British rule (broken, however, by the participation in representation, for propaganda and educational purposes); days of fasting designed as mass protests against the prevailing power group; boycott of British textile industry by use of the spinning wheel; the use of the hunger strike (employed on other occasions, however). These devices may be summed up in what is termed "soul force," by which is meant the use of moral pressure as against physical force or violence: the conquest of the lower through the higher nature. These constitute an elaborate and in many ways effective system of what may be called civil disobedience, within the borders of legality. The ingenuity with which these measures have been devised and the magnitude of the support accorded them have been puzzling in the extreme to the powers that be. Here again, however, the employment of crass violence only strengthens the impression of solidarity which these very policies are designed to foster and reenforce and in a sense drives the barb more deeply in.[11]

Of passive resistance Gandhi says:

> Its equivalent in the vernacular, rendered into English, means Truth Force. I think Tolstoi called it also Soul Force or Love Force, and so it is. Carried out to its utmost limits, this force is independent of pecuniary or other material assistance; certainly even in its elementary form, of physical force or violence. Indeed violence is the negation of this great spiritual force, which can only be cultivated or wielded by those who will entirely eschew violence.[12]

[11] Mahatma Gandhi, *Sermon on the Sea,* Chap. XVI, "Brute Force"; Chap. XVII, "Passive Resistance."

[12] *Mahatma Gandhi, His Life, Writings and Speeches,* pp. 95–96.

The range of possibilities in this direction is very great, and has never been thoroughly explored even by the most adventurous student of tactics or of political organization. The opportunities are as wide as the sphere of social relations, including sex, the social amenities, religious relations, business contact, sport relations, and recreation generally; in short, the caste situation reversed by the pariahs as against their masters.

The continuing will to resist, however, may not be present. Leaders may be won over, the fainter hearted may give up, the fearful may yield to force; and the counter propagandas and pressures of the power groups themselves may wear away the attitude and the behavior pattern which began so bravely.

Just as the official who attempts to exercise power outside the field in which he "belongs" may encounter difficulty, so the resistant who has back of him no large social interest which he reflects or represents, or who is not skillful in his devices, will find himself in a difficult position. Instead of appearing as a social benefactor or a martyr, he may find himself classified as a common nuisance, deserted and derided by his friends, while he is punished by his foes.[13] Neither the arrogance of the unrepresentative official nor the impudence of the unrepresentative resistant is any guaranty in itself of a successful outcome; for the group is not primarily interested in either, and indeed looks upon them both as excrescences upon the body politic.

The history of the conscientious objectors to war offers many illustrations of the tactics of nonresistance. For centuries, in the midst of military activities which have aroused the emotions of their communities, these groups have maintained their determination not to support directly the institution of war.[14] Little effect has been produced upon this group by the severest measures, including not merely physical punishment but social obloquy as well. The earlier resistance was based largely upon religious grounds, so that

[13] H. Ibsen, *Enemy of the People.*

[14] C. M. Case, *Non-violent Coercion;* R. Niebuhr, *Moral Man and Immoral Society.*

the individual was reenforced by his conscience and by another member of the family of power which came to his aid. Most governments have, indeed, found it expedient to recognize these groups in some fashion or other, and accord them some position of tolerance in the community, even in the progress of war, as notably in the case of the Quakers.

In more recent times the theory of resistance has been shifted from religious grounds over to that of general opposition to war as an institution. War, now outlawed as a crime, may be opposed as unreasonable and intolerable both in particular instances and in general without regard to the merits of any particular controversy. The modern struggle turns upon this phase of the problem, rather than upon the more specifically religious aspects of the question. With this is also entangled a type of resistance, not to war per se, but to war not justified by certain economic or other considerations. Communists, for example, are not opposed to war as such or violence as such, but to any war not directed in the interest of the communist ideology.

The long and varied history of passive resistance to war presents, then, one of the most interesting chapters in the wide gamut of types of quiet opposition to the policy of the politically powerful. The annals of Western countries are full of the many subtle problems of law, conscience, and administration that are presented under such circumstances by those who are determined to hold out against the use of organized violence.

The present-day outlawry of war, the organization of the League of Nations and the World Court—and, on the other hand, the intense development of national interest in expanding armaments—is an illustration of the fundamental contrast in the sentiments of the Western nations, and the inability to arrive at an equilibrium respecting the employment of violence *inter se*.[15]

These, then, are fragmentary examples taken from a great wealth of cases in which the incidence of authority upon various individuals and groups produces resistance and may

[15] John Dewey, "Force, Violence and Law," *New Republic*, vol. 5 (1916), p. 295.

result in the failure of the proposed rule of behavior. It is clear that the rebel has his opportunity and his satisfactions as well as the regular. In truth the possibilities of resistance to law on the part of minorities with tenacity of purpose are very large, assuming willingness to pay the price and a fixed will to win at this particular point. Given these qualities the rebels may encyst themselves in the body politic in such a manner as to make removal very difficult and painful, and even dangerous, for the political power holders.

The beginnings of revolutionary movements offer many illustrations of the border lines of power, and in these situations is often clearly indicated the weakness of authority under a variety of conditions.[16] When does power cease to be power; at what moment does the rigidity of authority begin to crumble; what are the key points in the defense of the nominal government; what are the lines of attack upon it that are most feasible; and how far may these be generalized and how far are they limited to special conditions found in the social and economic background of the moment? What are the situations that break the will of those in command and substitute the will of the opposition? These and related questions are close to the problem of the poverty of power.

We have considered in the preceding pages the underside of authority and the defense mechanisms of those outside the circle of the nominal government. They include:

1. The constitutional defenses built up against arbitrary exercise of authority without some form of check—the apparatus of constitutionalism and especially of civil rights.

2. The mechanism for peaceful overthrow of the government through the agency of responsible representation and of the electoral process.

3. The wide range of other devices not reflected in formal institutions, including low-level deference; organized disobedience without violence, incidental or purposive; organ-

[16] See L. Trotzky, *History of the Russian Revolution;* Arthur Rosenberg, *Geschichte des Bolschewismus;* P. A. Sorokin, *Psychology of Revolution;* C. Malaparte, *Le Technique du coup d'état.*

ized resistance; and organized noncooperation, without violence.

These devices are not so different as might appear, however, in that they all relate to a system of general understandings, to a form of political psychology, to an emotional balance in the community, to the functioning of the power situation as a whole and the benevolent attitude of the family of power. If these conditions are not found, the formal mechanisms do not stand for long. They may be easily swept away, and another type of arrangement substituted. It may even happen that authority is like the hard-boiled, hard-faced person who is in point of fact compensating for an inner shyness and timidity. One with insight realizes that some faces are harder than humanity can possible be, and the same may be said of governments with the same rigidity. There is a way behind and through the defenses, we may readily conclude. The unamendable constitution, the unappealable decision, the inexorable official of whatever rank, may be found putty instead of granite if the right point is reached.

Power that demands insistently and uniformly the deepest subordination may in its turn be found equally servile to the next higher rank, and, indeed, these relations may be regarded as concomitant. The king's underling may be found more authoritative than the king himself, since the assured position of the latter may render him less likely to endeavor to impress his subordinates with this power, which is not in dispute. Indeed, in power personalities one may observe from time to time that nature has not conferred upon them the externalia of authority, the voice of command, the eye of command, the mien and bearing of command, but forms of gentleness and simplicity, as in Lincoln and Gandhi.

All formal systems contain safety valves for their own modification or partial suspension, to meet military or other emergencies. But what constitutes an emergency? This will be determined partly in the light of precedents and juristic considerations, but mainly in the light of the general understandings of the time, the emerging balance of power set over against the old. If the will is present, the interpretation may be found and may be made acceptable to the bulk of the community, particularly if it coincides with some great group of interests—economic, religious, racial, or otherwise. Power is never, therefore, as forceful as it seems, if looked upon as an institutionalized irresistibility. It must always be examined, if one wishes to make a careful appraisal of its significance, from the back and from the underside: banks sometimes exhibit to the public impressive doors of heavy steel which seem impenetrable but may have rear walls only two bricks thick or under surfaces or upper surfaces which are easy to break through; a military situation may seem impregnable when attacked by a frontal assault but may readily be taken from the rear or flank.

Power is not an illusion, but its omnipotence and permanence are, its existence away from the frame of social interests and values from which its life is derived. Punishment and even death are not effective in moments when the counter values surge up against them and lead men to despise suffering and defy death. The very challenge of death which power itself throws down in moments of greatest social tension may be used against it by the very same logic. Over and over in human experience rebels and resistants have gone cheerfully to their death or to the prison, defiant to the last gasp of the formal authority around them, but sometimes surviving to see the prison gates swing open and the convicts come back to the seats of authority.

The personal aggressiveness of the governors who administer punishment may be matched by the counter aggressiveness of those who are punished; and, when this is true, the oppressed may derive as much satisfaction from their side of the experience as do the power group from theirs. The rebel and the resistant build up their own world of miranda and credenda, their own symbolism of action. In secrecy and darkness they may develop their own world of satisfactions; and from within this inner world of resistance they hurl defiance at authority. Paul and Silas sing in chains at midnight, and masses acclaim the great prisoners as leaders or martyrs if need be. These groups may either thrust power back in defeat or force excess that in turn defeats authority by its atrocity.

Power is not strongest when it uses violence, but weakest. It is strongest when it employs the instruments of substitution and counter attraction, of allurement, of participation rather than of exclusion, of education rather than of annihilation. Rape is not an evidence of irresistible power in politics or in sex.

We cannot exile and imprison and execute many, after all; so why not draw them in rather than cast them out of the community in which there may be offered substantial advantages and emotional satisfactions? So reason the more prudent rulers.

From the side of omnipotence authority is an illusion; from the side of anarchy it is a reality.

From the side of arbitrary individual authority faced in naked granite, power is also an illusion; from the side of social functions, however, it is a reality.

From the side of permanence, at least in individuals or in special groups, power is again an illusion; but from the side of social adaptation and adjustment it is a living reality.

But power attempts to crystallize and perhaps fossilize itself, whereas in point of social analysis its true life lies in change, in a form of function growing out of the need of adjustment from time to time. If there were no social change, a case might be made for automatism, or for what might be termed anarchy, or for a type of social organization like that of the termites. It is precisely in the adjustment and composition of shifting interests that a great part of the vitality of politics lies.

The poverty of power is a characterization of one side only of the authority. For power possesses a wealth of social force and influence, when it does not attempt to draw out more than there is available in the given situation and regard itself as the end rather than the means. Centuries ago Plato undertook to prove that the just ruler was 729 times happier than the unjust tryant. Whether his mathematical calculations were correct or not, it is true that the power group understanding its own limitations and its own intimate relation to the social groupings of its time is indefinitely stronger than the group that identifies its leaders with arbitrary authority, as the owners rather than the trustees of the community. The authority may continue but its morale will be weakened, and some other interest or idealism, some other formula, may more readily overthrow it, when the moment arrives.

But are there not situations in which the absoluteness of authority is so firmly set in law, custom, and symbolism that any form of resistance is practically impossible? Yes, when the social insight of the ruling group is so keen that it anticipates and renders nugatory or needless the opposition of those whose interests it interprets. But, even in the most absolute system, individual or group, there is constantly encountered a form of resistance which may arise either from the general morale which sags or from those who bore within the system while rendering apparent conformity. In such instances the individual salutes the system, but objects to the special methods of power practiced in the particular situation. He agrees with monarchy or democracy or communism or fascism, but he differs as to the expediency of the government's action in special cases. His motives cannot be doubted, and his criticism can with difficulty be repressed, at least within the inner circle where there must be preliminary disagreement, no matter how united the front in the end. From within, then, he may carry on resistance, the legality of which cannot be contested.

He may be discouraged, demoted, exiled, or perhaps imprisoned, but others will arise to carry on the same process of criticism of the government—leading, perhaps, to its overthrow. In its inner chamber power must listen to opposition, to divided counsels, to divergent plans, in peace as in war; and, while the particular decision may be final, the case may perhaps rise again and must once more be fought out within the circle, assuming that none of the dissent escapes the frail walls of the king's bedchamber.

Thus the power situation, invincible as it may seem, is, behind the scenes, full of divergence and perhaps disunity, as for that matter the mind of the individual tyrant may be, even when he seems to consult no one but himself. But, through the back door if not from the front, from above or below, some counselor appears and helps to turn the scales of judgment; or in effect may become the master in disguise—some Rasputin, some Madame Pompadour, some kitchen cabinet, from whence authority really flows in an underground stream.

Embedded in the poverty of power lies much of the liberty of the world, safe from the hand of the aggressor who would take it away. Rights may be defended by ideologies, by patterns of concrete interests, by institutional contrivances and procedures designed to hold back the arbitrary, but liberty is still more deeply intrenched. Naked hands and empty pockets may obstruct and antagonize the action of authority and with means can scarcely be successfully opposed without destroying the basis of human association itself. These forms of resistance are understood almost as well by the ignorant as by the learned—indeed, sometimes more perfectly—and their action may be spontaneous, unorganized, unled in emergencies.

The protective devices of the inferior in rank and status are, then, among the outstanding facts of the power world. These procedures may not find their way into books of law, but they are interwoven with strands of incredible tenacity into the ways of human life. This is the law of the weak against the law of the strong.

Chapter 7

The Survival of the Fittest

Some Techniques of Power

IF WE WISHED to give play to the imagination, we might ask, "What sort of a manual of power would the governors of the world prepare, if they were all assembled for such a purpose?" Would they merely agree to disagree? Or would they conclude that special situations were more important than any possible generalizations? Or would Stalin, and MacDonald, and Gandhi, and Herriot, and Hitler, and Roosevelt discover some inner groups of rules, maxims, principles which might be useful to know and follow?

Would they agree upon what constituted a great lawmaker or a "good" administrator, or a "good" judge, or a "good" leader, or a "good" general? Or whether this or that situation was well handled or badly handled? Would they find in the other's group types of personnel, of arrangements, of techniques which they would like to bring over into their own; or per contra mechanisms and devices in their own institutions and experience which they would think might advantageously be generalized? Or would they find their several situations so widely disparate that no common basis might be found? It is not to be assumed that all individual power holders must possess the same set of characteristics. Some are leaders; some are managers; some are adjudicators; some are warriors; and each class possesses a special set of qualifications somewhat different from each of the others. Political leadership is something different from management in the administrative sense of the term; and management is something quite different from the task of judicial analysis and declaration. In the power holder's group, however, all of these types will inevitably be found; and the group as a whole will unite and balance these characteristics in a system that will be known as the government, the responsible political agency through which a phase of the political will be administered.

And it is this group which might consult the maxims of a manual of power, with special reference to the more specific suggestions useful for their own more limited and special domains. Indeed one of the most serious difficulties may prove to be that of coordinating these special branches of governmental activity into a going political concern.

The means of preserving power have been considered in more than one treatise on government, although in more recent times these attempts have been relatively few. Conspicuous among these studies have been those of the Chinese, the Hindus, the Greeks, the *Prince* of Machiavelli, Montesquieu's *Spirit of the Laws,* a long series of mirrors of princes, running through centuries.

Assuming a personal government headed by a king, many of these discussions are filled with examination of the type of person or the set of qualities to be found in the position of authority. From this point of view the danger of governmental decline may be found in the failure to cultivate fully these indispensable skills, either in one individual or the group of individuals with whom authority rests.

In the Confucian system these qualities are set forth in great detail and their relation to special needs of the state examined fully,[1] while the outcome under such a system is described in glowing terms.

Confucius laid down the principles of "benevolent government," of personality, and the techniques important to political progress. The ten principles of political "development" he presents as follows:

1. Ching Tien, or distribution of social wealth.
2. Attention to technical invention.
3. Eugenics, meaning here the choice of mothers.
4. Benevolent government.
5. Criminal justice.
6. Li, which seems to mean a type of balance or moderation.
7. Music, including under that term art, poetry, rhythm, appreciation of beauty of nature, recreation.

[1] *Confucian Analects; The Great Learning; The Doctrine of The Mean.*

8. Religion, familial and divine.
9. Education.
10. Faith in progress.[2]

The Indian system presents an imposing catalogue of Hindu virtues as follows. The best qualities of the king are:

> Born of a high family, godly, possessed of valour, seeing through the medium of aged persons, virtuous, truthful, not of a contradictory nature, grateful, having large aims, highly enthusiastic, not addicted to procrastination, powerful to control his neighbouring kings, of resolute mind, having an assembly of ministers of no mean quality, and possessed of a taste for discipline—these are the qualities of an inviting nature.
>
> Inquiry, hearing, perception, retention in memory, reflection, deliberation, inference and steadfast adherence to conclusions are the qualities of the intellect.
>
> Valour, determination of purpose, quickness, and probity are the aspects of enthusiasm.
>
> Possessed of a sharp intellect, strong memory, and keen mind, energetic, powerful, trained in all kinds of arts, free from vice, capable of paying in the same coin by way of awarding punishments or rewards, possessed of dignity, capable of taking remedial measures against dangers, possessed of foresight, ready to avail himself of opportunities when afforded in respect of place, time, and manly efforts, clever enough to discern the causes necessitating the cessation of treaty or war with an enemy, or to lie in wait keeping treaties, obligations and pledges, or to avail himself of his enemy's weak points, making jokes with no loss of dignity or secrecy, never brow-beating and casting haughty and stern looks, free from passion, anger, greed, obstinacy, fickleness, haste and back-biting habits, talking to others with a smiling face, and observing customs as taught by aged persons—such is the nature of self-possession.[3]

Plato in his famous passage on the qualities of the guard-

[2] C. Hsü, *Political Philosophy of Confucianism.*
[3] Kautilya, *Arthásāstra,* p. 287.

ians of the law in the ideal state enumerated the sets of attributes which were essential for the philosopher kings of the coming political society.

> Then in our judgment the man whose natural gifts promise to make him a perfect guardian of the state will be philosophical, high spirited, swift-footed, and strong.[4]

> Then, as I said just now, we must inquire who are the best guardians of this inner conviction, that they must always do that which they think best for the state. We must watch them, I say, from their earliest childhood, giving them actions to perform in which people would be most likely to forget, or beguiled of such a belief, and then we must select those whose memory is tenacious, and who are proof against deceit, and exclude the rest. . . . We must also appoint them labors, and vexations, and contests, in which we watch them for the same symptoms of character. . . . And as a third kind of test, we must try them with witchcraft, and observe their behaviour; and, just as young horses are taken into the presence of noise and tumult, to see whether they are timid, so must we bring our men, while still young, into the midst of objects of terror, and presently transfer them to scenes of pleasure, trying them much more thoroughly than gold is tried in the fire, to find whether they shew themselves under all circumstances inaccessible to witchcraft, and seemly in their bearing, good guardians of themselves and of the music which they have been taught, approving themselves on every occasion true to the laws of rhythm and harmony, and acting in such a way as would render them most useful to themselves and the state. And whoever, from time to time, after being put to the proof, as a child, as a youth, and as a man, comes forth uninjured from the trials, must be appointed a ruler and guardian of the city and must receive honors in life and in death.[5]

Aristotle in his well-known discussion of revolutions in the

[4] Plato, *Republic*, Book 2, p. 376.
[5] Plato, *Republic*, Book 3, pp. 413–414.

Politics discussed the ways of preventing revolution both in general and in the various forms of states. These are not schematically presented but include such general precepts as guarding against the beginnings of change, the observation of proportionate equality, avoidance of giving anyone too many honors and of monopolizing honors, observing the "just mean" in all things, and education in the spirit of the government. In addition to these the Greek philosopher presented a series of special devices for the protection of particular forms of government, monarchy, tyranny, democracy, aristocracy, oligarchy.[6]

Machiavelli outlined the qualities useful for the Prince in a manner which aroused more controversy than any other treatise on a like subject. Along with this there may be placed the endless series of manuals for heirs apparent and for ruling monarchs—exhortations directed to the conscience of the king in the absence of any institutionalized form of more direct responsibility—mirrors of princes.

In a less personal manner, there has also been extended consideration of the best means of maintaining the position of power, either in general or in particular classes of cases.

The Machiavellian manual of power was in great part an adaptation of that section of Aristotle's study dealing with the means of preserving a tyranny, although the doctrine of Machiavelli might be applied to any state. In broadest form the Italian theory provided for the maintenance of authority by any means available, and that without regard to the restrictions of moral precepts. The end justifies the means is the short statement of this policy. That it is better to be feared than to be loved; that a prince is not bound by his promises; that injuries are to be committed all at once but the "Benefits should be distilled by drops, that the relish may be greater"; what sort of advisers to choose; whether it is better to have good qualities or merely to seem to have them: "Everybody sees how you appear," said Machiavelli, "but few know what in reality you are"; avoidance of becoming contemptible in the eyes of the subjects. Or again: "A prince is

[6] *Politics*, Book V.

contemptible when he is counted effeminate, light, inconstant, pusillanimous and irresolute," as over against magnanimity, courage, gravity, fortitude. The enumeration of methods of assassination, poisoning, cruelty of various forms as inevitable means of state support is carried forward in detail. These constitute the general framework of the scheme laid down by the Florentine philosopher as a basis of acquiring and holding political power.

Another basic effort to establish the methods of preserving power is that set up by Montesquieu in his *Spirit of the Laws*. The great principle emphasized by this philosopher was that of "relativity" among a variety of factors, environment, institutions, people, laws. This may be regarded as the main element in the perpetuation of government, namely the balance between the various social factors concerned in the composition of authority in a special situation. In addition to this, however, he presents a plan for preservation of several forms of government; "virtue" for the republic; "moderation" for the aristocracy; "honor" for the monarchy; "fear" for the despotism. The government will best be preserved by the maintenance of the special principle adapted to the particular type of rule, and the power will fall with the decline of its basic principle.

In the light of these discussions of the methods of preserving power, we may proceed to consider the essential elements in the maintenance of authority in the modern day.

Is there not a series of inner maxims of universal value to the holders of authority, the criteria by which the fitter may survive? Are there not precepts generally agreed upon or acted upon by the authoritarians, sage sayings that would be set down were they so inclined in their copy-books for the learners?

The power holder himself will probably deny that there are any inner principles, preferring to identify his personal success with his own personal traits, or even with some minor accident in his career which he may superstitiously regard as the cause of his success. He does not in fact always perceive the elements in the situation which have brought about his special advance, as a successful business man, poet, cardinal may reach out blindly for the underlying controls. He may find the solution in some fetish, some trifling incident, some foam which had little to do with the wave. The biographies of important political personages are full of eccentricities of this type, which obviously had little to do with the outcome.

The alternative is to follow through a series of power situations and endeavor to cull from them the tactics which seem to have been characteristic of the survivors, setting them over against the tactics of failure. There will be found difficulty in determining just what weight to allocate to the different factors in very intricate situations with many variables; and the outcome may readily be challenged. I do not profess to do more than set up a provisional list which others may improve with fuller data and more acute analysis. When other observations and hypotheses are set down, the accumulating material will be all the richer, and the opportunity for accurate generalization wider.

1. One of the first elements of survival is that of intimate knowledge of the social composition of authority in the given scene; its interests, groupings, and relations, the common understandings, ideologies of the moment, competing loyalties, significant personalities and their weight; the nature and use of social intelligence.

Is a ruler an encyclopedia then? No, but he is likely to be far better informed on the social basis of his authority than anyone else, or at least the knowledge lies within the special group in power. In many instances he rules because he knows the elements of a situation which the average man comprehends only vaguely. The personalia and the principia of the community are plainer to him than to his rivals or his subjects, though he may not catalogue these data. The boss knows his city; the dictator his country; the parliamentarian his electorate and his key men.

These facts must be ready for instantaneous action, as a baseball or tennis player moves almost automatically in accordance with a complicated pattern. The general in action, the parliamentarian, the orator cannot pause to study the general plan; he must know and use his knowledge in instant proceedings.

The power holder must know how to use the intelligence of the community; *i.e.*, the practical intelligence available for political control. Where did suggestions for new armament and strategy come from in the army? Or lawmaking or administration? History does not always record the influence of the silent figures who quietly went their way through the halls of state, busy with finance, administration, expertising as they went.

With the remarkable development of science and technology in our time, the manual of power may recognize the importance of expert information upon the basic problems of the state, upon the methods of administration, and upon the development of new policies and plans. Research and technology make deeper and deeper marks upon modern life, and the wise ruler does not permit himself to fall behind the advance of technical knowledge in its most modern form.

What is the relation of the power holder to the expert? Who has had the ear of power in historic times? The medicine man, the magician, the priest, the astrologer, the court fool, the elder statesman, and perhaps the expert in a special field. Broadly speaking the wisest kings and rulers were those who were advised by their wisest men. They did not govern without them, but found a place in their organization for the integration of special knowledge and skill. In the modern movement the benevolent despots were careful to provide for the organization of intelligence, as notably in Prussia and in France.

In the earlier times the government allied itself with magic, with religion, with art and culture, with such types of prudence and science as began to develop. Often to be sure there are strange minglings of brutality and violence with expert and technical ability, of intelligence and superstition, and these have obscured the relationship between rulers and formal intelligence. There are many examples of the superstitious suppression of intelligence by power groups, even in our own day. But the repression of intelligence is a process which requires intelligence itself in the long run, and thus the thing it is sought to banish may reappear even in the act of exile. The greater rulers, however, those whose names go down through history, have allied themselves with the technical ability of the society and have utilized it for the enrichment of their domains and the welfare of their community.[7]

In the earlier forms of political association, taboos and, later, magic supplemented the intelligence of the ruling group, and from time to time religion was intimately associated with both. Primitive governors were protected by forms of taboo which encircled them as effectively as a modern electric wire. A number of Maoris who lighted their pipes from the forbidden tinder box of their chief died of fright when they discovered what sacrilege they had committed.[8] In later periods this magic survived in the belief in the sacredness of the body of the king, in the efficacy of the king's touch in curing disease, and even yet lies at the center of the modern court ceremony, where knees still weaken in the great presence.

Philo Judaeus in Alexandria likened political life to evil magic, comparing the sophistry of politicians and statesmen to that of augurs, ventriloquists, and sorcerers, "men skillful in juggling and incantations and in tricks of all kinds, from whose treacherous art it is very difficult to escape."[9] Maimonides found a type of person in whom the rational faculty is imperfect and the imaginative preponderant, "Whence arises the sect of politicians, of legislators, of diviners, and of enchanters, of dreamers. . . ."[10]

Lawgivers derived their laws from some magic or supernatural source and rulers determined courses of action in

[7] Lynn Thorndike, *Magic and Experimental Science*, and Andrew White, *Warfare of Science and Religion*, contain rich material on this subject. Anthropological literature is full of illustrations of primitive practice.

[8] J. G. Frazer, *Taboo and the Perils of the Soul.*

[9] *De Somniis* II, 1.

[10] Lynn Thorndike, *Magic and Experimental Science*, vol. I, pp. 358–359. See G. Waudaeus, *The History of Magick*, Chap. III, to the effect that many eminent persons who have been accounted magicians were only politicians.

accordance with the verdict of auspices, oracles, and mystical persons of various types.

From early times the desire to obtain the fullest knowledge of the community has led to the development of elaborate methods of espionage and surveillance. These may supplement an intelligent knowledge of the social processes, but they are not a substitute for it; and if this is presumed there may be disaster. The Russian Czarism, for example, was indefatigable in the pursuit of secret-service methods, but far less intelligent in the comprehension of the social forces and their actual weight and momentum in the old Empire. The mysterious and exciting news brought in by spies will not take the place of penetrating intelligence regarding the nature of the political personalities and forces at work in the background of the governmental basis of the community; and may in fact distract attention from more important considerations.

The power holder is then likely to be a learned man, learned in the material with which he works, and learned also in the wisdom of action. He does not ignore and offend the key personalities; he does not run against the prejudices of special groups, if avoidable, and then as a matter of policy. He does not underestimate the possibility of combinations either friendly or unfriendly to his tenure. It is his special business to know the weight and direction of social forces, whether in group or personal form, in concrete profits or in abstract ideologies. The realist does not despise his enemies; or permit his hate to blind his eyes to activities.

It is important to observe, however, that there is a time factor in the knowledge useful for power purposes, and if this is absent the knowledge will have only an historical value, telling afterward what should have been done at a past moment. There must be swift fusion of knowledge with action in moments when the experience of years must be mobilized and hurled into action in a moment of decision; otherwise the hour slips by. "Time is of the essence of the contract" is an old phrase that is peculiarly applicable to the political world. There are tension moments which are imperative in their demands for action if a social equilibrium is to be preserved.

It is true that in all kinds of groups and in all sorts of processes there are occasions when prompt decision must be made and immediate action is imminent. The intricate power balance is such that many elements must be held in suspense, and the conjunction of factors must be seized while it is at hand; for otherwise the unusual moment may pass and may not return again for a long time. Politics is in a sense a balance of balances for the preservation of an equilibrium among them, a balance of groups of values, of personalia. It is not enough therefore to know perfectly the rules of the game, but it is imperative that they be automatically and promptly employed, since action is so essential a part of the whole process. The most striking of all cases of this sort is of course the military emergency, when prompt decision will determine the outcome of the battle and perhaps decide the fate of the nation itself. And complementary to this is the urgency of prompt decision in the negotiations ensuing when the hostilities have come to an end and the treaty is to be made. Or again in revolutionary moments there come occasions in which decision may determine the balance of power in the given political community, and when faltering and vacillation may be fatal to the régime in authority.

There are parliamentary moments of very great importance when questions must be answered and the arguments pro and con must be marshaled by the party leaders. On the skill with which this is accomplished the outcome of legislation may hang; or at any rate the effectiveness of it. There are crowd moments when orators and speakers must meet attacks, which if left unrefuted may inflict irreparable injury upon the cause of the group. True the broad bases of law and administration are not shaped in such manner, and indeed the difficulty may often be the precise opposite, namely a type of leisurely and indolent avoidance of decision for long periods of time, grown into bureaucratic custom and sanctioned under the high name of authority.

But one of the problems of the ruling group is to establish a balance between the need for deliberation on the one hand and the necessities of quick action on the other in such a manner as to ensure a steadily going concern. Much of the work of political leaders has gone astray through failure to function at this very point of balance between preparation and action, or violent oscillation between them, without sufficient concert of factors. This may seem like a reflection which might be made upon any phase of human life and especially of any associated life, but it is an especially notable aspect of political life because of the unusual conjunction of elements which are held in solution in the political balance of factors and because of their volatility in many cases.

And this is one of the paragraphs in the manual of the power groups, not to be omitted from the calculations of the power avid.

We may conclude then that one of the first commandments for the governor is to know his community, its personalities, its groups, and their interests, ideologies, values, and their relative weights in terms of political possibilities; and to know how to utilize the most advanced social and political intelligence and techniques of his time and cultural level.

2. Another skill of the power group is the accurate distribution of political rewards and preferments in accordance with the understanding of the social background of power, paying each group and person in proportion to its services and in the currency preferred, since there are many forms of legal tender in the world of power. The problem of the relative valuation of services is one of the unsolved problems of the economic world where not even the price system has been able to give the answer; but it is also a problem of government, although the commodities are not so readily measurable or prices so clearly marked. What is one group worth as against another in the family of power; or what is one person worth as against another in the market place of power?

Personal patronage and substantial interest satisfactions of a very material nature are of course the perquisites of the group in power, and they will be allocated and distributed in such a fashion as to combine the sometimes difficult factors of allegiance and efficiency. The rulers will attach to themselves a considerable circle of those who are employed in the service of the state or obtain important concessions or are the beneficiaries of significant policies of the commonwealth. In all systems these persons and the groups they represent, informally, constitute a center of gravity for authority, and the wisdom with which such a following is organized is an important test of the viability of the particular authority.

In all governmental systems there are arrangements of various sorts for the recognition of special forms of merit, orders of distinction which may be conferred upon citizens of the community, who for one reason or another are deemed worthy of being singled out. The perquisites and emoluments of substantial patronage may be supplemented by titles and decorations which, discreetly distributed, raise the morale of various individuals and groups in the society.

In hereditary systems these distinctions are of course passed down through the hereditary line of descent, although the boundaries of biology may be enlarged from time to time by royal decree of ennoblement. But the danger in this case is that the born élite may not correspond with the natural holders of power attributes and qualities, and that consequently discontent and sedition in the end may arise.

There is nothing to prevent, however, the organization of distinctions in a democratic or nonhereditary society, given the will and the ingenuity to do so.[11] The Legion of Honor in France is a striking example of the creation *de novo* of such an order of importance, designed to take the place of the distinctions developed under the régime of the nobility. In more recent times the Soviet rulers have undertaken the development of the Order of Lenin and other like titles of recognition in the field of proletarianism.

It is not only in the form of titles that distinctions may be found and distributed; for there are innumerable types of recognition of a less formal nature that may be utilized for the purpose of according some form of governmental honor to a wide variety of members of the community. Chairmanships, presidencies, secretariats, memberships on innumerable boards and commissions where the position is honorific rather

[11] Cf. Montesquieu, *The Spirit of the Laws,* on the nature and importance of "distinctions" in all hereditary groupings.

than technical; these are legion, and the distributive value of them is an important factor in the organization of authority, either on the part of the immediate holder of the power or of the system itself in the broader sense of the term. They serve as an important supplement to patronage of a more material character, to special interests, to ideologies, emotionalisms, all of which have their limitations, and none of which possess that flattering function of the special and personal recognition *causa honoris* so to speak, which may play so large a part in the pleasant adjustment of human relations and in the closer organization of authority.

On the other hand, these distributions of perquisites and emoluments are for the maladroit a source of worry and weakness, containing vast possibilities of dissatisfaction and discontent among the persons favored or omitted from the roll of honor. Incomprehensible errors may be made with ensuing consequences of the most unfortunate nature. These are not the cause of revolutions to be sure but the dry material which may be inflamed by the spark of discontent at the appropriate moment. But in any case they are not to be omitted from the manual of power.

These are often difficult decisions to be made. Some of these cases may be standardized, as in the form of the civil service or the courts of professional types. But many of the knots must be untied by political valuation, balancing legislation, taxes, tariffs, credits, patronage, concessions of a hundred sorts against each other, in terms of a political pattern along with personalities and groups. It may be supposed that these compromises and concessions are peculiar to parliamentary government, but in fact the identical situation is observed in any form of government, whether of one, of many, or of few. The scene may not be a parliamentary hall or a popular forum, but it will be the same play on a smaller stage and perhaps with fewer actors. The *aristoi* will divide into factions, the king's mind will have several compartments not sealed against each other, and his anteroom may be more confused than the noisiest parliament ever assembled. Whispering will take the place of shouting perhaps, but a world of whispers may be as noisy as one of resonant oratory.

Contrary to a common view, the politics of absolutism is as complex as that of any other form, indeed one might say even more so, since the arbitrary will of an exalted ass may enter into and upset the calculations at a vital moment. Even the simplicity of individual concentration of power does not change the complex social forces with which he must deal and the wide variety of their patterns.

Given the richest array of personal patronage and heaping granaries of substantial privilege, all at his disposal, the power bearer who is inexpert may readily find all his favors distributed, and yet the resulting combination of forces very weak. The key persons will have been overlooked or misplaced or underplaced; the key groups will have been, or enough of them, dissatisfied with their allotment; and the family of power, or too many of its members, will be sullen. As a fool with a fortune to invest will soon find himself bankrupt or loaded with unproductive investments, so the governor may find himself with all his credits out and little coming in. His enemies will watch the disintegration of his prestige with ill-concealed joy, if concealed at all; for they will instantly begin the chorus of discontent, and help to swell it louder and louder, if they can.

There will never be enough loaves and fishes to satisfy all those with power hunger and privilege hunger, and the task must always be that of performing a miracle, or somehow without a miracle satisfying enough to prevent a general rebellion of those who are left outside. But of course the dealer may trade on expectancies and recollections as well as present realization, and thus expand his political credit.

What is this shrewdness or craftiness in distribution of recognitions and rewards which so often characterizes the skillful ruler? Is it possible to analyze it more nearly? From one point of view it is not unlike the skill of the trader, who knows how to buy low and sell high and maintain the continuity of commercial intercourse. In politics especially the transaction may be well oiled over with personality and prestige. One politician's "no" may be as good as another's "yes," and his "yes" gracious and winning; the half must pass for the whole sometimes, and still be legal tender. In some situations, and judgments may differ as to how many, the kind word and the pleasant smile, the majestic and gracious manner may answer the human purpose as well as the delivery of the coin, within certain limits, that is.

The "shrewdness" lies partly (1) in the keener knowledge of the materials, partly (2) in the quicker reaction time in bargaining, partly (3) in the superior *empressement* of the accomplished trader in things political. A good horse trader knows horses. Among skilled diplomats the "fast thinker" in a bargain situation, and there are many, will survive as against the duller and slower in perception and suggestion. But this is not the only type of political situation and there are others in which the tempo is far slower, and longer and more solid calculation may be even more effective.

Nor can it be forgotten that there are also traders among other members of the social groupings. The church has her diplomats by no means without experience and ability; business has produced great bargainers of whom a professional member of the power group would say they might have made great statesmen; labor is not without its traders in these later days who understand the art of concession as well as any others. And they are likewise fully informed regarding the stuff with which they deal. The battle is waged not with amateurs alone but with a great array of competing ability, equally bent upon the attainment of its goal, and equally capable of combination within or without the power group. It is only in the generality of information and in superior experience with a wide variety of competing loyalties that the political diplomats may have an advantage, if any.

There is also the value of the *pis aller* for the politician; if nothing can be done in the way of compromise, well what then? If there can be no agreement then the *status quo* continues and the power holder goes on, for a government must be had whether the special new demands of all the classes may be met or no. He may live with a *status* only, whether it be *quo* or *ante*. If he cannot make a combination of his own, he may survive by preventing a combination against him, for in that case the rule continues for the time.

It is in this inner field of balance and bargain that the

governmental group not only displays rare skill from time to time, but also renders an important social service. Yet dangers lurk here. One is that habituation to balance and compromise may produce a type of mind or tactics which will be satisfied to remain within the circle of the diplomatic procedure; and fail to take cognizance of the outer world where other forces may be gathering, of a type likely to overturn the table even, and set up another of its own. The limits of verbal compromise or round the table infighting are set by the narrow frame of reference in which the whole situation exists, and the bargainer may lose sight of the larger adjustment of the less visibly represented factors in the power organization of the community or of the resources of those who may project a wide appeal outside. And the will to power of the opponent may count upon tactics of compromise, having in mind further action, if necessary, on the outside.

The ruler may conclude that politics is a game of chess, when it may in fact contain an element of poker. Or he may assume an orderly game of poker and discover that his rival carries a gun and is likely to "draw" on him. What if the table on which the game is played is rudely kicked over, as sometimes happens, and shooting begins? In short the compromiser may fail to function as a fighter in a world where compromise will not always solve the equation. Appeals to the electorate, to public opinion, to the sword may always be made.

The rating of social and political values is then one of the tasks of the power group not wholly unlike the intervaluation of services in the economic world. The trader in political commodities may be compared with the trader in economic goods. Upon his perception, his shrewdness, and skill, his way of "carrying off" the affair, will depend much of his success. Armies and gold and ideologies and utopias, and personalities and groups and interests and traditions, and all the other complex factors in a political situation are the material with which he must deal and show himself a master.

3. A common principle of the manual of power is that of moderation. This was clearly expressed by Confucius, by Aristotle, and again by Bagehot. The great Grecian developed

an entire philosophy both of ethics and of politics based upon the "golden mean" as the essential principle in both.[12] Bagehot presented as the characteristic quality of British politics what he termed "an illogical moderation." This principle is as valid today as it ever was, and I can merely elaborate somewhat at this point what has already been said long ago, but sometimes forgotten.

The wise ruler does not press too far his principle, his policy, or his personal or tactical advantage. This is perhaps the greatest temptation of any successful individual or group come into authority. Like intoxication power destroys the usual inhibitions of the individual, and at the very moment when he should hold back, the gates are thrown wider open. Are we not victorious; and is not the world at our feet, or at least our dearest enemy, personal, class, national? Vengeance and vindictiveness are in the air in these wild moments when pride and power take charge. But out of these events may come the insult or the atrocity which festers for long periods in the memory of those upon whom the blow fell. There may spring up that feudism in which the opponents of authority may find refuge.

Prudence provides that there be left a margin or factor of safety, between what might conceivably be done and what might reasonably be done. Not every possible element of power is exhausted, except in the great tension moments when the last reserves are thrown into the breach in some desperate effort to save the day. But on other occasions too high a price may be paid for the achievement of an objective, too great a loss may be incurred, and some other way may be found. Not all the patronage need be taken; nor all the honor, perquisites, and emoluments; not all the extremities to which the law or its enforcement might go are to be employed. Leave something to be lost, it might be said. Otherwise the "outs" may criticise the fairness of the proceeding, the emotional may rage against it, sounding new depths of action. Despair may nerve the outcast to make the last desperate throw, since he has now nothing to lose. Evictions,

[12] In turn an adaptation of Plato's doctrine of harmony.

prisons, exiles, martyrdoms, may kindle fires in the hearts of those who deem themselves oppressed, fires hard to reach and smother as they smoulder deep down in the emotions.

Hate is one of the most powerful driving forces in human nature and especially in government. Hence every effort is made to prevent the formation of its dark centers of infection in the body politic with all the evils and dangers that may result. It is precisely at this point that the function of moderation is most evident. Rivalry of equals or superiors may be avoided and even under favorable circumstances be turned into alliance and mutual advantage. The jealous hatred of the unequal or the slightly inferior is the most difficult of all to avoid, and likewise the most dangerous in its fuller development. Moderation may avoid the dark bile of hate, and turn some forms of constraint into tolerance or even combination. The problem involves perhaps priorities of position or claim, and here the way is never clear, although it may be helped by good will and intelligent invention of alternatives, or sometimes by good-natured muddling of the situation.

Absorption rather than exclusion may be the policy of the power holder who seeks to strengthen his hold upon authority. He may draw in his foes rather than drive them out. He may make them a part of his organization, rather than an irreconcilable group preparing sedition from outside. To be sure there must be moments of righteous indignation and unarguable conviction in a group as in an individual. But not too many.

The expanding political powers of which Rome and Britain may be taken as illustration adopted a policy of absorbing their enemies within their own ranks, as people after people were given recognition in the larger empire to which they had succumbed. The same policy has been pursued by other successfully growing states, uninterested in setting up institutionalized hatreds against them.

But is revolution a moment for mildness and moderation or for ruthlessness and irreconcilability? In a revolutionary movement the danger lies in impatience and the neurotic demand for instant results in fields where crops must be grown and not merely willed. The firebrand finds his easiest release in the denunciation of all others less immediate and direct than himself, for in truth they interfere with his personal program. But after the revolution is achieved the clamor for vengeance and proscription rises loudest and that in the most intoxicating moment of success. The old prisons are opened but they must be filled with new victims of the state. Punishment must be meted out to those who resisted or came into the parade only tardily and reluctantly. Reprisals and revenge must be satisfied perhaps in an orgy of blood and vindictiveness. But when once revolution has taken possession of the halls of state and raised its own flag and commands its own army, then the left wing is almost invariably slowly elbowed back to a position where it is impossible to dictate the policy of moderation.[13]

But after all, it may be said, is so vague a principle as moderation valuable as a rule of conduct, or is it rather not in the nature of a counsel of perfection? Who knows what moderation is? In definition moderation may be argued at great length, but the practice of moderation is readily discovered in a political community. Those who are moderate in temperament recognize and approve it; and others recognize and perhaps admire or hate it, but there is no great practical difficulty in discovering the presence or the absence of a reasonable moderation among the power group of a country or in the character of a man. A manual of power could not in the nature of the case provide a complete set of rules, but rather the broad generalizations or attitudes that might characterize conduct, the type of conduct pattern to be admired and adopted in a great variety of situations which cannot possibly be described in advance.

Even in military moments of direct personal combat, blind hate is inferior to balanced intelligence in the struggle on which life or death may hang. The fighter does not lose his temper; he controls it to direct his force. It is an old trick of the ring, of the court room, of the parliamentary conflict, of

[13] Cf. L. Trotzky, *History of the Russian Revolution,* which in no sense confirms the policy of the continuance of revolutionary leftism; also Emma Goldman, *Living My Life,* the experience of the anarchists in Soviet Russia.

the committee room or conference, to irritate an opponent to a point where his rage inhibits intelligent action. Righteous indignation is harnessed to moderation when most successful. Finally, moderation is not an evidence of weakness or mildness but of strength. It is not to be confused with mildness or softness of a gentle nature that knows nothing of storm and passion. Moderation is in the nature of a balance between opposing elements, perhaps of great force, of attractions and aversions, which finally meet in an equilibrium, avoiding the extremes.

4. Avoidance of congestion of authority—the zoning of power. One of the paragraphs in a power manual might well be directed toward the dangers of overconcentration of authority in a single individual or organ. A distinction must be drawn here between structural or legal concentration of responsibility and legality, and the actual consolidation of working powers, which is quite another matter. The danger lies in the latter, in the possibility that the congestion in the power center becomes so great that authority fails to function effectively.

The intoxicating influence of power, however, is dangerous to its holder. Power may breed the desire for yet more power. This may be due partly to the sheer lust for personal aggrandizement of the power holders, the expansive impulse of individuals who reach out greedily for more and more worlds to conquer—raw will to power. Or it may arise from the very information and intelligence of power in a given situation. I have the superior knowledge of facts and forces, says the ruler, more experience than any other. I can solve this problem better than anyone else. And indeed this may be literally true in a given case. Hence the power holder will not abdicate to any other. But in the end the overcentralized system kills itself, crushed down by the impossible burdens it has tried to carry. All its good intentions will not avert catastrophe.

The experienced holder of power understands how to delegate and supervise, without abdication on the one side or undue assumption of function on the other. This is the *pons asinorum* of rulers. The inexperienced attempts to hold every element of authority in his own grasp, fears to trust any subordinate, destroys the spirit of responsibility through his organization, and ends by abdication, formal or informal. This is as true of an individual as it is of a class, and equally true of a national organization as against a local one. Overcentralism has been the cause of the overthrow of many an individual and government, by concentration against it of all the disaffected elements of excluded authority. The circumference is always against the center, even when there is no good functional reason why it should be; and when there is really sufficient cause the situation becomes most serious. In a period of specialization of activity and of specialization even in the art of management this tends to become increasingly true, and to place all the greater obligation upon the holder of authority to adjust himself to the changing conditions.

How to find a field for the periphery of power:—for personalism, for the individual, in the large-scale systems of modern power, whether political or industrial, is one of the outstanding questions of our day and all days and has caused innumerable controversies of the most serious description. The avoidance of excessive personal centralization is a question constantly confronting the holders of power, and is not unrelated to the larger territorial question which has been raised in countless forms in almost every state. Centralization of responsibility and power in the last analysis may be readily distinguished from personal reluctance to delegate or deputize authority within the bounds of any system, local or national. In political leadership, where constitutional and juristic forms have less ready application, the type of control is determined by the attitude of the power bearers and may be broad or narrow, jealously personal or generously inclusive of a considerable number of allies.

The zoning of power is then one of the major problems of government and administration, from the point of view of territorial, group, and personal adjustments. It involves the maintenance of an important equilibrium in a vital world of struggling forces, and it is not contained wholly in laws, rules, or decisions. These may provide for the balance but fail to secure it; or they may provide against it, and yet the balance may emerge by virtue of the skillful adjustment of the holder of power at a given time.

The special subtlety of the problem lies in the delicate and perhaps confusing interplay between juristic absoluteness and practical concentration of authority. There may be juristic completeness of centralization and practical flexibility in adjustment; or there may be elaborate juristic division and distribution of power and practical concentration of the most despotic sort.

Trust in a considerable group of men is a condition of success in most enterprises, and nowhere is this more evident than in the field of governmental power, where so many of the rewards are in terms of prestige, and relatively so little in profits. This is one of the points where the practiced hand of experience and assurance makes itself most effectively felt.

5. Planning and leadership. The manual of power might contain paragraphs regarding the importance of some obvious leadership on the part of the rulers, some program of activity, some evidence of inventiveness in the general interest. Power cannot well be personal, even if incarnated in a specific person, but must be generalized as authority in trust for others. Even if it is my government, or my patrimony, or my army, in legal title, there must be an element of trusteeship in it, a recognition of the importance and value of the interests held in trust. "Ich bin der erste Diener meines Staates," was the utterance of one endowed with despotic power, but disposed to emphasize the functional relation of his authority. The question of the type of responsibility of the guardian to the ward was quite another matter, and the institutionalization of responsibility was resisted by the power holders, partly for personal reasons of opposition to a check, but also for fear of interference with the large purposes of the state. The responsibility most sought is that to God or one's own good nature, and not to a legal mechanism of any sort, except perhaps as a camouflage for uninterrupted control.

But the recognition of trusteeship is another thing, and the skilled ruler emphasizes and reiterates his deep sense of responsibility for the general welfare of the people he serves, and frames himself in this large scheme of values of which he is the champion. The benefits of the power system are constantly kept before the eye of the community, in terms generally understood and approved when understood.

This may be done in terms of substantial interests, economic or otherwise, in terms of ideologies, social and political, in terms of symbolisms and ceremonies emphasizing the sense of participation in the government and proprietorship in the nation. The various classes and groups discover distinct benefits from a form of rule, the ideologies fit in with the run of advantage, and the symbolisms cover all this with artistry and emotional satisfaction.

In government as in industry it is important to have not only production, but also salesmanship, for the goods are useless unless they are known to be good and there is an effective demand for them. The general advantages of government, the specific benefits derived from it, and the special relation of the existing personnel of rulers must all be made clear to the community by an unending process of adult education, which will run like a red thread through the ways of life. This may be termed showmanship, as an adjunct to statesmanship or even in lieu of it. A cynic might say it is more important to appear to serve the people than actually to do so, but in the long run it may prove difficult to avoid an accounting to those whose interests are presumably served, and the reckoning may be all the more severe if it is not accurate. However it must be conceded that from the short-time point of view, it is as useful to appear as to be serving in actuality, and some new form of advertising may take the place of the old and forgotten. At this point the tempo of change is important to know, for this may weaken the force of memory and quicken the spirit of invention.

But it may be said that, after all, the pretensions of the ruler have historically been merely the screen of an exploiting class, which has not genuinely served the interests of the whole community upon which it relied for support but which it in fact officially robbed. In very many instances it was unquestionably true that professions of love were cloaks of lust. Wave upon wave of invaders has swept over weaker peoples and compelled them to submission by force temporarily and perhaps later by absorption or adoption, or may have held them as slaves, helots, serfs, *Untermenschen* in one form or another. This may be seen in the case of racial groups, of religious groups in less degree, of agrarian classes, and of industrial classes in the ascendancy. In many instances, however, the power group still proclaimed its rule as useful for the entire community, the under as well as the upper class, and attempted programs of reconciliation and advantage as to time and system, first of all for individuals who might be drawn into the ruling group, and then for the mass of the outsiders. Considerations of military necessity would inspire this policy under some conditions, of industrial productivity in others, of general morale and convenience in still others.

These considerations linger even in the case of castes,[14] which have played so large a part in the world's experience, and of slavery, which has likewise long been characteristic of power relations, even in cases where the slaves were taken from an equal or even superior culture, as in Greece and Rome. It was from the Grecian bastards that there emerged the world's first great philosophy of freedom, born of the outlawry of the expatriate. Even here an effort is made to instill the idea of benevolent paternalism of the master over the slave, by processes of emancipation and improvement of status, and recognition of the more capable among the under group to hold back the tide of hate, without too much reliance upon the force of fear.

One may well ask, How is a man ever persuaded that he is justly a slave? I shall not enter here into the historic rationalizations of this process. Some perhaps believe; some are not reflecting; and some are wise but helpless; and perhaps their very reflectiveness has made them soft. Implicit obedience in a hierarchy of social orders may be ingrained into human nature so deeply that it becomes an automatic process, and in fact one which the participant may even enjoy. The slave of the great one may lord it over the slave of the lesser one, the higher slave over the lower, satisfying his sense of com-

[14] C. Bougle, *Essais sur le régime des castes.*

mand if any. There may arise a government within the world of slaves as among the pariahs, and within this the old relations may be reestablished for some of the stronger leaders of the undergroup. But slavery has been abolished in most Western states for many generations, and where it still prevails perhaps in modified form the responsibility of those who are in control is duly recognized; and the care of their bodies, minds and souls, together with the promotion of their ultimate economic interests is fully set forth, in words at least and as part of the power program.

In democratic countries the need of recognition of governmental trusteeship is expressed in institutional form; in political theory; and in the tactics and professions of the leaders of the movements. However loosely the *persona* may fit, it is always assumed, and never cast aside. And indeed the wiser rule, following the manual of power, seeks in truth to assume a functional leadership in the community within the field by general consent accorded to the governing power group. The limits of the program are not so much trickery and hypocrisy as ignorance of what might most advantageously be done, without of course interfering with the basis of the power group, thus recognizing the intimate relationship between personal power and functional power.

In other systems the idea of trusteeship of the government for the people is emphasized in differing manners. The lords proclaim their leadership of the mass and their ability to interpret mass desire and interest more accurately than is done through the electoral process. They insist upon their basic representation of massism and adherence to the mass will and interest.

It is commonly found useful, then, for the power group to make an impression of community service rather than personal aggrandizement, of broad social utility rather than greed and raw power hunger. Whether all power holders have in fact actually been benefactors of their communities may well be disputed by an outside and objective observer, but the profession of such benefaction and the persuasion of important elements in the community that this is so have been significant factors in the maintenance of authority. For this purpose attitudes, ceremonies, ideologies, prejudices, emotions, misrepresentations, and false persuasion, all have their place in the picture, as it appears in a given political society. That monstrous injustice and vast frauds may have been perpetrated under such pretences is well understood, but from the point of view of an analysis of the elements of power, the basic situation remains unchanged.

6. The balance between justice and order. Two great pillars of the state are justice and order—basic purposes of the political association. At a given time one or the other may seem to be important, but by and large both are indispensable to the operation of the community.

The state must maintain a system of order, a framework within which the other members of the family of power may carry on their activities without too great or frequent interruption. The ruler or rulers who are not able to bring this about will find their power slipping away, for they are working outside their foundation principle. It is this broad guaranty or assurance upon which the generality of the community or the effective members of it (from the point of view of power reckoning) rely; and if this is not produced they have no abiding interest in the thing that miscalls itself a government. They will turn elsewhere for the security they seek. Or they will help to break the situation avowedly into what it is—a state of civil or other war. The difficulties of maintaining such a balance under some situation are obviously great, but this is a function of the state which cannot fail; and the government must find the ways and means of compassing it.

It is just at this point that the qualities of power will assert themselves and deal effectively with tough situations, insoluble though they appear to be to the inexpert, with problems in conciliation, diplomacy, administration, persuasion, intimidation, or other agencies available in a given milieu.

But the other element in the balance of power which is no less indispensable is that of justice. For power without justice rests upon an uncertain basis, and its days are numbered. If we ask what is this justice, the answer is not ready;

but the sense of justice in the community is easy to find. It is only necessary to outrage or violate it, and the intangible becomes real, the indefinable evident and effective in terms of authority and of morale.

Justice is the great popular support of any political group, and without it the association is weakened alike in peace and in war. The feeling of justice, it is true, may be deviously derived; as from some divinity, some type of credenda of dubious origin and value; some ideology transparent to all except those who hold it. But this is immaterial from the point of view of power, since the important consideration is the feeling that justice in general prevails.

It is easy for the authoritarian to regard order as more important than justice, especially as he looks at a short time and an immediate situation confronting him; but if he looks forward the significance of the establishment of a feeling of justice throughout the community will become larger and larger. It is to be observed that two of the greatest of governing groups, the Romans and the British, both were able to combine for a time these two factors in their government. Roman and British order, Roman and British justice, were widely celebrated.

Order makes possible an integration of external behavior in patterns that may be counted upon; and justice makes possible or facilitates an inner integration of the personality in terms of adjustment of the individual to the group in which he lives. They both presuppose adaptation, adjustment, management, balance of various factors otherwise engaged in forms of struggle that make difficult the conduct of affairs alike in the world of the material and the ideal. And the balance of the two, again, is a double balance.

The manual of power will therefore contain an admonition to watch constantly the gauges recording the pressure of these factors so full of meaning for the state. They are diagnostic symptoms as important for power as pulse and respiration for the physician dealing with the human organism, although by no means so easily and accurately read. Yet there are indicia by which the power group with social insight may learn the condition of these basic factors in the political association with reasonable enough precision to facilitate the necessary adjustments in tensions and torsions.

In any consideration of the nature of political power, various questions inevitably arise—what is the attitude of the governors toward morality, and toward the use of violence? Are immorality and force a part of the weapons of authority, and under what circumstances may they be most effectively employed?

Is the ruler wisely limited by moral considerations? The well-known treatise of Machiavelli has presented the doctrine of the liberty of the ruler from the canons of the *petite morale*, and this doctrine has been followed in practice in many instances by individuals and nations.[15] If the life of the state or the ruler is at stake, should he be bound by his agreements or the common consensus of moral opinion, if such exists?

A part of the difficulty with this historic and much-disputed question lies in the meaning of the word morality, and not merely in the verbalism itself, but in the broader understanding of the concept morality and of its implications. Morality in the sense of social morality is a body of practices and customs which have become behavior patterns in a particular group, and which are enforced by various sanctions of custom, chief but not alone among which is the loss of prestige, the lowering in the scale of social approbation, which individuals reckon among their assets. Morality in a socialized frame signifies that the conduct impinging on the welfare of the group is a signal for loss of esteem, for an unfavorable judgment. In this sense no ruler can be continually immoral or typically immoral, for this would involve antisocial tendencies incompatible with the exercise of the social trusteeship which he professes. As to an exceptional violation, the power holders are in the same situation as other individuals outside their circle, namely that of license for occasional violations of a social code, but not for general emancipation from it,

[15] Cf. F. Meinecke, *Die Idee der Staatsräson in der Neueren Geschichte*, for the best summary; also Friederich von Wieser, *Das Gesetz der Macht*.

except on penalty of outlawry. One who rules in terms of common welfare cannot claim immunity from the basic principles upon which that welfare presumably rests; he violates the very understanding upon which his authority is based.

There may be situations, however, where there are competing moralities, that of religion, that of race, that of class, and any one of these the ruler may defy if it draws him out of the line of his general pattern of action. He may go against the moral interpretation of the church, if that leaves an interpretation in terms of the community; he may defy the racial charge of immorality under like conditions; he may defy the bourgeois or the proletarian canons, if that again fits in with another scheme of social responsibility. But he does not defy all the ethics of all the members of the family of power, of all groups and classes alike; or the inner circle of maxims that lies within them all.

The power holders may in fact more safely violate the morality of their own political group than that of others, on the ground that they presumably understand better the interpretation of their own subject. Thus it might be possible to violate a constitutional or other restriction and make the impression prevail that this was a legitimate interpretation of perhaps a dubious sentence; more easy than to break the code of the church which is subject to another authentic and professional interpretation, or that of the racial, business, or working-class world. In view of the political function of group and personal adjustment, a wide range may be given the governing group in shading of statement and promise to various competing elements, providing this is not too obviously done. It may be recognized as a form of sleight of hand, which is understood to be some form of deception, but which the eye cannot follow. We know the politician cannot perform miracles, but we may be amused at the magical skill with which he may appear to do so, drawing, let us say, coins from every point his fingers touch, or cutting in two the living woman who is immediately made one again.

In international relations the situation is much more difficult, chiefly because of the incipient quality of the morality of the world order. In war relations the lie becomes the rule, and spy may readily become a martyr, celebrated because of his untruthful avocation, although even in war there lies a realm, an inner realm where good faith prevails, as with the white flag of truce and the red cross of mercy.

In world relations a code is slowly developing, but in the absence of a jural order, thoroughly established, or a firm and general understanding, there is a far wider opportunity for the violation of rules accepted by many. The governor who does so may lose no prestige among his *entourage*, but on the contrary be acclaimed as a great statesman, if he succeeds in his enterprise. There is a double standard of world morality, and a policy of ruthlessness may perhaps steer a way between them, but the good will of the world has become an important economic and military asset and carries with it prestige value not only abroad but at home. This must be balanced against the temporary advantage of defiance of international rules of behavior, even in a life and death struggle. Since the adoption of the agreement regarding the outlawry of war, the practical application of which is of course still undetermined, the course of the power group, advancing over the overthrow of morality, has been made all the more difficult. Good faith in short begins to have a more realistic basis than in the preinternational-law period.

In sum we may say that the ruler group is more closely bound by the considerations of morality than any other, with the exception of the church, if we interpret morality in terms of social forces. Sharp turns may be and have been made by those with power hunger highly developed. Deep insights into emerging moralities may enable other rulers to combat an old while championing a new morality; but all these moves are made at the risk of the entrepreneur, and their only justification is success in terms of some group profiting by the adventure. Broadly speaking, the common understandings bind political power perhaps more closely than any other, for these are the bases upon which morale and discipline rest; and they cannot be destroyed without removing the base upon which the whole situation itself rests.

There still remains, however, the Machiavellian thesis that

the ruler may appear to be moral but in fact profits by breaches of the professed code, especially in the case of religious attitudes. This is always possible, but it represents a difficult juggling with the elements of power, and if it fails the end is disastrous. There is no denying the possibility, however, and the actuality in many historic instances which come to mind. Political and other fortunes have been built upon a breach of faith, upon a sudden coup, which resulted in a triumph, capitalized and institutionalized.

In reality the ruler's relation to political morality is little different from his relation to social morality. Theoretically an absolute ruler can do anything; take what he will, destroy whom he will; pursue his absolute pleasure; crush, castrate, torture, kill; but in practice he cannot take very much, or imprison very many, or destroy many of his enemies; for this will precipitate his downfall. He has a margin of free will, but not after all a wide one, and always narrower than it seems. Omnipotence is one of the recurring illusions of authority. In like manner the power hungry may violate individual canons of the code of ethics from time to time and apparently with unlimited license. But not too many, or too often; for otherwise he rouses against him the very social elements from which his authority is woven. If he deceives everyone, he is no longer a good deceiver; if he breaks all of his promises, no one will accept his word in consideration of anything; at best he can claim only an occasional license which does not carry him too far away from the circle of social custom, given the time and place.

Another question relates to the use of force and violence. To what extent does the manual of power recommend the employment of these factors in the establishment and perpetuation of authority? Or is this so general a question that no answer is of any special value in any particular situation? Clearly there are so many different types of situations and of violence that no counsel can dictate yes or no in every instance. But there may be general attitudes and tactics of value developed.

The army and the police are temptations to the exercise of authority in its crassest form, for the results seem so indisputably immediate, direct, and incontestable. The crowd is dispersed, the recalcitrant is carried away shouting perhaps and protesting, but firmly held. The prison silences his voice or perhaps the firing squad. A softer course may increase the discontent, it is said; the little flame becomes the great fire, if it is not quickly quenched.

The sword is the symbol of authority, the sign of the short way to rule. And many rulers counsel its ready and free employment. Yet force may be regarded not as the highest expression of authority but its supreme confession of failure in modern times. It is not so much the brutality of force that makes it incompatible with modern civilization as its asininity, its inadequacy to accomplish its purposes within the pattern of the modern world and its ways of living and its devices for control.

Or from another point of view, violence is the appeal to the lower level of human and social control as compared with the higher; the appeal to high explosives which are the device of modern chemistry instead of the remolding influences of the modern social scientist which are almost as important now and destined in the future to be still more so than at present. Psychologically the sword is not in our day the symbol of intelligence but of impatience, of the killing impulse of hate thwarted in its appeal to reason and unable to await the outcome of more subtle and less brutal methods.

Even at the moment when outbursts of violence are most common and at the time when the revival of force seems most generally imminent throughout the world, as between nations and as between classes, violence sickens. The processes of social technique and control, coincident with the advances in modern intelligence and science, begin to make their way.

Brutality will not cease merely because of the physical pain it causes or because of the deaths it causes, but because of its disutility and the substitution of more effective measures based now upon modern techniques of social and political control, the substitution of education, organization, adjudication, in lieu of the arbitrament of arms.

In a world dotted by prisons and heavy with armament this may seem a preposterous conclusion, likely to be drowned at any moment in the roar of artillery arising from some new struggle for world supremacy. But to those who penetrate beneath the surface into the harder realities of social evolution, the conclusion is inevitable. The present day idealists are those who dream of a return to the golden age of violence, the doom of which has been struck by modern civilization. The realists know that brutality is ignorance, violence is relative failure, there are other and easier ways for the adjustment of human relationships which are emerging even out of the thunder and lightning of war clouds gathering around.

The essence of government does not lie solely in the monopoly of brute force, but in the organization of community action on wider or other scales than those of most associations of which the individual is a member. The emphasis on coercion has historically been evident, but in modern times the situation has very materially changed. The basic purpose of the political association becomes clearer than before, when it was obscured by military purposes and organization and the conspicuous nature of the elements of police and slavery, using police in the broader sense of the term here and not the recent organization of this service. The regulation and stabilization of industrial organization, the organization of education and recreation and cultural opportunity; all these emerge in our own time as among the primary tasks of the political group. These may be colored by violence, it is true, from time to time, and in periods of transition with heavy doses of brutality, but on the whole this factor tends to recede into the background and the larger cultural and constructive purposes of the community to emerge into broader and more common recognition.

Viewing the present state of the world's armaments, and looking back at the world's greatest military struggle, no one can contest the widespread availability and tendency toward the employment of compulsion in its extreme form. Ready weapons command the strategic points all over the world, and within every community. The muzzle of a gun is never far away or the uniform of an officer of some type. A special class of professional warriors, a system of vested interests in war materials, a ringing propaganda of militarism reenforces the tendency. The warriors indeed may compete with the statesmen—the "frocks"—for popular appeal, on the emotional side, in the broad stream of public interest and attachment and undertake to determine the lines of the power pattern, except in the more democratic countries. Are not these the hard realities which sweep away all idealisms, all ideologies, and provide their own rationalizations? The efforts to set these gigantic forces in a framework of effective jural order have thus far been only partially successful.

Attention cannot be long diverted, however, from the subjective nature of power, using subjective in the absence of a better term to indicate the social basis of authority found in motives and drives as well as in special instruments of material power, such as artillery or navies.

The power hungry have always to consider whether the army will fight or with what enthusiasm or for how long in such a cause. The mass army is itself a mass phenomenon, in which propaganda, organization, morale become essential factors; indeed the very life of the group. What if the army lays down its arms, and what, if still more distressing, it turns them in the other direction? Modern armies in Western states at least tend to include the able-bodied adult male population. They include many persons with education under a universal and obligatory system; they are vast organizations to which the principles of industrial organization of the new school apply rather than the military tactics of the old times; their morale is deeply affected by propaganda and by mass feelings which come streaming in from behind the lines, even from the enemy masses with whom they may fraternize across the lines at times, in the friendly comradeship of common soldiers; they are affected by the propaganda of human brotherhood, which makes this all the easier.[16] Thus the uniform and the bayonet must be regarded from the point of view of the subjective as well as of the objective, and with the closest regard not merely to numbers and equipment but also to morale.

What all this signifies is that the gap between violence and

[16] For example, the fraternization at Caporetto and the demoralization of the Russian army.

intelligence is not what it seems to the inexperienced. There is a difference, but in modern times it is not so wide as it once was. When the use of the army is considered, the problem is not one of military tactics in the narrower sense of the term, but of social strategy in the broadest meaning of the term. The other members of the family of power must be consulted before the battle begins. Will the soldiers fire upon the workers; will the church approve or stand aloof; will the industrials come forward with ready loans or require coercion; will the general sentiment of the community approve the cause or remain indifferent; what will be the sentiment of the civilized world, and what will that involve in war materials and in loans and in the more abstract but yet effective moral support? These are problems for the power holder to consider before the sword is drawn or the shot is fired, and it is plain that these are all social problems, not so different in quality from those already considered in examining the possibilities of the exercise of authority.

When war is declared, what is mobilized is not merely the troops but public sentiment, a force incapable of the same discipline, and likely to make itself felt in the ranks of the army itself, no matter what the generals may determine and decide. Labor, and gold, and press must be in line to ensure success, and these are not under military control, under any system for any considerable period of time.

Nor is the internal situation any more secure than the international unless the social forces are in balance. What will the police or the army do against the strikers? Will they fire on the workingmen, or will they falter and perhaps go over to the other side? What will they do against the priests or the clergy? What will they undertake against those of a kindred nationality; how far will they proceed in the enforcement of an unpopular law; to what extent may they be honeycombed by the agents of the opposition leaking information and anticipating every type of tactics?

Here again the police are a part of the social system, enmeshed closely in its sentiments and aspirations, its attitudes, and how far they may be willing to go against these streams may well be questioned. At the very moment when the conflict is sharpest and their guns are most needed, they may be low in morale, and unreliable in the sharp struggle ahead. What seems a solid wall of blue or gray or green turns out to be an inoffensive group of uninterested men, or of half-hearted officers mildly struggling with their fellows and reluctantly taking steps against them. Here too the impulse of the authoritarian for swift and decisive action may be checked by the thought of the social basis of his power, and the insecurity of authority working against its own social origins and relationships. Who knows what the outcome of the struggle may be, either politically for the temporary holders of power or permanently for the power régime itself?[17]

We may conclude then that the use of violence is by no means so simple a problem as in the more primitive times, but has become inextricably intertwined with the whole problem of social interests and sentiments; and that force is no longer what it seems. In last analysis it tends to become subjective; instead of brute force it tends to become brain force, with the weapons as items of secondary consideration. True the more modern guns are more effective than the earlier, but the inventive faculty which makes this possible is again a phase of the cultural level of the group and an index of their technological ability; and the same might be said of the more disastrous forms of chemical destruction in its latest styles. Powerful and deadly weapons of destruction may unquestionably be set in motion by the holders or seekers of power, but their relation to the intelligence of the community is so close as to make it necessary to look upon violence in its social setting, and not as a thing by itself.

Violence in government as in other relations is a confession of failure; it may be inevitable, given the situation as it is; but looking back the observer might discover a better way out or around, less painful and expensive. The punishment of a child may often be the condemnation of those who made the result possible, when sounder tactics might have reached the goal by another way.

[17] Moritz Hartman, *Revolutionäre Erinnerungen;* Emil Menke Gluckert, *Die November Revolution 1918.*

Violence is not the first thought but the last, the final effort to solve an otherwise insoluble problem in a crude manner. Many great events have been determined in this fashion, and perhaps will be again; but this does not detract from what has just been said. The wisest ruler finds a minimum of coercion necessary; the expanding group or state may effect its ends by organization and education and the activity of pressure groups, as well as by sword and fire.

The spirit of war and violence is deep ingrained in human experience, from the days when the chase of beasts and the killing of the enemy were the standard pursuits of mankind. War is to many the great adventure which falls athwart the monotony of their drab lives, and lifts them up to exaltation, especially between wars, and particularly for those who have never passed through the agonies of prolonged and sanguinary struggle. War seems to present the alternatives of death or glory, and in this sense satisfies the *Todestriebe* of which Freud advises us, the suicidal impulse which lies deep in so many constitutions. Comradeship, courage, sacrifice, glory, adventure, these are powerfully animating impulses in human nature, and war calls them forth, until the war weariness comes surging back again. That this war spirit is extinct no one looking around him at the array of military establishments or observing the military enthusiasms of peoples could conclude, and there is reason to believe that this instrument will be invoked in many instances for the settlement of conflicting claims which do not seem at the moment to be justifiable, although at the end of the war it might seem more feasible.

But the broad principle laid down I should prefer to leave standing in the manual of power, with whatever exceptions time may bring. In the long run the army and the social group tend to approach each other under modern conditions, and through propaganda, morale, education, mass organization to interpenetrate and to condition each other. And the network of adjudication and factual determination of disputes to spread quietly over the areas of conflict.[18]

[18] On this point see further in the last chapter, on the emerging tendencies of authority.

The cruder forms of force have already disappeared from many of their ancient haunts. The lash is no longer wielded by the head of the household over his wife in most countries; the whip is relatively little employed in the school, where other methods have supplanted it; the church lays far less emphasis on the physical terrors of the future world and the realistic presentation of the pains of hell; in the world of labor the personal chastisement of the worker lingers only on the outposts of civilization although once regarded as an indispensable adjunct of industry. The lash tends to disappear from the criminal law in great measure; and from the penal institution itself as a means of discipline. Even in the army corporal punishment tends to disappear as a means of discipline of the private soldier. In medicine the earlier punishment of the insane and the feeble-minded through custodial restraint alone has almost disappeared; and the physical pangs of suffering have been assuaged or removed through the influence of various forms of anaesthetics and drugs.

In war itself the efforts of three hundred years since the thirty years' struggle have been directed toward the minimization of the cruder cruelties of conflict such as poisoning wells and using dumdum bullets, a recognition in principle even if offset by the increasing number of severities that may be inflicted upon armies and population through the more recent devices of high explosives and chemical combinations.

It is only in certain circles of authority that the tradition of the necessity and inevitability of violence still continues as an actual basis of conduct and at times even as an ideology upon which society may be rationally constructed.

In general the world is committed to the principle of the elimination of the lower forms of human suffering as a means of social control; and definitely pointed toward the substitution of other modes of control better adapted to the level of civilization and scientific attainment in which society now begins to find itself. Other forms of pressure are developing and will continue to evolve, and perhaps mentally they may occasion as much suffering as the older types; but they will operate on a higher plateau of behavior, and involve less of the historic brutality than ever before.

The type of intelligence required to organize and maintain the modern army and its mechanical equipment, all in competition with other armies in a period of revolutionary changes in technological technique, dictates that the war becomes one of intelligence on the higher levels; and this tends to overshadow the actual application of brute force on a lower level. In other words intelligence tends to take over the use of force, and substitute its own technique and choose its own field of battle—which is on a different level from that of destruction of life.

These then are some of the maxims of those who survive the storms of political struggle, referring now not merely to specific individuals but to the groups of individuals who constitute the government from time to time. Individual qualities are for the moment thrust into the background, such as industry, courage, persistence, determination, and the other traits attributed to leaders in earlier paragraphs.

These are the broader canons of the power group of common application throughout a wide variety of systems externally different in the type of organization and in their functions. They are equally applicable to democracy or monarchy, to the rule of the élite, or the government of the soviets, and they may be found useful in the employment of a considerable variety of power techniques. Not all of these qualities may be found in any one man, or perhaps in the whole group at a given moment, but in general they may be held as characteristic, and in general the lack of these qualities has brought groups down to ruin or loss.

Not to know the community and to utilize its experts, not to be able to distribute rewards wisely, not to exercise moderation in government, not to be able to delegate and divide authority, not to have or appear to have plans of responsible leadership for the community, not to be able to maintain a system of order through which the principle of justice permeates; these are the conditions under which rulers often fall. Not that all of these situations must coincide, but a sufficient number of them in an impressive enough combination may precipitate the loss of prestige and power.[19]

If the margin of brute force is wide enough, almost anything may be done, as those who have witnessed deeds of cruelty in this world may testify, from a strong boy pommeling a weak one, to a strong nation beating a weaker and defenseless one; and the long roll of history gives countless pictures of cruelty and brutality crushing down the weaker with blood and terror and death.

But when we reach the zone where the balance of power is more nearly even, then the types of skill just discussed bcome of immediate meaning in the life of the political association, and have a practical bearing on the struggle for power. The big man may push the small or weak man around at will, but when he is matched with someone of his own size and weight and experience, he must begin to consider the finer points of combat and the elements of survival, and it is here that such general precepts as have been considered have their application. Under these conditions of struggle, those who are fittest in the techniques described—they are the survivors.

[19] See Chap. 9, "Morbidity and Mortality of Power," for further discussion of this topic.

Chapter 8

Abnegation and the Road to Power

IS THE WILL to political power stronger in human relations, or the abnegation of power; the spirit of conquest or the spirit of devotion; Tolstoy or the Czar; Gandhi or Mussolini?

Here we approach an area of vast importance to the understanding of authority, but one thus far little cultivated by the students of government. In modern times, Nietzsche has glorified the will to power, and has made it appear that this is the key to domination. Thus he declares: "What is good? All that enhances the feeling of power, the Will to Power, and Power itself in man. What is bad?—all that proceeds from weakness. What is happiness?—the feeling that power is increasing—that resistance has been overcome."[1]

In wide contrast, however, is the doctrine of Jesus: "But he that is greatest among you shall be your servant. And whosoever shall exalt himself shall be abased; and he that shall humble himself shall be exalted."[2]

Where does the truth lie, as between these views?

Without attempting to decide which among several elements in the composition of power is most important, it is plain that the factor of abnegation is one which cannot be neglected in any comprehensive survey of authority. There is an element of truth in the analysis of Nietzsche, but this is by no means the whole truth, and those who rely upon this factor alone are certain to be disillusioned in the course of political experience.

There are qualities of sacrifice and surrender in the power complex, both on the part of the leaders and on the part of the ruled, which unquestionably play an important role in the understanding of the political process. There are idealistic and utopian elements, which influence deeply the course of

[1] *Twilight of the Idols,* p. 128.
[2] Matt. 23. 11, 12.

political events in many important moments. Those who dislike these attitudes or movements prefer to disregard them or to minimize their importance, but it is the part of an objective study to endeavor to put them in their appropriate place in the larger framework of the political.

It may lightly be assumed that altruism, mysticism, sacrifice, martyrdom, belong wholly in the field of religion, and have no place in political discussion, but this is obviously contradicted by an examination of what actually occurs in the political world. The idealism of politics is not unlike that of religion in outward appearance or in inward significance and origin. In the modern world the enthusiasm of class and nation has at times acquired more spirituality than the more formal and institutionalized religions themselves.

We cannot conclude that authority rests wholly upon the "will to power" of the rulers, upon aggressive tendencies and dispositions alone, as it has seemed to some. The power holder assumes that in the community there is the impulse to surrender and sacrifice. The germinating principle of politics is not found in the will to rule, but in the will to sacrifice, in a broad satisfaction in the generous impulse of community devotion. The ruler is a function, an instrument, a means of the community, not an end in himself. He cannot command, however harsh his voice or hard his hand, unless he reflects the very opposite of what he seems to stand for—unless he incarnates sacrifice as well as self-assertion; unless he incorporates altruism as well as egoism. If he rules by divine right, he must reflect that divinity; or if by custom he must embody the traditions of the group. He may be so intoxicated by his apparent authority that he forgets or despises the gentler impulses upon which all his pride rests in last analysis, but the community does not forget its own basic purposes and doom dogs his footsteps.

Patriotisms of all lands build upon a spirit of sacrifice and devotion, as well as upon conquest and acquisition. They assume the principle of surrender on the part of great masses of individuals. Without ability to reckon confidently upon this willingness of men, political sacrifices would quickly come to a standstill. They call and not in vain for the surrender of comfort, convenience, industry, profession, home, health, liberty, perhaps life. And this appeal is made to a reserve of unselfishness which is confidently assumed.

Public spirit in times of peace is a form of altruism in part, and makes heavy drafts upon the time and energy of those who contribute to its maintenance, and without this great fund of available service all movements involving organization and effort would be hopeless from the beginning. The keynote of all the appeals is couched in terms of sacrifice and devotion, and the same may be said of civic enthusiasm and of party spirit.

When a state reaches a position in which its members lightly say, "Why should I do anything for my nation? What has it ever done for me?" the end is near. What the citizen typically says from time to time is, "I offer everything; I reserve nothing." And it is on the assumption that he will say this and do likewise that nations rest.

But are not material interests the basis of group cohesion rather than the loss of interests? In a sense, yes, there must be some material advantages in the association, and these are a part of the enterprise, a very important part of it. But this is not all; for there are paradoxically noninterests. Or, more accurately, there are material noninterests which are also interests themselves. There are satisfactions in terms other than the commodities which have a market value in the social organization; and among them are the qualities of sacrifice and devotion which are expected in the political power group.

Is there indeed a pleasure in sacrifice or is this an illusion covered over with flowers? The answer of enlightened selfishness may not be adequate, perhaps, but from the point of view of the total situation, an explanation is forthcoming which better satisfies the requirements. The sacrificial impulse or attitude, or whatever it may rightly be termed, has its organic justification on an equal basis with any other human impulse or attitude, and the intellectual calculation involved is relatively unimportant. It does not matter whether the satisfaction is mental or "constitutional," biological, or whether it is called an "illusion" or a "reality."

The function of sacrifice is clearly evident in the religious rites in which it is most clearly expressed.[3] It effects a release of impulses which play a great part in the operation of the human constitutional arrangements, an atonement, a reconciliation, a reorientation.

Sacrifice is a type moment of expiation, perhaps for oneself, perhaps vicariously for someone else, but in any case it wipes away the stain, it blots out the feeling of guilt which plays so great a part in human feeling. But this reorientation, this reopening of the books of life does not limit itself to the ceremonials of religion proper, for it may be found in other groups, in the family par excellence, in the class or race, and in the state as well. In the political world the individual "owes something" to the community. He may have sinned against it; in fact, it is almost certain that he has at some time or other fallen short of his legal duties and obligations; and he makes up for it after a fashion by the attitude of devotion and the penance of service. The course of justice represents one aspect of the penitential aspect of the political process. There the guilty may atone for his crime, and be restored to society again, but in fact more likely to be branded for life literally or figuratively. The penitentiary, unfortunately, does not wholly purge and is a poor substitute for the great realities of the ceremonial world of government and of religion.

But in some of the rites of the state, in its great demonstrations and celebrations, there is a combination of the confessional and the penance of religion. The individual is at once released from his burden, and exalted once more. There is a likeness between the revival meeting of religion and the great political assembly. In both, many long- and short-time converts are made; and many others are filled with holy zeal to go about doing good. If one shuts his eyes and listens to the impassioned voice of the great political orator, he might be preaching some gospel. If one looks at the flushed faces and sometimes tearful eyes of the participants, he might be witnessing some great spiritual uplift, although the subject matter may be taxes and tariffs. There is a therapeutic value in the moments of collective zeal; the participants "feel better";

[3] See Marcel Moess on the function of sacrifice for illustrations of this principle.

their tonicity is finer; a glow of good feeling courses through them; their spirit rises. Wickedness and selfishness drop away and for a moment the group is borne up on the voice of the orator or with the tide of song, or the delirium of the moment never to be forgotten. The common feeling in such moments is indeed so powerful that one might question whether such experiences are not to be classed as among the most enjoyable in human life.[4]

In some of the early tribal rites the worship of fertility (of soil and sex), of political power, and of religion were all combined in one ceremony and perhaps in one rhythmic movement, a dance. These have fallen apart now, but the political celebration survives as a tribal ceremony, doing for the modern group what the other did for the earlier. The symbolism of sex and that of magic in its more obvious forms are absent, but the ritualistic character of the tribal demonstration remains and is perhaps equally effective. Sex survives in the love and affection for the fatherland or motherland, as the case may be, and possibly in the attitudes toward the virile leader with caressing voice and manner, while politics is itself a form of religion easily interchangeable. Magic is now found in the legerdemain of verbalisms and the juggling with logic which is so common a feature of mass assemblies, for obviously many of the orators' verbalisms are incantations rather than arguments, intoned for the benefit of the mass as a part of the music of the occasion. There is also a form of magic in the ceremonies themselves with their weird impressiveness and their incalculable forms of influence upon the great masses assembled.

There may occur indeed something not so far removed from a miracle in the proceedings of a mass demonstration, an incredible transition from one attitude to another, leading to a fundamental change in behavior on the part of individuals. The healing and restoring effect produced in mass phenomena is well known in more than one way of life and is not confined to the religious alone. The impressive ceremonials and results of Lourdes may be matched by the

[4] In local revivals there were certain persons who were always converted because "it felt so good."

patriotic rites and festivals in which like restorations have been accomplished, and similar reconditionings. Maladjustments in social and political attitudes, emotional fixations, may be "cured" by exposure to the rays of the vast assembly and to the waves of sound emanating from the orator or from the crowd itself. The art of Trotzky or of Hitler is not so unlike that of Peter the Hermit or of Savonarola. Intense preoccupation with a specific and compelling object may possess a degree of therapeutic value in some types of cases, and among the objects of concentration there may be the forms of crowd action. In these mass demonstrations strange changes may be effected in the balance and disposition of the participants or of some of them, which may have the effect of transmutation of behavior. What is called a physical "cure" or a spiritual "conversion" has its analogue in the reorientation of the political attitude and conduct from that time forth.

These political miracles, then, are a part of the basis of power, as much as are the decisions of courts, the decrees of the administration, or the guns of the army. They condition fundamentally in many situations the nature and limits of authority in general and in individual cases, and cannot be neglected in any serious study of the political.

It is not necessary to know the language of a mass demonstration in order to catch its spirit or be impressed by its ceremonies, especially if it is within a near-by cultural level and not too far removed from the forms and rhythms to which one is habituated and conditioned. Its cabalistic quality is impressive, and its light, form, and movement require no special impression in order to produce the grand general effect desired.

Or, without any crowd movement, the brooding individual may attach his melancholia and his obsession to a specific political cause or object to which he may henceforth devote his best efforts. Thus there emerge the leaders and the staff of movements which may shake the foundations of the established orders, Mazzinis, Lenins, Cromwells, Calvins, Garrisons, who emerge from obscurity with dynamic force projecting themselves into apparently impregnable positions.

Abnegation is found in all the members of the family of power as a basis of authority, and not merely in the political groupings. In the family and the church this quality is developed on a large scale and is perhaps more emphasized than in the state. But in other social groupings as well the same spirit is manifested on many occasions and in many different ways. The life of the group is conditioned on the spirit of altruism on the part of the bulk of its members. The techniques and the spirit are transferable and interchangeable in many ways.

Thus a Mohammedan who gave up his life in war might expect to awake in Paradise surrounded by houris. Or the Christian knight to find his home in the glory of the after world. Or other groups may combine group satisfaction in the rescuing of their special society. While in one sense there are competing loyalties in any series of societies, there are also supplementing loyalties, which may reenforce and strengthen each other notably. If the church, the state, the labor group, the business society, the cultural group, all say the same thing, the combined social pressure that may be brought to bear upon a given focus is vast. While they may not always be found in happy accord, yet there is an agreement upon the value of devotion in the abstract as a desirable quality in any association. The individual may be especially patriotic in one group and less so in another, but the meaning of abnegation is well understood throughout all the groups united in organized forms, including, as has been shown, the outlaw societies themselves. The sacrificial attitudes and rites are to be found, then, in all the family of power, and the presence of them is fully understood and appreciated throughout the kingdom of associated life.

The element of abnegation is also important in the leaders of power movements as well as in the rank and file of followers. Whatever the personal ambition of the power leader may be, he must always profess the altruistic impulse and present a picture painted accordingly. If it is a life of early struggle and sacrifice, so much the better, for then he may appeal to the sympathies of the other sacrificial participants in the group devotions. But if not, he may make up for this by subsequent sacrifices for the common weal, moral, political, economic, or whatever the category may be in a special instance. To be imprisoned in a just cause is an admirable preparation for a public figure, if it is perfectly clear that he was right, or that he thought he was and made the sacrifice accordingly.

Perhaps no darker blot can be cast on the escutcheon of a leader than to characterize him as selfish in personal disposition. He may be ambitious, or ruthless, or reckless, but he must not be classified as self-centered, with the connotation of "selfish." Or at least this quality must not be brought into obvious conflict with the general good, as commonly understood. The public will not condone the selfishness of the commander who will not accept an inferior post from personal pique, or of the statesman who refuses all service because the first position cannot be accorded him in a given crisis. This is almost the unpardonable sin of the political leader.

Not only is this true, but many of the world's greatest leaders have been men marked by the surrender of the will to power and by martyr-like devotion to a principle involving the common good, as interpreted by them. This is a road to power which the power hungry cannot comprehend, but which may lead in that direction by a reverse process. Few men have had greater power than Gandhi, whose life of simplicity and frugality brought him no material rewards and whose imprisonment was a decoration that blazoned him as a sufferer for the community, regardless of the wisdom of his policy. By what title does this little person take the throne? The Franciscans and the Dominicans, beginning as begging friars, gave up all, and received in return property and power of vast proportions, on the strength of which arose the arrogance of some of their successors who no longer begged but now commanded. Count Tolstoy wielded wide influence on the political life of all the Western states, and upon Gandhi. The national history of every land contains the names and the deeds of great men whose sacrifice was conspicuous. In prison, exile, contempt, they wove the fabric of later years. Masaryk is a conspicuous example in our time of the type of a wandering patriot who at last came home to power in a dénouement not always seen in the lives of sufferers for a cause, for often the exiles do not come back.

The mystic type may of course turn in upon himself and find his satisfaction in abnegation, nonintercourse, meditation to the point of autointoxication. The annals of Buddhism, of Stoicism, of Christianity, of all religions, are full of the sacrifices of men whose devotion developed no relationship with political power processes.[5] They find within themselves a world almost self-contained, a grouping of interests, ideals, ideologies, a formation of power types, if they may so be characterized, a government within the self; and this they rule, detached from the external world as far as possible. In this mystical hypnosis, trance, whatever it may properly be termed, they spin the web of their existence. Indirectly they may have helped to shape ideologies and influence behavior by precept and example but without special connection with the political. In other instances, however, these types have exercised a profound influence upon the course of political events, particularly at points where the religious impinged upon the governmental.

There is established in the relation between the sacrificial leader and the sacrificial citizen or member of the society a rapport of the utmost value in the formation of a power situation. The two elements are brought in combination, with the resulting fusion of attitude and aspiration. The individual sees in the leader the picture of himself, perhaps enlarged and idealized somewhat. One speaks from his experience to another in the fellowship of shared experience. As the common phrase runs, "The heart of one speaks to the heart of the other"; and here the symbols may be of far more importance than the verbalisms. In the great moment of emotional ecstasy the two, the orator and the listener, are one, in the political sense of the term.

The individual has also been misunderstood, he also has

[5] Franz Alexander, "Buddhist Training as an Artificial Catatonia," *Psychoanalytical Review,* 13: 129–145.

been persecuted; he also has suffered and failed; and so he may readily fall into sympathy with the leader who has likewise experienced some of the bitterness of life. At this sacrificial point the religion of politics may make itself manifest in a form of mystical rapport between the crowd or members of it and the leader who for the moment becomes their representative, the bearer of their burdens, at once their fellow and one whom they are ready to follow.

In may also be pointed out that there are those who rejoice to follow a leader, who find pleasure in surrender, those with passive nature who are always looking for a master. They may be far happier when sacrificing for another than when achieving for themselves; indeed their chiefest joy is this very surrender to the will of another. Abnegation is for them almost an end in itself, a *summum bonum.* There needs only appear a situation in which this relationship is set up to arouse their devotional interest and inspire their affection and allegiance. They throw themselves out on the great mysterious tide of mastery on which they float in supreme sacrificial abandonment. In such instances the appeal of the ruler is not to gain, but to loss of all—to supreme surrender, to ultimate sacrifice.

It may of course be pointed out that the sacrificing leader is not in reality "suffering," but may be giving expression to an urge the release of which is fundamental to his nature. There is no internal struggle in his constitution, but an unchecked flood of irresistible sacrificial (masochistic) impulse, even the *Todestriebe* of which the Freudians speak. The martyr may thus be explained as a type, but from the point of view of political behavior this does not change the basic situation. His conduct remains in fact what other men regard as sacrificial, and it operates upon them just as if it were what it seems to be, even if it is something else; and the relations he sets up with other men as followers remain the same. We may understand better the types who are thus available for functions of this nature, but the functions go on, undisturbed.[6]

[6] H. D. Lasswell, *Psychopathology and Politics.*

Opposed, then, stand the raw assertions of the will to power and the abnegation of power, yet each may be the road to power, leading over another way. Religion has perhaps contributed historically the largest number of sacrificial types, but the political world is by no means devoid of examples, most of which are less dramatic, but which involve the identical principle seen in religious devotion. The fact that renunciation may bring recognition; that one may give up all and find more; is for some a hard saying, the truth and application of which are stubbornly resisted, because it seems so diametrically opposed to the basic principles of power. But the truth of it stands out unmistakably on close examination of the power process.

Just as sacrifice may not be conceded as a part of the power acquiring process, so the appeals to idealism and utopianism may be disregarded by the practitioners in the field of government, or dismissed as unrelated to the process of actual government.[7] But in point of fact they have an important bearing on the organization of power groups. The fact that they are impractical immediately may make them practical. That they present works of imagination not adapted to a momentary situation does not disqualify them for use in the real world, although that use is a different one from the ordinary. That they are dreams may only the better fit them for a world of reveries. Plato once declared, "I am the only statesman of my time," meaning that he was outlining the course by which the ship must be steered to reach the harbor, rather than managing the workings of the crew and the wheel.

The utopian is a dreamer, an inventor, allowing his imagination to play freely over masses of data and to assume some new form of organization, some new action pattern or constellation. He may allow his temperament, or his personal experience, or his wishes to influence his reorientation of the political facts and institutions, to such an extent that society recoils from his picture of the future. And in such a

[7] On this topic see Karl Mannheim, *Ideologie und Utopie,* on "Das utopische Bewusstsein."

case his reverie may be passed by and not even find a place in recorded history. But in other instances these dreams become the basis of a new authority. Thus the ideas of a Mazzini, or a Marx, or a Mill may come to play a large role in the affairs of the power holders and seekers.[8]

Individual citizens, or many of them, may be dreamers, and in a manner inventors, framing new shapes of power from the material at hand, on lines indicated by their discontent and the free play of their imagination.[9] The citizen is not averse to some degree of free fantasy with respect to the arrangements which circumscribe him. The imperfection of reality may disturb him and inspire plans for betterment; or the very efficiency of regimentation may irritate him to think of some other scheme or organization in which his role might be more pleasant. It is to this element in human nature that the dreamer, the inventor may address himself, and may project and promise a reorganization in which material improvement may be the outcome. He may, in short, present utopia with an appeal to groups of persons, reaching into their inner life and releasing impulses for change in personnel or organization of the political order. These appeals and these responses may be entirely outside the boundaries of the existing political system, may even be banned by the existing authority, and indeed so completely crushed externally that they survive only underground. But they may yet become the elements from which a new order is shaped, as the Marxian ideology, or the democratic, or the racial, or the religious. Their impossibility, practically speaking, does not

[8] "Verdienstvolle kulturhistorische Forschung hat festgestellt, dass menschliche Sehnsuchtsprojektionen erfassbaren Gestaltungsprinzipien unterliegen und dass man in bestimmten historischen Perioden die Wunscherfüllung mehr in Zeit-, in anderen wieder mehr in Raumbilder projiziert." K. Mannheim, *Ideologie und Utopie,* p. 183. He discusses as types of utopias: (1) Der orgiastische Chiliasmus der Wiedertäufer; (2) Die liberal-humanitäre Idee; (3) Die konservative Idee; (4) Die sozialistisch-kommunistische Utopie. See also H. Freyer, "Das Problem der Utopie," *Deutsche Rundschau,* v. 183, p. 321; A. Doren, *Wünschräume und Wünschzeiten.*

[9] Jerome Davis, *Contemporary Social Movements,* Book II, "Utopias."

prevent them from becoming possible eventually, and political power is wielded by those who transform the *status quo* through the development of the new impossibilities.

The dreamer does not abdicate authority, but he chooses the final phase rather than the immediate, and finds his satisfaction in another field outside of formal juristically accepted political power. But this detachment from the ceremonials and responsibilities of authority may paradoxically render him all the stronger with the mass of the community. He cannot be charged with the evils of the existing régime, nor is he regarded as inspired by power hunger and the power satisfactions which may come from it. This relative irresponsibility he shares with the mass, and also his sacrificial attitude toward the social situation. Hence if the utopian's dream is not so far removed from reality that it cannot be comprehended by his fellows, he may acquire a renown and a prestige which cannot be gainsaid, and which is as real as that of his power holding critic. His martyrdom may involve the beginning of a movement toward a new order. "The blood of the martyrs is the seed of the church," is an old saying.

The utopian in the nature of the case has a freer hand than the responsible governor, and may draw a picture with more regard to a broad situation and with less attention to questions of detail, indeed with a degree of unfairness to those charged with the responsibility for detailed administration. From this point of view he may readily capitalize the defects of any going concern, and start with the inevitable impetus of inevitable discontent with the given order.

These utopias are in turn subjected to equally savage criticism; and the criticisms of utopias are received with equally bad grace. For the new ideology seeks to protect itself by all the devices employed by the régime which it seeks to destroy. Each ideology, being true and just, defends itself against falsehood and injustice, by whatever means may prove expedient.

We may conclude, then, that the will to power is not the only road that leads to Rome. There are other ways which start in the opposite direction, and wind their course back to the imperial city by circuitous roads, along unbeaten paths, with weapons other than stone and steel and high explosives. Their success is an unending surprise to the established and authentic holders of authority, who view with perennial amazement the success of this ancient technique of power.

And yet this need not be, for we may say, looking at the power process and its mass background, that abnegation, sacrifice, surrender are the basis of all authority. Eliminate the possibility of an appeal to the spirit of sacrifice and a sure mass response and authority is gone. The army does not come; the taxes are not collected; the law is not obeyed; the spirit of the community dies; and the nominal power withers away. What the power holder builds upon, the continuing basis of his authority, is not only selfish interest but sacrifice, although he may not recognize it as appearing in other and unorthodox types. Sacrifice is indeed a form of personal interest.

But to the student of political power this situation is of profound importance, for it enables him to see more clearly the inner nature of authority and the tenure by which it is held, outside the formal books of jurisprudence, outside the ring of inner power.

There is steel in power, but there is also soul in power; and neither can deny the other a reality in the realm of the political. There cannot be sovereignty unless there is a spirit of sacrifice in the community—an abnegation and devotion that transcend the bounds of the formally juristic. Both armies and gold melt away—for they are both built on claims of service—unless they can find support in the impulses of the many to risk life, liberty, and the pursuit of happiness for the political community, and to find a pleasure-pain in the great renunciation.

Chapter 9

Morbidity and Mortality of Power

WHAT ARE THE situations under which power, political power, sickens and dies? This query may refer to a given territory and people, to a given political system, to particular rulers, or to a great variety of tension situations.

First of all it may be said that the various efforts to arrive at a form of government which will be perfect or will never change, the view that ways and means may be devised so carefully that power systems may be made perpetual have been generally abandoned. Both Plato and Aristotle hoped to find the final form in which sickness or at least death would never enter, and with this in mind they resorted to extraordinary measures to ensure the health and prolong the life of authority. The Greeks located their ideal city back from the sea so that disturbing contacts with sailors or other strangers might not operate to upset the equilibrium of the community. Plato extended his meticulous care even to the games of the people and to their music, fearing that some change in rhythm, jazz perhaps, might subtly communicate itself to the seat of power and overthrow it. Since the days of Bodin in the sixteenth century this search for the perfect and unchangeable form of state has been abandoned, and the task of politics has been conceived as that of making the necessary changes as smoothly as possible, and with the least community loss. A study of the best means of maintaining the health of authority may be made, as in Plato, Aristotle, and Montesquieu, but this need not be addressed to the perpetuation of an ideal condition.

Threats to power may arise from a very wide variety of sources: from outside the community—alien source; from a combination of outside elements with those on the inside; from inside in revolutionary form; from inside without threatening the existing system, but only a change of personnel of rulers.

From any one of these points of the compass, a hostile movement may develop at any time and threaten the position of the existing régime. And of course all of these factors act and react upon each other. It is in the light of these various angles of attack that the power policy of the dominant group must be laid down.

As against the outside enemy, rulers may usually count upon the support of the entire community. But where there is internal dissension among the members of the family of power, the difficulties are very great and may at any moment develop into disaffection of the most serious description. Race, religion, class, may place their interests ahead of that of the political group and may be willing to make the most serious sacrifices to overthrow it. Thus the local balance is menaced not only by the strength of the local factions but by the possibility of external agreement on a wholly different basis than that which appears on the surface of things. The powerless local group may overnight become a serious threat to morale and military strength.

The race, the class, the religion may find a more pleasant status in some other political framework or may even be reenforced by a foreign power. More than one great state owes its establishment to the aid of a power not personally friendly perhaps but interested in the weakening of powerful antagonists, as in the case of the recent succession states. Disturbances in the family of power may thus assume an importance quite out of relation to their local weight, if conjoined with the aid and comfort of an alien or outside authority. To this point the eye of the cautious power holder must ever be directed. In more recent times this problem has centered chiefly around racial differences, with increasing emphasis on the economic classes, while historically the major interest for a long time centered around the position and tactics of the church.

The balance is thus a highly complicated one, as between the family of power, the shareholders in the political power group, and the outsiders whose intervention real or implied may upset the local equilibrium from time to time. The possibility of new combinations and constellations of authority is always in the background and may at any time sweep forward with unexpected violence, under the influence of an interest, an ideology, a personality, or a combination of these factors in some new pattern of authority.

In the broadest sense, the situations under which power sickens and dies may be uncovered as the obverse side of those under which it comes to birth and vitality. Obviously the reverse of the forces that produce integration in the political society will bring about its disintegration. The unbalance of the social groups whose combination has produced civic cohesion; futility in the adjustments of various types of personality patterns; failure to perform the basic functions of the political society, such as successful defense against external attack, the maintenance of a generally accepted system of order and of justice; the accompanying weakness of the general morale; or the inadequacy and weakness of the governing personnel; all these are among the indicia of disintegration—the signs of morbidity and perhaps of mortality. Collapses and catastrophes may be diagnosed on through malfunctioning, the source of difficulty discovered by the political doctor.

What happens when the power group "runs down," as it were, is often a failure of adaptation to the trends of social change. Power systems are in a sense interpretations of social interests and values, and if the interpretation lags behind the emerging realities, its accuracy, its validity, its force are weakened *pro tanto*. The perfect equilibrium of one period may be an unbalance in another, and the power system based on such an equilibration will lose its utility and finally its prestige. If the local balance is weakened, following the same reasoning, it becomes easier for an outside foe to conquer and destroy the local pattern of authority.

As the power group weakens, the faltering operation for an essential organ or organs becomes evident. Interests, mechanisms, attitudes, personalities are inextricably intertwined in the power situation, and the failure of any one of these elements to fit into the general pattern may cause the whole contrivance to suffer.

The members of the family of power may readily fall out, and if they do not all agree or if any one of them is dissatisfied the power complex is weakened. Any class, race, religion may raise the flag of dissent or even of sabotage and upset the balance of political power in the given community. If they carry their opposition far enough, the whole basis of civil order may be threatened or may be maintained only at a heavy cost to the net output of the community.

The Catholics in Italy, the Irish in Britain, the Poles in Germany, the three (five) groups in old Austria-Hungary, are illustrations in modern times showing the possibilities of a disturbance of the power equilibrium in the social groupings. Switzerland offers a striking example of a successful policy under difficult conditions. The balance is often more delicate than appears, and a slight disturbance may overthrow the system before it seems possible that it is tottering. This inner weakness may become evident in case of an outside attack and lead to the downfall of the state, as in Austria-Hungary.

Racial differences, religious demands, and above all economic conflicts contain the seeds of destruction, and it requires the utmost art to maintain the central organization without falling over some one of these factors of disturbance. Especially dangerous is the situation when two or more elements of the family of power act in concert. Religion and race, race and region, race and economic class, may contain the possibility of overthrow of power groups, and the combination of more than two is a signal for extraordinary vigilance if the state or the ruler is to be saved.

Much depends upon the vigor and effectiveness of the minority groups and upon the skill of their organization and their propaganda, for there are examples of far-reaching territories held together loosely but surviving for long periods of time, chiefly because there seemed to be no effective center of opposition around which discontent might rally.[1] The

[1] R. B. Dixon, *Building of Cultures.*

inertia, indolence, ineffectiveness of great masses of population may make easy the success of a weak central power group, which could not hold its own against earnest and organized opposition. In such cases a small ruling class with an army, a bureaucracy, and a religion may preserve a status favorable to them for a long time, as in old Russia. Another type is the Chinese, held together, in so far as it is together, by different bonds of interest and compulsion.

The decay of the older value systems, seen either in the form of attitudes or, on higher cultural levels, in the decline of systematic ideologies, marks the weakening of the dominant power system and group, unless it is found possible to assimilate, reconcile, reintegrate the older pattern with the new. Along with these doctrines go the symbol systems of authority or revolution as the case may be. It may be assumed that theories have little bearing upon power systems, but the jealousy with which new systems of theory are watched and the readiness with which they are banned and if possible suppressed indicate the force which is really attributed to them by authority. Ideologies are almost as much feared as armies on cultural levels where systematic thinking is carried on.

"Subversive" ideas are always assailed as deadly foes of the state, and extraordinary efforts made to suppress them, except in the case of the more habile and flexible power groups, who have learned how to assimilate and reintegrate the new in such a manner as to restore the validity of the state.

The symbol systems of interests and ideologies are almost as bitterly assailed as the forces back of the symbol. The faces, forms, emblems, rhythms, memorials, not consistent with those of the dominant power group are ruthlessly barred or torn down, so that only the symbolism of the authoritarians of the moment may be observed or heard or felt.

The cross, the crown, the red flag, the swastika, the old flag, the new song, the monuments, the statues, the emblems; these are all involved in moments of political tension; and alternately pushed forward and back by the struggling forces in the community.[2]

From the functional point of view, which may be looked upon as the measure of group and individual interests, the sickness of the political society may be observed by attention to the effectiveness with which the political group serves the purposes attributed to it. Does it provide for the defense of the group against external forces, so that the members of the society are not subjected to tribute or made the victim of discriminations or indignities? If not, the political society is ill.

Of all the diseases that threaten the ruling groups, perhaps the most serious are failure in war and hunger, failure in production or distribution of economic goods. When the promise of military glory clearly fades, and the hour of national humiliation strikes, the power of the ruler is threatened; and there comes a moment when the army itself becomes a source of danger to the throne, if it is a throne. In the last hundred years the list of rulers who have lost their crowns with their wars is a long and impressive one, that may well induce the prospective warrior to look before he leaps. France, Russia, Germany, Austria are among the list.

The breakdowns of the system of order and justice are indicia of the weakening of the political power in the given group and point to its dissolution.[3] Indeed if an orderly society cannot be maintained, outside powers are ready to intervene for the protection of their own subjects, and may remain longer than was expected or perhaps intended. Failure to maintain order is a menace not only to particular power holders, but to the whole system and to the identity of the state itself.

But what is order and how may its presence be determined in a society? This is not an easy question to answer with precision, but common sense may frequently provide an ade-

[2] See S. Tschachotin und C. Mierendorff, *Grundlagen und Formen politischen Propaganda,* for a valuable account of the recent struggle in Germany.

[3] See James Bryce's study of the canons of government in his *Modern Democracies.*

quate answer. Neither is it easy to say exactly what is a state of war.[4]

In recent times types of criteria have been provided, however, by the action of international powers. When there is sufficient "provocation," intervention on the part of one or more powers is justified by the "common consent of mankind," if the interests of these powers are not adequately protected by the political society under consideration. In the sharp competition of nations for new territory, any such situation will be carefully observed, and indeed intervention may occur when there is no sound reason but only a pretext for aggrandizement of some power. But the underlying principle is there, namely that of the necessity of preserving some system of orderly procedure under which human relations may be carried on, if the society is to claim recognition as a member of the family of nations. Other states may not be primarily concerned with the nature of the system of order, which may follow many diverse patterns, but with a degree of certainty and regularity in its operation. Likewise from within there is no greater reproach to a political power group than the failure to establish and maintain some system of public order, however crudely conceived or roughly executed.

The weakening of the function of justice may also upset the health of the political community, and produce the most violent fevers and other disorders, threatening the very existence of those in political power. Justice as between individuals and justice as between social groups is a matter of fundamental concern, and the temperature of the society in such tensions is of very great importance. The morale of the community depends in large measure on the sense of justice in the political society, and the widespread feeling of injustice is the deadliest foe of political power. This is equally true whether we refer to individual instances or to types of intergroup injustice. It is true of groups as of individuals that "no rogue e'er felt the halter draw with good opinion of the law," but the generality of the community are never

[4] Clyde Eagleton, *The Attempt to Define War.*

rogues, or if they are then the appearance of a new political power group may safely be forecast. If too many cry "unjust," not at a particular decision, but at a system as a whole, then the decay of that system is well under way.

One may ask again, but what is justice?[5] Justice is not a quantity which may be carried to the tenth decimal point, but common-sense understanding of it is not difficult to hit upon in a given political community. It rests basically upon an assumed generality of a system of values in a community, allotting recognition to individuals and groups under a regularized system. If there is not such a fundamental agreement upon values and recognitions and upon what constitutes consistency in distribution, there is no generalized sense of injustice. Indeed many of the political conflicts arise just at this point, where competing value systems and competing ideas of recognition are not fully integrated and come into collision. It may again be pointed out in passing, however, that this aspect of human relations is no exclusive characteristic of the political society, but is common to all forms of association.

The residual function of the political power group is also of vast importance and relates itself closely to the general morale of the association. The leadership displayed by the governor, the type of satisfaction they are able to produce, will determine the attitude of the community toward their tenure of power and the extent of their recognized authority. The government must "produce results," which will not be specified in advance, but which the subjects will appraise most critically, whether openly or covertly it matters little in the end. Political power groups are in serious condition when the public is either cold or hot. Power cannot live long with either sub- or super-normal temperature, accurately read with the clinical thermometer of the expert politician. If the ruler can only wring his hands and lament the impossibility of action, some other will rise to show the way to "recovery."

[5] See Aristotle's *Politics,* Book III, Chaps. IV and XII, for discussion of types of justice in the generalized sense of the term.

And again one may say, but what are "results," and how shall we recognize them? The unskillful cannot, but the eye of insight can determine these within reasonable limits; and, as in the old fairy tales, the one who guesses wrong loses his head.

In tension periods the common interest seems to intensify and becomes persistent in some demand for action, perhaps in the economic field, perhaps in the religious or other cultural domain. In such moments of sharp interest, danger rides for those in authority, whether they perceive it or not; and to measure rightly its force, or to put in motion the appropriate remedies for dealing with it—on this may hang the outcome of the balance of power. At this very point the most serious blunders are made by the authoritarians; they minimize the opposition, they are irritated by the new situation; then impatiently they apply too late the remedies that earlier might have been effective. These concessions are now spurned as evidence of weakness when a little while ago they might have been accepted with jubilation. Complaints are trifling in their scope and content; opposition is the bile of malcontents; revolutions are riots; these are the formula of prerevolutionary periods, when those set within the well-wrought frame of power are confident that no force can shake them. But tension moments are not merely signals for repressive measures; they may be opportunities for constructive reorientation of the whole situation, for a display of inventiveness and leadership in a difficult hour. What is demanded is not necessarily a new power group but an alleviation of a difficult situation, a way out.

Hunger on the part of the mass, economic insecurity and lagging progress, more broadly speaking, weakening of economic advantage, may become the basis for a change in the basis of authority; some larger territorial unit or some different personnel in the ruling power group may be the outcome. Hunger and distress will destroy the morale of the group, and leave the door wide open to a rival candidate for authority, while economic interests will not permanently be restrained by considerations of patriotism if they can count with confidence upon superior advantages in another jurisdiction. The tie of loyalty will hold for a time in the face of adversity but it cannot be counted upon forever, and there is a point beyond which allegiance will not stretch.

Significant pressures of this sort are observable in the plebiscites in border cases such as in Schleswig and upper Silesia. In these instances the power of social elements may be observed and measured—the relative force of economic advantage, of religion, of race, of political affiliation. The flag, the pocket-book, the church, the family perhaps, the ancestral inheritance of tradition: between these a hard choice must be made. The competitors exhibit their wares before the prospective buyer, so to speak, and argue their respective claims upon his attention and interest. The propaganda literature of these struggles is rich in material illustrative of the essential nature of political allegiance, and exhibits in clear form the crude and naked considerations which determine choices among groups of men.[6] "The nation," said Renan, "is a daily plebiscite."

Somewhat the same case is presented when the prospective emigrant considers the relative advantages of the old country and the new. What passes through his mind as he reflects upon Germany or Brazil, Hungary or California, Italy or Argentina? What are the social elements that enter into the determination of his choice to go or to stay, to elect one flag or the other?[7] Some are found to be economic; others domestic; others libertarian and political; others pertain to social prestige and opportunity. What determines whether a German, English, American workingman decides to throw in his lot with the Soviet Union, or remain where he is? Are the considerations drawn from religion, family, pocket-book, flag, liberty? And what finally casts the deciding vote in this

[6] Sarah Wambaugh, *Plebiscites*, especially documents cited; also *La Pratique des plébiscites internationaux* in *Recueil des Cours, Académie de Droit International; Plebiscite and Referendum*, British Foreign Office.

[7] See Harold F. Gosnell, "Non-naturalization: A Study in Political Assimilation," *American Journal of Sociology*, 33: 930–939 and "Characteristics of the Non-naturalized," *ibid.*, 34: 847–855.

little election held by the individual in his own little personal parliament where so many elements are represented?

An examination of such factors as these may indicate what it is that determines political cohesion; what elements hold fast and longest in general and in what types of individual and experience; what elements surrender most quickly to the appeal of the opposing loyalty.

An even clearer case is seen in the instance of a migrant who having lived in two countries now weighs the whole question of relative advantage, all things considered, intellectual and emotional, traditions, dollars, living conditions as a whole, religion, family, all together; and out of this shapes a decision as to a life course. It is not to be assumed that he sets up a careful hedonistic calculus in which all elements are carefully put over against each other, but if we examine the basic presuppositions, his social experience, and his temperament, we are in the way of finding something important about the inner elements of power and the situations which affect its hold upon life. The same considerations do not operate with equal force upon every individual, but in masses of cases the relation between individual types and social pressures is very clearly illustrated, and this is of the essence of political authority, the penetralia of power into which the political student has not yet entered very far.

But it is just here that there appear most clearly the integration and disintegration of the elements which taken together constitute a given power situation. Which of them are most tenacious with respect to various types of experience and temperament, and which are least resistant to types of experience and temperament? Scientifically one might suggest that the power holder might well take a sample from time to time from among the marginal migrants and ascertain what the political *Stimmung* is among the citizens and subjects. It must be assumed, of course, that he penetrates under the surface of the verbal reactions of those questioned, into their behavior as determined in other ways. And these inquiries might reveal not merely the relation between social factors and individual type and experience, but also the dynamics, the genetics of the case, the moving process of individual development through age groups, the role of habituation, the inner meaning of nostalgia.

One might also study the qualities of the special types of allegiance in their sub- and super-forms. The martyr type and the traitor type are widely separated extremes which illustrate points of view with respect to the power group and raise the question, what are the situations under which these types are developed? How does the martyr come to be such? How does the traitor come to be such, with relation to this power pattern? Is it temperament, social experience, ideology, calculation of interest, conscious or subconscious attraction and aversion?[8] The Freudian explanation of some of these cases seems adequate, but in others inadequate and somewhat naïve, as if operating on one string only. The Freudian and the Marxian dialectics are excellent illustrations of the danger of carrying one single principle all the way, even against its own protest and to its own confusion. Pocket-book and sex will explain much that resists publicity and light, but not all life is so simple.

Written large in the temperament and experience of these extremist types in relation to the symbolism of the power group lies something of the secret of power itself; for here are seen the traits and tendencies of great groups of the population, trends out of which the pattern of authority is woven. Here may be observed the instruments of symbolism, force, ideology, personality, directed by those with the power hunger. The seeker and the holder of power may wish to understand them.

The perennial problem of individual personality adjustments is also important in considering the illness of a particular society. Groups and ideologies are important but also individuals with their private systems demanding recognition and expression within the framework of the political society. Individuals are constantly appraising and reappraising the behavior of those in authority. Little parliaments

[8] See H. D. Lasswell, *Psychopathology and Politics,* for case studies.

in themselves, they discuss and determine their attitudes toward power holders and systems. Criminal, rebel, deviate, disaffected, indifferent, disloyal, types may emerge from social situations which are unfavorable to the growth of stronger types of civic cohesion and allegiance. Rough-handed holders of power may increase the tension at this point by repression and brutality, while those with greater insight and prevision may remove the causes of disaffection and avoid the growth of counter individuals.

These verdicts taken singly and alone may well seem unimportant, but their cumulation is impressive and becomes the basis of the popular morale upon which the power system rests. Each individual impression is a drop in itself, but taken together they may produce a storm.

In tension periods these individual attitudes and appraisals take on even greater significance, for out of these personalities are recruited the fiery centers of allegiance on the one hand or resistance on the other. In moments of doubt a number of these persons may easily turn the tide one way or another, for their influence is determined not merely by their number but their dynamic energy, radiating in every direction.

A long series of trifling incidents may have a bearing on the extent to which individuals identify their interests with those of the leaders. Flaming ideologies, brilliant personalities, vivid propaganda may also accomplish the same result, and succeed in drawing into the fold of the power group great masses of citizens. But the more quiet, day by day, appraisal of government and governors is of far-reaching moment in the shaping of public morale.

The personal qualities and aptitudes of the power holders are important in the consideration of the morbidity and mortality of power, although they may be overestimated by emphasizing too strongly individual blunders of individual potentates at moments of revolution. If the selective process by which rulers are chosen produces types who do not as a whole embody the traits and skills of leaders, the situation will be serious for the maintenance of the power group, and if projected for any considerable period of time will inevitably lead to a collapse and the substitution of other types. The aristocracy may die from inbreeding, the élite from lack of circulation, the electoral process may fail to place in authority the fittest for the given situation. If the weakness of the rulers coincides with a period of great tension in the community, the discovery of the ineptitude of the governors will be all the more readily and quickly detected by those for whom they are presumably functioning.

The personal conduct of the power holders is nevertheless one of the significant elements in the perpetuation of a régime of authority. The types of behavior discussed under the caption "The Shame of Power" may readily affect the tenure of the rulers, if the balance in their favor is small. Brutality and arrogance, treachery, outstanding incompetence, cowardice and rashness, immoderation, indolence are dangerous qualities to develop in governmental behavior, especially if these qualities are not balanced by other outstanding indicia of courage or talent. Much may be forgiven the ruler who on the whole promotes the acknowledged interest of the community, but little if there is doubt of his genuine value to the group he represents.

A particular ruler finds it important to avoid transgression of the basic taboos of the community, whatever they may be in a given period. And in general this will be true of all the taboos of all the members of the family of power. He will not defy the code of the church or of business or of labor, or the common run of the customs of his group.[9] The more immoral he is politically, the more moral he may be in other respects, with regard to other canons of conduct than those of the particular field in which he is strongest.

It was Machiavelli who said that it is better to appear to be religious than actually to be so, on the ground that too highly developed a conscience might cause a fatal hesitation at the critical moment when action should occur. This is not wholly true, however, for the most promising type is one who actually is highly religious and interprets all situations which are to his own advantage in terms of religion, and that

[9] See the sage comments of the ancient Greek, Aristotle, at this point, *Politics*, Book V.

without any trace of hypocrisy but as the result of the conceit of his nature and his confidence in the infallibility of his own religio-political judgment. He may be able to find moral justification for material advantages.

In any case the ruler cannot be known, for example, as a coward in military situations, unjust in administration, doctrinally irreligious or scornful of religious ceremonies in a religious community, unsympathetic with the masses, without seriously endangering the basis of his authority. And from period to period other points of danger are outlined on the chart of the particular time and place—reefs and shoals which the wise and prudent governors avoid.

High up among the causes of morbidity in political society, as indeed in many other societies, is the failure of the system of selection and succession of the responsible governors, whether one, few, or many. It is not without deep significance that so much of the attention of students of government has been devoted to the discovery or defense of some principle of selectivity—age, heredity, special merit, election, by many or few or by cooptation, even by lot or magic.

In a special tension moment a ruler or rulers of eminence and capacity may be found, but the choice of their successors presents a problem of enormously greater difficulty. The comparison of the methods of the state, the church, the army, business, labor, and other cultural groups shows that all groups are obliged to struggle with this perennial difficulty in preserving the continuity of authority. The breakdown of the accepted system of selection, or its weak functioning, is the recurring cause of malaise and perhaps distruction of the *status quo* in political power. If the old men display senility instead of sagacity, if the hereditary lion produces an ass, if the electors choose a fool or a demagogue, if the self-selected élite are incompetent and untrustworthy, if the army chieftains produce bravery without might, then the way is open to the sickness of the society. Upon the technique of the continuity of power within a given system lies much of the burden of the maintenance of political equilibrium and morale.

Progress has been made by the isolation in whole or in

part of public administration from the function and personnel of political leadership through some form of merit system; but the direction of the political community continues as a problem of the first magnitude in every society. No community has yet been willing to accept a system in which the choice of leaders was made in accordance with predetermined criteria of availability, as Plato suggested in the proposed guardians. The intense specialization of knowledge and the rise of the expert and advisor tend to limit the field of the leader or to delimit his choices to well-considered alternatives, yet the basic question of the continuing selection of the responsible holders of power remains as an unsolved problem.

The determination of the metes and bounds of responsibility of ruler to ruled is likewise one of the power situations in which many systems come to grief. The ways and means of holding governors to an accounting are many, resting upon custom, religion, morality, public law, complex schemes of institutionalized responsibility in modern government. Rulers concede their trusteeship as fathers, proprietors, divine representatives, defenders and protectors, interpreters and guides, or other terms employed to indicate the fiduciary relation. The formulation of the common understanding upon which this relationship rests and the instrumentation of its application are basic problems of organization in political groups and indeed in other societies as well.

It is precisely at this point, however, that misunderstandings may arise to cloud the sky and engender storms. Just what is the arrangement with the governors, and is the ruler's action within the scope of this understanding? These are questions which constantly arise and if not answered successfully may set fire to an edifice of power.

Here authority may well set an unsleeping guard to observe the rise of discontent, not merely for the purpose of harsh repression, but to observe and deal with the causes of the immediate focus of infection.[10] In customs, ideologies, institutional contrivance, discontent may spring up and wax

[10] See Aristotle on the beginnings of change, *Politics,* Book V.

strong, unless care is taken to deal effectively with these evidences of nonfunctioning of the basic principles of the governmental association. In periods of rapid or sudden change, this task becomes all the more urgent and at the same time difficult, and at this point governing personnel without insight, intelligence, inventiveness, determination, may totter to its fall. The higher wisdom will recognize the realities it may not like and proceed to the organization of a new pattern in which the effective social elements are included or enough of them to make a combination strong enough to endure.

But power long continued often suffers from what might be termed hardening of the arteries, and in a crisis shows high temper instead of high intelligence—the frown of the authoritarian, rather than the smile of the diplomat or the poise of the statesman in the true sense of the term.

Or the inept will mistake an attitude of unlimited compromise for a balanced pattern of yielding and aggressiveness; and abandoning its position prematurely opens the way to another form of unbalance from the other side.

The typical combination, however, is that of pride, stubbornness, and unintelligence, which utterly misinterprets the position of leadership as trustee for the community, and falters through misunderstanding to misfortune. At the simplest never an easy task, this task of interpreting the general understanding as to the nature of responsibility in its more complex forms has been the Waterloo of many a power system and power personnel. Not only is the allocation of material advantages a failure, or the reading of the signs of ideology or custom wrong, but the community loses faith in the ability of the rulers to play their ruler role at all. They decline from the place of *maestro* to that of amateur, and jeers arise where cheers once resounded.

The morbidity of power may be sought then in:

1. Poor social functioning of the given system for groups and individuals.
2. The weakening of civic cohesion.
3. Weak personnel of the leaders.
4. Defective techniques of organization and action.

5. Low morale.
6. Weakened ideologies and symbolism.[11]

In sick political societies it will be found that the members of the family of power are not in accord, in short that the power holders are not performing their function of adjustment and balance in the given society. It may be found that the process of selecting leaders has not produced types who possess the requisite qualities necessary for those who wield political authority, or not in sufficient numbers. It will be found that the standard techniques of obtaining cohesion and allegiance have not been thoroughly employed by those who might have utilized them. The old ideologies and symbolisms have lost much of their force. And finally it will be found that the mass relations, especially in modern times, have not been brought into rapport with the general scheme of the existing order, its interest combinations, its ideologies, its personnel. Outside powers may of course upset the political order through the intrusion of other elements, powerful enough to crush a system otherwise well organized and adjusted.

What happens in the sickness of political society is then the weakening of its functional services, whether from the personal ineptitude of the power holders or because of a transition to another and widely different type of integration which no personal effort could perhaps compass. Great racial, religious, economic, cultural movements sweep along, bringing with them new sets of values, new urges for new orientations and patterns of social prestige and preferment. Or outside groups bear down with irresistible might, conquer the weak, and reintegrate them in another political power world, as the Persians engulfed the Grecian power or the Huns the Roman political structure. In such instances the territorial unit, the political system, and the ruling personnel may go down together.

In many cases, however, the sickness and death of the power group arise from the failure to adapt the existing

[11] Compare the English, French, Russian, and German revolutions for impressive illustrations.

order to the social demand for new patterns of power, new social functions, new forms of distribution of social esteem and recognition. The power holders either do not see or will not learn or misjudge the strength of the new elements of power, and there ensues corruption and perhaps disintegration and death of system and personnel as well.

A more profound and penetrating study of political forces and relations will perhaps show us underneath the surface of class and group problems (1) the deeper meaning of the relation between individual cravings and satisfactions, in the field of what may be called "constitutionalism," (2) the interchange of symbolisms, as an interpretation of experience, and (3) the invention of mechanisms of association and control based upon these fundamental factors in social and particularly in political life. A new science and art are on the way, which will provide another point of departure for the power problem and will supersede or at least supplement in a very important way the preceding systems of ideology, interests, and organization. This will not be a panacea for morbidity and mortality of power, but may indeed lead to more mobility than before in the combinations of power holders.

In revolutionary movements the diseases and death of political power are portrayed at times with astonishing vividness, as in a flash of lightning the actualities of authority are illuminated.[12] In transition moments the factors that fall and those that stand or stand longest are observable. In the tactics of the power groups both within and without, the revolutionary and the governmental, may also be seen the power points and the processes at which attack and defense are concentrated.

The vital elements in the revolutionary moment include the material equipment for the use of force; the nuclei of organization; means of intercommunication and transportation; the possession of the elements of public confidence and

[12] Cf. L. Trotzky, *History of the Russian Revolution;* P. A. Sorokin, *Psychology of Revolution;* L. P. Edwards, *Natural History of Revolution.*

its instrumentation. These strategic points differ from time to time and place to place.

The force points in modern times are the army and the police and their equipment in stone and steel, assuming for the moment that the mechanism will function at all, public buildings, intercommunication including railways, telegraph, telephone, radio, press, street circulation, and the central nerve points in the economic organization, such as electrical plants, water, basic food supplies, and materials of production.

But what determines whether the army, officers and men, will fight at the critical moment, or for whom they will fight, and likewise the police? What determines whether the mass will actually come to grips with force at the last moment? Or whether they will flee in headlong panic?

There is a whole technique of the suppression of revolutions on the one hand and the advancement of them, on the other, little described in formal literature. Police headquarters and revolutionary centers have more information.[13] Authoritarians have made elaborate studies of the tactics of revolutions both past and present, and of the detailed ways and means of dealing with the various devices that may be summoned against authority. And likewise the prospective revolutionaries have made detailed inquiries into the opposite tactics, and have devoted themselves to the development of new forms of strategic attack in case of an open clash between competing power groups. The inner archives of several groups contain a mass of important material bearing upon this transition strategy and particularly rich in studies of individual cases of success and failure.

Precisely what are the most important power centers, both material and personal; and how may they be seized and defended most successfully? This is one of the recurring problems of government. What is the importance in such situations of the mass meeting, the demonstration, the press, the strike, the conference and committee organization? What are modes of infiltration into police and army on the one

[13] See C. Malaparte, *Le Technique du coup d'état.*

hand, or incipient revolutionists on the other? What are the possibilities of wide-reaching espionage on either side?

What are the accepted boundaries of legality? What types of resistance may be permitted in a given community? What are the tension psychology and tactics on both sides? The tactics discussed under the head of the poverty of power suggest innumerable modes of sabotage so differently shaded and so difficult to regulate as to indicate a wide field of civil disobedience short of actual overt acts which might come under the head of treason. The imprisonment of leaders, the suspension of publicity, the intimidation of crowds by force; these are powerless against the subtle forms of resistance which may be conjured up from the resourcefulness of social experience. These passive resistants may indeed become *agents provocateurs,* matching those on the other side, and they may force the authoritarians into acts of violence and atrocity of such a nature as to provide new fuel for the flames of rebellions. Martyrs can with difficulty be denied burial, and funerals may become demonstrations difficult to suppress without crashing through the solemnity of religious ritualism, again opening another flood of emotional resistance.

Again, power faces the problem of repressing violence without such counter violence as will constitute atrocity; how to deal with sabotage and provocation without such roughness and unfairness as may forfeit the good will of the community; how to meet revolutionary propaganda with counter propaganda equally colorful and inspiring; how to compete in the struggle for preferment in promises of security, recognition, euphoria. The common law of these struggles and the appropriate tactics vary widely with different times and places, and, especially in periods of transition, present great opportunities for imagination and inventiveness in social techniques.

At the very crisis of power, its social composition is most important and most evident, looking backward at the event at any rate. From one point of view and perhaps the most dramatic one, it might seem as if some individual deed of courage, daring, or some blunder or delay had caused the outbreak to flare up into revolution or die down in ashes. But a closer view shows that these moments had been prepared by a series of events reaching down much more deeply into the social soil. It will appear that the power techniques, already discussed in preceding chapters, have not been observed. The power mechanism has fallen into disrepute and inefficiency. Members of the family of power have fallen away, in disaffection; churches, races, classes perhaps, have weakened one side of the power structure. The mechanisms of morale have been neglected, the principles of power behavior have been violated in important respects. The basic power functions, its instrumentations, and its *esprit* have all been eaten through, until there is only a dead tree standing. A strong wind throws it down.[14]

The army itself as an instrument of power is still there, but the army personnel may be shot through and through with disaffection, with the same electric currents that are sweeping through the community or great sections of it. If the army is alien, the citizens dislike it. If it is native and sympathetic, it cannot escape the influences of the group from which it springs. What determines now at the critical moment whether dread of treason and fear of death cast the decisive vote, or indignation, despair, the hope of a victorious outcome? Each successful revolutionist has a formula by which he determines this, but his conclusions, like the observations of the successful leader, may not be the real ones, or may not be of general application if true in the particular instance.[15] Few revolutions come as total surprises. They are preceded by long periods of clear indication of social and political malaise, the signs of which are not difficult to read for those skilled in political analysis and diagnosis. Conceit rather than the lack of courage on the part of authority may shut it off from information as to what is actually occurring, but secret conspiracies without a broad basis in the family of

[14] See the interesting account of the Putsch in 1923 by Leon Feuchtwanger in *Success*, Books 4 and 5; also examples of other unsuccessful uprisings and how they were frustrated.

[15] Cf. L. Trotzky, *History of the Russian Revolution*, at this point.

power are not common. David knew that Absalom was sitting at the gates and fomenting revolution as well as the Kaiser might have known the morale of the German people and the impending military collapse.

Ignorance, stubbornness, reliance upon what seems the invincible arm of brute force are the equipment with which many power holders make their exit from authority, while the more flexible retreat has saved the nominal throne of many a ruler otherwise in exile. The moment may come when the ruler will be obliged to choose between actual power and nominal prestige, or between peaceful retirement and violent overthrow. The power situation and function is in itself flexible, adaptable, adjustable; this is indeed one of its outstanding characteristics; but the power holders may be inflexible, unadaptable, stubborn even and may find themselves separated from the basis of their functionalism. But it will be found that in many instances this inflexibility of the power holder reflects the attitude of a class, of a vested interest, which will not bend to the storm, but prefers to ride the waves, as it has done before and will do again—until the last time.

The insight of power into social situations is often clouded by the very atmosphere of authority itself. Power is surrounded by courtiers and flatterers; by those who look for favors, perquisites, emoluments, at the hands of the governors. The aspirants hope to make themselves agreeable by saying what pleases the rulers, even if it is not true. They may not intend to deceive, but they aim to be acceptable. Thus power breeds its own destruction.

It further follows that the weaker the rulers the more susceptible they may be to flattery, to overstatement of what they themselves may secretly doubt, if they suspect their own incompetence or mediocrity. If overconfident, megalomaniac, the recognition of this greatness by others only rejoices them the more. The strong may endure criticism more readily than the weak; and courtiers are not slow to discover this, to the weakening of the weak.

What has just been said may seem to apply only to personal governments as in the case of kings, nobility, dictators.

But in a sense all governments are personal, and flattery and sycophancy may accomplish their work under one system as well as under another. A dangerous atmosphere envelops all authority, which may befog the vision of those caught within the clouds. Or taking another analogy, power may act as heroin upon its holders, inducing dreams of grandeur, moods of heroic posing and dreaming, which may fall fatally short of the stark realities.

Revolutionary moods seldom compass the whole field of human behavior, but they leave great areas of surviving traditions untouched, sometimes with amusing results. It is said that in one German Putsch communists were caught by the police because they would not run across the grass, but went around and were captured. The peasants once rose against the lord, armed themselves and advanced to the attack. But they were stopped by the toll-gate keeper who demanded a *pfennig*. "We have no *pfennig*." "Then you cannot come through." So they returned to their homes. Forms of mores not merely social but political survive and are found in strange proximity to the newer developments. The Soviets undertook at one time to abolish all legal precedents as bourgeois, as to do away with handshaking, dancing as bourgeois, and, still more difficult, to discourage kissing as unsanitary.

In earlier times, the power holders were perhaps in more fortunate position than now. Their subjects and their *entourage* accepted the doctrine of class or caste[16] and were less disposed to assert their own dignity or to challenge the position and perquisites of their masters, and at the same time the small class gathered around the chief were somewhat conscious of their exclusive status and might stand by the ruler to the bitter end, except as against one of their own number. Social change was less rapid, and custom benevolently affirmed what was.

Further, in the earlier periods it was possible to employ soldiers of fortune from outside the political community, without adverse comment. The ruler might and did rally to

[16] C. Bougle, *Essais sur le régime des castes.*

his cause professional soldiers of career, who might be depended upon, even against the streams of local sentiment, to which indeed they might be largely immune. This employment of outside mercenaries was indeed the commonplace of political life for centuries, and, until very recent times, aroused little comment and apparently affected the morale of the political community relatively little.[17] In addition to this, it was possible for the head of the state to fall back upon the friendly intervention of outside potentates who might be persuaded or otherwise induced to come to his assistance. Family relationships might be helpful in bringing this about, or the common cause of authority based upon nobility as against the upstarts without this background. The Holy Alliance was an outstanding example of the mobilization of "legitimacy" against "revolution," but only an illustration of what had happened many times before upon a smaller scale. Racial and economic ties may of course operate with much the same strength in other situations

The modern electoral mechanism makes it possible to gauge roughly the strength of the various political elements in a community from period to period, and to analyze them by various groups and classes. In this manner both disaffection and allegience may be statistically depicted and the power group well advised by blue prints of the location and type of resistance. It is true that this is not an absolute index of what might happen in a power struggle, but it is in any event a useful approximation of the political weather and is more dependable than any of the earlier indexes.

The electoral mechanism may indeed act as a preventive of violent revolutions of authority, either personal or more broadly with reference to an entire system. And it has the advantage of drawing into its contests and habituating to its methods those who might prefer the appeal to other forms of power. Even while advocating other than electoral appeals and while awaiting perhaps the hour of the appeal

[17] R. Michels, "Zur historischen Analyse des Patriotismus," *Archiv fur Sozialwissenschaft und Sozialpolitik*, 36: 14–43, 394–449.

to arms, they become habituated to the techniques of the elective system, and may come to prefer it to the less highly organized appeal to arms in revolutionary manner. It is for this very reason that leaders of revolutionary movements have at times attempted to draw their followers away from the political struggles at the ballot box, fearing their entanglement in the other system. At this point the electoral system as one form of mass organization must compete with other forms as reflectors of mass opinion and sentiment. But when once an opposition force has come into power it is of course possible to employ again the mechanism of elections either to make an appearance of general support or in fact to measure the degree of resistance developing in particular sections of the community. Striking examples of this are seen in Italy and in Soviet Russia.

Revolutions are not limited to the zone of politics but may be found in the domain of any other of the members of the family of power, in the church, in the labor group, in the industrial centers. And the principles and situations are not so widely different as would appear, except that brute force is not so readily applied because of the state monopoly. But the same indicia of revolution may be discovered, the same malaise, the same disaffection of balanced interests and values, and often the same conceit and stubbornness of authority. In the church there are not only rebels individually but also rebellions and revolutions on a broad scale. Here again the spiritual pains and penalties may prove ineffectual in types of situations not widely different from those described in the case of the political. The types of danger zones are not unlike those in government, and the basic causes not so widely different, given the variation in purpose and method of the group. In these smaller areas of authority indeed the shift in power may be most clearly seen and the elements of power discerned. One authority dissolves into another in an unending series of small committees, conferences, bureaus, administrations of innumerable types, where function, mechanics, technique, personality play much the same role as in the more distinctly political jurisdiction. If we press the question what causes the overthrow of A or B or C in any club or society, we may find the elements of transition in factors not unlike those observed in the case of kings and potentates—lack of touch with the social *niveau*, its personalities and values, defective mechanism of adjustment, indolence, conceit, and stubbornness at the end. The cloak of prestige no longer covers the poverty of the wearer, and the rival aspirants acquire courage to attack, and perhaps to overthrow.

The morbidity and mortality of power illustrate the reversal of the situations in which power is born. Disintegration takes the place of integration; adaptation to changing conditions and interests is resisted; social function is misinterpreted and misjudged. The orientation which included interest groups, individual differentials, ideologies, symbols weakens as the selective process no longer produces leaders with adequate insight, inventiveness, adaptiveness. Order, justice, morale arising from satisfaction with "results" broadly construed, no longer adorn the record of the rulers.

Out of all this, the state itself may disappear from the family of nations; or the special political system may be overthrown; or the particular rulers may be replaced by others. The world is full of the graves of independent principalities and powers whose "little brief authority" came to a close in some tragic moment of collapse of the power system. Politics cannot guarantee immortality to any political system or set of rulers. Wisdom, however, may weaken the force of the shock of change and avoid the vast losses that come in years of blind and futile struggle for balance and adjustment. Knowledge of the patterns of political equilibrium, and insight into the actual process and personalities involved at any given moment, may aid in the avoidance of many reefs and shoals and help to weather many storms.

Chapter 10

The Emerging Trends of Authority

WHAT ARE THE emerging trends of political authority in these later days? What are the inner tendencies observable in the whirl of contemporary social phenomena? Some of these trends have already been anticipated in the discussion that has gone before, but will be drawn again into the summary of the power situation as it is developing in our own times.

We may approach this problem by examining:

I. The underlying factors in the social situation and their trends in relation to power complexes.

II. The social composition of power.

III. The common underlying problems.

IV. The ideological trends regarding authoritarianism.

V. The new instrumentation of the power process.

And we may then undertake to appraise the total influence of these various factors on the emergence of power patterns, in so far as this is susceptible of determination by the relatively imperfect instruments we possess. May I suggest again that this is not a final analysis of power but an attempt to state what has been found out about power down to this time—a free play of reflection on the data at hand.

Underlying Factors Affecting Social Action and Process

First of all, there are no recent indications of basic alteration of the biological inheritance of mankind in the near future. The growth of eugenics might ultimately lead to material modifications of the human breeding process, but thus far there is no development in this direction indicative of any substantial change in the immediate future. The natural environment of man has been materially modified by the substitution of secondary environments in defiance of "nature," as in urban centers and colder climates, but on the whole the great physical environmental factors in the conditioning of human growth remain much as they were thousands of years ago.

In social heritage, however, and in penetration into the knowledge of the processes of nature, there have been and continue to be revolutionary changes which have a direct bearing upon the organization of power situations. And of all of these elements the following may be viewed as of greatest significance: science, industrialization, urbanization, leisure time, education.

The key to the emerging world is found in science and its many by-products, the rise of intelligence as a factor in human relations displacing ignorance and tradition as the great facts in human existence. The ultimate implications of this for power patterns have not been clearly observed but are just beginning to dawn upon the advance guard of the new generation. In reality the change about to be wrought in human relations is far more fundamental than has ever occurred even in the most deep-reaching revolutions of the most sanguinary nature in historic times. Control passes from the realm of tradition and force to the realm of constructive intelligence. This is the greatest of all the emerging trends in the organization of authority.

The scientific attitude itself is the most revolutionary of human forces, for it respects neither law nor morality. It involves the substitution for the older traditions of the modern types of adjustment to changing conditions, an open-eyed rather than a blind adaptation.

The most striking emerging factor is that of invention, most conspicuous in the field of mechanical contrivance, but also, although less impressive thus far, in the field of social relations. Invention, mechanical and social, materially modifies the conditions of social living, and thereby precipitates power problems of the greatest perplexity in the modern period.

The growth of communication and transportation alone has overturned the boundary lines of authority, geographically, and has in effect set up a new world. The aeroplane has broken down the old lines of states at many points, and destroyed the traditional military defense in many states. The units of organization have been upset. We may ask, what would a map of the world show if it were reconstructed by some bold hand, endeavoring to reorganize the social and economic realities of our time within new political boundary lines? Or what would the map of almost any of the individual nations be if its organization were shaped in accord with the social facts of the present time?[1]

Modern technology and social techniques have overturned many of the ways of life. Famine has been driven back in civilized states, pestilence has been beaten into retreat, production has advanced to a point where an "economy of plenty" might be set up. Industrialization has thrust agriculture into the background in great sections of the race, while urbanization has transformed the conditions of living for millions of mankind; and with urban-industrialism there came new problems of security, equilibrium, leadership.

To these facts, catastrophic from the older point of view, the modern world of power remains largely unadjusted, employing many of the attitudes and artifices of periods that have passed forever, and celebrating the glories of the old world as it was.

In addition to these factors there must be taken into consideration, for the purposes of observing whither the power trend is carrying us, the major fact of the emerging new leisure of mankind and the new education of mankind, for these will construct a new world from the point of view of power. Education and leisure may bring at first the cruder forms of mass appeal and control, but what will eventually emerge in the form of critical and constructive intelligence when once the new opportunities have been more fully adapted and adjusted?

And what bearing have these situations upon the problem of emerging authority as compared with a world in which most men were uneducated, slaves, agrarians, parochial, traditional, haunted by magic and superstition, beset by fear of pestilence and famine?

[1] See *Recent Social Trends* for analysis of these developments in the United States.

These mighty changes, unparalleled both in scope and in speed, have profound and far-reaching effects upon the whole structure and process of power. The family, the church, the industrial organization, the state, the whole political attitude, structure, process, and behavior are fundamentally influenced by these new elements which must be woven into political patterns of a new type.

Social Composition of Power

The social composition of the power situation changes its form from period to period with varying degrees of complexity and with emphasis on different aspects of human behavior. The relative simplicity of the last century has tended to break up in more recent times, with the rise of organized groups of great importance, until the power problem has become externally one of far greater intricacy than heretofore. The pluralism of the middle ages may have been more complex than the modern situation, but the pattern of that day has long been forgotten in the power manipulations with which we are familiar.

The great main lines of conflict in our day are manifold: between economic "classes"; between "races"; between "nations"; between church and state; and between all four of them. The problem of establishing jural and political relations becomes increasingly difficult, and the development of the general understandings upon which government rests hard to set up or to maintain.

Obviously a party or parliamentary system is difficult to operate if there is too wide a disagreement on the fundamental rules under which the game is played, if the parliamentary system is sabotaged or revolution begun. Under such conditions new forms of the power pattern will begin to emerge and new institutionalizations will appear. Just as on a larger scale the clash of competing nationalities, not willing to cooperate in the construction of a jural order, creates types of association of a new form and fosters the growth of new power patterns quite different from the earlier organization of authority. They make possible the construction of "bastard" forms of interrelationships such as those encouraged in international law and relations, and the larger and more flexible forms of association such as the British Commonwealth.

The clash between the competing behavior systems represented by the religious and the political is less severe than in some earlier periods. In recent years the renascence of a social policy in the church and of the stimulation of social activities under the auspices of the ecclesiastical unit, with the entrance of the church into the field of party politics, has enriched the variety of combinations and orientations. In the background, but not far behind, are the conflicts of the competing "race" cultures, which divide the allegiance of the members of the human family and which may stake their claims upon the necessity of political independence or some wide range of autonomy. The possible combinations of chief importance are:

Nations..............	50 plus
Races................	3 plus
Religions.............	Western and Oriental
Economic classes........	3 (or in Marxist theory only 2)

One might make a map of the world in which organization was expressed in these terms, or four maps, and endeavor to superimpose one upon another. This might seem like an impossible task, but it is precisely this which the power groups in the world are undertaking to bring about. Or, more accurately, each group seeks to develop its superior pattern in priority to all the others. And this not only from the world point of view, which may or may not be held in all groups, but from the point of view of a special locality in which the power combination is especially strong and where its dominance may be anticipated with some show of plausibility.

In and through these shifting systems the power competitors weave their way, organizing and magnetizing as they go. The outworn political and economic formula and systems are reshaped and reassembled by the inventors and pioneers of idea systems, as dear to the heart of the conservative as the radical. For the golden days of the one reach forward, and the other backward; and each performs its function as a frame of reference for a set of interests, ideas, and attitudes which are loosely thrown together around them. The whole process is in a sense a gigantic competition of advertising and organization, in which communists, capitalists, Catholics and Protestants, Americans, Japanese, British, Germans, Italians are at present the chief producers and distributors of delectable and useful wares.

The infallibility of the church, the Marxian dialectic and its assertion of "scientific" unassailability, the Nordic supremacy based on claims of superiority, the superior productivity of capitalistic enterprise, the divinity of nationalism, the dreams of world order: these are among the more common slogans of the combat to which millions of human beings are committed and to which they are ready to devote their energies to the extreme limit of sacrificial enthusiasm.

It is not my purpose to indicate which of these forms is developing the greatest strength, but to show that it is out of such changing material as this that the future power patterns are emerging, and to demonstrate the strong possibility of the emergence of entirely different forms of institutions and attitudes in the not distant future. The power hunters most likely to impose their plans upon masses of persons may well reckon with the pluralism of life and the sharp conflicts which now divide the race, and adjust their power systems accordingly in such a manner as to comprehend the largest possible terms of satisfaction. It is always possible that some one of these competitors may impose its features on the whole world, but it is also possible that the new patterns may be such as take cognizance of variety in unity.

From the geographical point of view, centralism and pluralism carry on a battle upon many fronts. The economic and the scientific tendencies of the time press forward toward a form of unity in which the wastes of duplication are eliminated and higher coordination of action is obtained. At this point these elements coincide with the unity of a monotheistic religion of universal application, and with the aspirations of the proletarian group toward world-wide organization of the workers. Against these tendencies are localisms with deep roots tapping the traditions of communities, strengthened by the fear of outside domination over affairs of the local group, nationalism and tribalism of wide variety which have developed their chauvinism to a height of fervor sometimes greater than religion itself. By these groups unity, or what is termed internationalization, is regarded as an infringement of special and local prerogatives.

The emerging power pattern is one that points a way through powerful nationalisms toward (1) a jural order leaving no disputes between political groups unjusticiable and (2) an outline of an economic order systematizing and stabilizing the elements of production. Both these are aimed at the elimination of obvious types of waste and loss for the human race.

Once these are attained, and not in spite of but because of them, it will be possible for a wide variety of pluralisms to assert and express themselves within the general framework of the large unity in which they are set. With the threat against the group removed, whether that of political extinction or of economic depression, the qualities of the special association may unfold with far greater freedom than before and without constant diversion of social effort to prevent the domination of other groups over their inner life and aspirations. This assumes that such groupings are not inconsistent with the development and operation of the larger jural and economic framework of the race. Herein may lie the possibility of unfolding a far richer social life than hitherto possible.

Common Underlying Problems

Running through these competing systems there are like elements with problems much more similar when analysed than the externalia of the forms of organization, just as we may find like ideas veiled behind the obscurantism of language. What are some of these basic problems?

1. The problem of adequate production of commodities

and utilities such as food, shelter, clothing, and standard social services.

2. The problem of the interchange and intervaluation of human services.

3. The problem of morale.

4. The problem of central control in the given unit in the midst of changing situations.

5. The problem of the check upon control. In what manner shall those who are entrusted with the authority of decision and execution be held to an accountability by those in whose name they function?

6. The problem of the expert, the broker, the consumer.

These basic questions are asked in each of the power forms and systems, whether economic, political, racial, religious, or other cultural form. In moments when the rancor of partisanship is laid aside the striking similarity of these fundamental problems is clearly evident to those who are not blinded by the dust and excitement of the struggle in which they are engaged.

1. The problem of adequate commodity production runs through all of the power systems, whether of one economic complexion or another, or of one nationalistic group or another. Germany, the United States, Russia, are interested in large-scale, quantity production, while France employs another system and Italy and England another. When the experts of these various units come together they speak much the same technical language with variations of dialect. Furthermore, the experts are interchangeable to a great extent. Communists employ capitalist and nationalistic experts, and capitalists observe with interest the technical experimentation in communistic situations. Each studies not merely the mechanical organization of the other, but also the human organization for purposes of efficient production, whether agricultural or industrial, in the framework, to be sure, of a special system, but with broad general lines of undoubted common interest. Colonel Cooper's 800,000 horse-power dam and the organization by which this was constructed is an object of general interest to those who have the bourgeois psychology as well as the Marxist, and to the Japanese as well

as the Nordic. And since the conquest of man over nature has reached a point where it is possible to produce adequate amounts of commodities sufficient if properly distributed for general use, the organization of the human services becomes more than ever a matter of the gravest interest and the deepest concern. At this point of commodity production, each system is willing to scrutinize all others, and perhaps borrow from them if this can be done without too great danger to the power group.

2. The problem of the interchange of services and their intervaluation is a fundamental in all of the power systems, whether capitalistic, communistic, nationalistic, or even religious.

The human differentials are a problem in Moscow as well as in Berlin, or Rome, or London. How shall the services of the doctor be exchanged with those of the steel worker, or the manager with those of his clerk; or how shall the services of individuals in competing occupations or industries, as the farm and the factory, be compared and exchanged with those of others? Neither the form of government nor the form of the economic order can finally determine this automatically, except by an act of generality not yet undertaken for any long period of time, although there are striking illustrations of this principle in the army and perhaps in Russian military communism.

There arises not only the problem of what these differentials shall be, but also the problem who shall determine this or how shall it be determined? Trade union, employer, party, government, combinations of these, as they may be developed? No system in the whole family of power offers any complete formula for the solution of this recurring problem, although in specificity those of the church and the communist are the simplest.

When the experts and power holders come together, they are able to discuss these basic questions with far greater objectivity than in the case of their respective ideologies and their power pattern, nationally or otherwise. When the interchange of services as between national groups arises the ease of intercourse breaks down and other considerations interpose their disturbing influence. Basically, this is an old-time economic problem, waiving for the moment the establishment of a general principle of distribution, a ground line, as it were, from which calculations may be projected.

3. A third principle is that of morale, which is a grand concern of all systems, and a question of equal moment in great capitals and smaller centers of either economic, religious, or political power. How shall the indispensable degree of good will and good feeling be obtained and secured? On this point again it is possible to set up a form of objectivity, which may enable the various power holders to match experiences with some degree of comparability. Good will is a problem in all political systems, in all economic systems, in all religious systems. The morale experts can understand a common language, and they may develop like lines of action even through the most diverse systems. Mussolini and Stalin might interchange their problems with some degree of mutual advantage; and Stalin might compare notes with the head of the United States Steel corporation or the steel industrialists in the Ruhr.

Neither commodity production nor interchange of services can proceed without the lubricating influence of this important element in social organization, whether economic or political. And there is something to be gained by the careful comparative scrutiny of the various systems in vogue, some material for the better adjustment of the important human relations involved in the satisfactory adjustment of this most serious of all problems in a going concern. Like the atmosphere, morale is not noticed until it begins to disappear.

4. There is in every unit a control system, or, perhaps better, a constellation of them, centered, however, around a central sun of inner authority, with recognized power to make the essential decisions which must be made within the functional radius of the group, which must be presumed to have some *raison d'être*.

Some of these decisions are "economic" and some are "political" and others are moral, but they cannot be too far apart in their types if the system is to function with a degree of smoothness. There is at least a clearing house of control, or a consultation among the members of the family of power. To some extent the policies of the social group may be allowed to drift and determine themselves without control, but there must be decision and determination of types of alternatives. And a part of the authority will be vested in a political center which will be recognized as "authoritative" for the moment at least. The relations of this "authority" to other forms of power will vary widely, as has already been pointed out, and in some cases the weight will seem "economic," and in other instances "religious," "racial," or "cultural."

In all the modern systems, regardless of economic class basis, of racial trends, or of religious affinities, this problem recurs, and earnest efforts are made for the adjustment and adaptation of the control system in the changing relations of the time and place. This problem is an object of interest in Russia as well as in Italy, in Germany as well as in France, in England as well as in the United States. The precise form in which the problem is put is not quite the same, but the basic relations might well be studied in any other system. In Soviet Russia it may take the form of a query as to the relative position of the party, the soviets, the trades unions, the centralism of the bureaucracy, and the mass feeling of the proletariat. In Italy the problem may be that of the interrelations of the syndicates, the party, and the government, and, remotely, the electorate. In Germany the question may be that of the balance between the economic, the religious, and the political elements in the construction of a political and economic order.

But in all cases there is the problem of political centralism and of the relation between political and economic or other control systems. These are technical problems on which the judgment of experts may to some extent be regarded as interchangeable, modified of course with reference to the special situations in the several communities. But through all runs the like question as to the organization, scope and methods of the central control system, for the moment viewed from the angle of authority.

5. And closely allied with this aspect of organization is

the problem of control over control. In what manner shall the control be held responsible to those in whose interest it is presumably and avowedly exercised? What is the system of representation, virtual or vicarious? What are the explicit or implicit terms and conditions upon which power is held? How far are these institutionalized and in what manner, and with what degree of direct and indirect mass control over the nominal control? Dictatorships do not solve control problems. They may simplify them for the moment, but for longer than that they constitute an over-simplification which does not function. There springs up within the dictatorial system itself a new hierarchy of authority, which embodies itself in general understandings or in more specific institutions and procedures, varying from place to place and time to time.

Not only must there be some recognized mode of calling to account the established authoritarians, in whatever order of life, but there must be a way through which the non-established and nonrecognized elements in the community may find a method of advance, independently of the central bureaucracy by whatever title known.

For example, one of the great central problems of organization in all institutional settings, political, economic, religious, is that of delegation and deputization, the surrender of initiative for the moment at least. No matter how complete the set of rules and regulations, there will be found occasions not covered, there will be found play for the individual or group (smaller than the central) initiative, if the organization is not destined to quick decay. Even in an army, which seems the embodiment of stern and inflexible discipline, this is true; and place is given for the initiative of the individual under certain circumstances.[2]

In the close-meshed organization of the Jesuit order, provision has been made for individual enterprise and responsibility, along with rigid discipline, and indeed one of the triumphs of this remarkable order has been the ability to combine the elements of individuality with those of complete central discipline. Such a type of man is selected by the

[2] Cf. Lieut. Mayer, *La Psychologie du commandement.*

system *ab initio,* and the status is maintained through his life.

Central control is one fact in organization, but difficult as it is for authoritarians in many cases to recognize the opposite principle it has equal validity. A place for noncontrol, for irresponsibility, is as important as central control. The function of initiative and criticism and opportunity for a free hand within certain limits is just as essential to a successful system, as is central control and unquestioned command in a crisis moment, and general control at all times.

And whether we look at the Catholic church, or the United States Steel corporation, or the administration of Germany, or the operation of the Soviet Union, or the group over which Mussolini presides, the same underlying situation will be observed and the same inevitable problem will quietly emerge—from the opposite corner of authority, perhaps, but still peeping out.

Selection and succession of control personnel is a common problem of various power systems, economic, political, religious, cultural. Alike they face the perennial question as to how their directing personnel shall be selected, and how continuity shall be preserved in their directors. London, Berlin, Moscow, Rome, and Washington must each develop a general understanding as to procedure at this point, and struggle with the difficulties of successful operation of their system. Indeed this is just as true of the nonpolitical units within or overlapping state lines as of the political group. In the choice of political leaders who are publicly acclaimed as policy determiners, there is the greatest difficulty in agreement among the representatives of the several power systems of the world. But in the somewhat narrower field of public administration, the various power holders are more easily able to understand each other, and to discuss the differential advantages of the competing plans which from time to time are tried out in different groups.

6. Another basic power problem running through various systems is that of the balance between the three groups which may be characterized as the expert or technician, the ruler,

and the consumer-producer. In all large group plans the relative position of these factors is of great importance, and constantly a subject of discussion among the responsible. How to adjust and balance them has been the theme of authority in all times. More recently with the rise of science and the technologist, the problem has become still more acute, as the importance of trained intelligence has become increasingly evident. Management has become as important as the possession of title either to property or to political power, and its recognition one of the outstanding problems of the time. In a way the nominal rulers may be regarded as brokers, operating between the mass on the one side and the experts on the other, and interpreting one to the other. What voice finally decides or in what situations? The voice of authority, or expertness, or of mass determination?[3]

The Soviet Union must consider this question as carefully as the government of England, or as the Catholic church, or the government of Germany or Japan. In small committees and in the wide range of international affairs, the same problem recurs, with varying outcomes in different cases. What is the power pattern here developed and what is further developing in our own day?

This is an inquiry which arises in each of the several members of the family of power, and in the political balance is of great and continuing significance. If authority shifts heavily over to the side of religion or of business or of labor, the question is raised there in the same way, and the control system must find a mode of operation, none the less. And when the institutional form no longer reflects the actualities of social and economic life, a reorientation is already on the way. This is no less true in the Soviet Union than in the fascist system, or the British or the American types of control, and it constitutes a staple and recurring topic of grave deliberation in all power systems. The streams of mass influence and the special qualities of leadership are perhaps more difficult to understand from the outside, but the inner

[3] Henry Dennison, *Organization Engineering;* H. T. Moore, "The Comparative Influence of Majority and Expert Opinion," *American Journal of Psychology* 32: 16–20.

problem is not unlike underneath the surface of race, religion, and economic class, regardless of the superficial differences.

It is in the light of these basic common problems of modern power systems that the emerging trends of authority may well be observed, and it is possible through the more detached observation of the leading tendencies a clearer view of the inner meaning of the authority patterns may be acquired.

From the scientific point of view, the scrutiny of the power complex must not be disturbed by the emotional deflection of class, race, nationalistic, religious elements in the situation, for these may only obscure the inner workings of the power relationship and elements in their naked clearness without reference to the specific ideological factors in the struggles or movements of special forms of groupings. To those who are concerned with the penetration of the problem of power development and organization, these basic questions which run through all of the competing power systems are subjects of technical study, which the technicians of all groups may discuss and upon which they may interchange experiences and skills, at many important points.

Further, the examination of what goes on in the inner circle of the common power problem is of importance, for it may aid in the formation of attitudes and the cultivation of skills necessary for the elaboration of new types of organization. This might be accomplished by stressing the essential forms and limits within which the power organization may be adapted to the needs of mankind, assuming the determination of the end goals or purposes, the specific values, it is desired to make effective in life.

The problem of production, the interchange of human services, the establishment of morale, the setting up of the central control and the control-control; these are the common property of various systems now in many instances furiously warring upon each other—capitalism, communism, religion and state, nationalism and internationalism, for these groups and types can achieve their ends only through the instrumentality of the ways indicated, and with due regard to the problem lines that must be passed before success can be achieved. It is idle to deny the fundamental similarity between the ground lines above indicated, in all of the main forms of social organization operating at the present time or in the emerging future, as far as we can see.

In viewing the trends of power, it is plain that the outworn forms and institutions, and with them outworn ideologies, are gradually being replaced by new patterns of institutions and of theories; and this, to be sure, is no new aspect of social and political organization.

Is there anything new in all this? It would seem (1) that the tempo of change is more rapid than ever before and (2) that basic changes attributable to science and invention, both natural and social, are more fundamental than ever before.

The combination of these factors produces situations in which adjustment and adaptation must proceed at a more rapid rate than has been customary. If not, disintegration sets in and mal- or non-functioning begins. It is precisely in this field of reorientation that new power patterns are likely to appear. The way is open therefore for the creation of new types of control, new inventions in construction, new adventures in imagination and in administration as well, directed toward the formation of new power points, new power centers.

Whether these power centers are nationalistic or worldwide, whether they are capitalistic or communistic, whether they are religious or secular, whether they are Nordic or otherwise racially; such questions will loom large in the near future of the power struggle, and rationalizations and techniques will be employed for the advancement of the respective power efforts.

Ideological Trends Regarding Authoritarianism

The modern patterns of power theory are not so firmly set as those of a century ago, when the nation-state had just emerged from the long struggle with feudalism, and when democracy brought a wave of enthusiasm and morale into the nation. Just at that time it was difficult to find a vantage point from which to defy the power group, or to organize other and competing political patterns.

But more recently the authenticity of authority has been challenged by fundamental changes in the general attitude toward authority itself and of obligation or duty toward it. Among these basic influences are:[4]

1. The doctrine of the economic interpretation of history.
2. The struggle between legalism and violence.
3. Pluralism and pragmatism.
4. Attacks upon religious authority.
5. The rise of internationalism.

It is unnecessary for this purpose to do more than indicate the relation of these doctrines to the central problem of authority in the political domain, and to show how deeply they are concerned with the underlying position of the power groups.

1. The economic determination of history asserting dogmatically that all forms of ideology are fundamentally reflections of the productive process, or of basic economic processes, affected vitally the doctrines of both law and morality. The one had been resting upon the theory of contract as a foundation of legal right, and the other upon the divine sanction or upon reason or social utility. In the new doctrine the phenomena of law and of all political institutions and authorities were traced back to the basic economic system under which they developed, and accorded no higher or lower position than the validity of this economic order itself may be given. And since the economic determinists who followed Karl Marx characterized the dominant system in recent times as capitalism, and announced the coming collapse of capitalism, the basis of political authority was to that extent placed in jeopardy. Even those who did not accept all of the conclusions drawn by the Marxians were deeply influenced by the assertion of the new basis of judging authority, and became critical of all forms and manifestations of any power, searching for implications other than those made evident by the prima facie claims of the legal and governmental system.

[4] See Merriam and Barnes, *op. cit.*, my Chap. 1; Otto Spahn, *Der wahre Staat;* Heinz O. Ziegler, *Die modern Nation,* and also *Autoritarer oder totaler Staat;* Carl Schmitt, *Der Begriff des Politischen.*

Thus the foundations of political and legal obligation were placed on the level of the economic institutions and tendencies of the period.

This was followed by the organization of a wide-ranging movement based on the proletarian class, aiming at the establishment of a new economic order without a state, to be effectuated by a process of revolutionary struggle in the course of which the old legality must go under. Theoretically no new legal or political order at all was to emerge, but only an economic system in which government faded away with the capitalistic class of which it was the tool, and without which there was no *raison d'être* for the political community.

2. Another phase of the weakening of authority is seen in the attack upon the validity of the legal order, the demand for its violent overthrow, and the development of new justifications for violence. The seventeenth and eighteenth centuries witnessed a struggle between the *Machtstaat* and the *Rechtstaat* in which the Legal State emerged triumphant. The principle of legal responsibility of governors was affirmed and widely established; still more widely in the nineteenth century. But another situation arose in the nineteenth and twentieth centuries in which the value of the legal order was challenged.

The earlier forms of attack upon legality took the shape of theoretical anarchism, which denied *in toto* the validity of legality in any form. Legality is morally illegal, it was asserted, and the solution of the problem the abolition of all legality, the elimination of the entire system of government. Authenticity of social control may be established only when coercive government ceases to exist. These doctrines variously stated had a vogue for a hundred years, but have tended to disappear in more recent times, although not without important survivals and restatements.[5] The sharpness of the economic struggle drew over many of the anarchists or rebel types, and they were absorbed in the proletarian movement. New types of anarchism may emerge out of the regimentation of life, but thus far the neoanarchism has not yet come over the horizon.

But while anarchism, as represented by Proudhon and

[5] Emma Goldman, *Living My Life*, is a good example.

Bakunin, was unable to make headway against socialism as represented by Marx and his followers, the early anarchist influence was reflected in the doctrines of the inevitability of social revolution and of violence as a necessary concomitant. The doctrine of the necessity of revolution as developed by the left-wing Marxians was directed at the authoritarian systems of the time, and in theory at least against all systems of political authority of any description whatever, whether capitalistic or proletarian; and at this point connected with the position of the anarchist likewise directed against all authoritarian systems.[6]

While the Marxian group attacked the state as the tool of capitalism, the capitalists attacked the state as a menace to their vigorous and successful conduct of business, and sought in many ways to curb its activities, and to throw into doubt if not disrepute the general idea of governmental activity. The doctrine of laissez faire was directed at the interference, as it was called, of the agents of an expanding government. In a sense there was set up a boycott of government, especially in the United States. Here government was reduced to the level of a necessary evil, the better the more reduced its functions and the less aggressive its personnel. And the value of the present-day forms of government, at least in their democratic and parliamentary form, was either challenged or tolerantly encouraged as in fascist experiments and theories of the new form of political organization.

Thus the authority of authority was attacked both from the right wing and from the left, for diametrically opposite reasons.

Additional aid was given by the systematic development of the theory of violence as an instrument in social reorganization, and of the morality of violence in class struggles. The most striking formulation of this doctrine was that of the French engineer, Sorel, whose *Reflections on Violence* organized the protest doctrines in a systematic defense of anti-authoritarianism through coercion, and proclaimed the legitimacy of illegality, even its ethical quality. In a sense this

[6] See Arthur Rosenberg, *Geschichte des Bolschewismus,* for elaboration of the Soviet theory upon this point.

was merely a revival of the older natural philosophy of the right of revolution which had been a commonplace of political theory for some three hundred years. But with this difference. Whereas the older doctrine had developed the justification, political and ethical, of revolution when necessary and expedient, the new doctrine developed the theory of the necessity and inevitability of revolution and of accompanying violence, omitting the possibility of important change through any other channel or instrumentality.

These doctrines have been developed in still more recent times through the glorification of force in the theory and practice of the fascist group, German and Italian.[7] Here violence becomes a joy in itself, an ultimate expression of the virility and expansiveness of life, a challenge to weakness and futility, a protest against words without "deeds," almost a *Ding an Sich*. Legalism, slightly paraphrasing Nietzsche, becomes decadence, and should not stand in the way of the many purposes of "red-blooded man," using now the American terminology for the moment. Great movements, it is held, are not brought about except by great and violent deeds; by bloodshed, suffering, and the loss of life; for out of these evidences of devotion are constructed the great works of social and political organization.

Here again, however, we find not a permanent doctrine but a phase of a revolutionary movement; for after the new régime is set up, resistance will be crushed out with ruthless determination, and without consideration of libertarian protests. In the developed form of the new authority, the right of revolution will not exist, for the new order is legitimate as against the illegitimacy of capitalism. It is now the proletarian type, or fascist type, the final form of organization, and there can be neither a right nor a duty to oppose it by violence or otherwise. This idea is fully developed in the organization of the Soviet Union, Italy, and Germany, which came into existence by violence but against which further violence is inadmissible. The monopoly of legality is vested in economic legitimacy, and there can be no further justification for

[7] See writings of Spahn, Mussolini, Hitler, and others in the same vein.

resistance. Theoretically it still remains the accepted doctrine that the state will yet disappear, and that only an economic organization will endure. But the fact that all but one national unit is capitalistic in form leaves open the question of new power patterns in all the other states, and presents a whole series of problems for the reorientation of the forms of authority throughout the world.

3. Along with these ideas came the less widely known and adopted, but none the less significant, doctrine of pragmatism.[8] The essence of the pragmatic theory is that of the relativity of values to their working utility at a given time and place. The test of institutions, of behavior patterns, is not a rational or supernatural sanction, but their works. The question is not whether the pattern has a logical basis, but does it operate? If so, it is true and right.[9] The sense of duty, then, or of obligation, whether political or otherwise, is transferred to the basis of working validity, and inherited reverence must give place to present-day appraisal and valuation in terms of the value of the instrumentality in our own lives. This is fundamentally a doctrine of challenge of prestige by present-day standards of utility.

Not wholly unrelated to this is Duguit's doctrine of the functional basis of the state and of all authority, the denial of any special sanction for state activity, the insistence upon the appraisal of every form of state activity in terms of the social solidarity it affects to serve.[10] This likewise provides a new method of challenging the essential position of authority, and of calling in question the whole range of action of the power group, except as far as it may be able to justify itself in specific situations.

4. The principle of authority in religion received a severe blow in the Reformation period when the revolt against the mother church shattered its prestige and split its power into

[8] See writings of John Dewey, especially *The Public and Its Problems* and *Human Nature and Conduct*.

[9] C. W. Morris, *Six Theories of Mind;* William James, *Pragmatism*.

[10] See L. Duguit, *Law in the Modern State,* and other publications.

fragments. But still more disastrous was the later weakening of religious authority through its conflict with science, which questioned the validity of many of religion's assertions and which reached out to substitute a world of law for a world of arbitrary will, of scientific analysis and reconstruction for a world of miracles.[11] The sense of duty, of obligation, of authority in social affairs was materially weakened by the crumbling of religious sanctions, not merely in government, but in all the ways of social behavior. The older supports of morality were threatened in the flood of scientific doubt and criticism, and with difficulty were able to maintain themselves. Not only was this true, but morality in the sense of the mores of the time was rendered uncertain of perception and recognition by reason of the swiftly changing ways of life and the lack of time for the maturation of new codes and standards of business behavior, sex behavior, social obligation at very many points.

Thus the validity of the religious pattern of authority was seriously weakened, and, notwithstanding vigorous efforts toward readaptation to modern social conditions, has not yet been able to regain its former position in the lives of men. In one great country religion has been officially condemned, and in others has suffered heavy loss in prestige. Many of the earlier functions of religion have been taken over by the school, the state, the medical profession, the technical social workers, while new forms of holy zeal have clustered around group movements other than those developed under the auspices of the ecclesiastical institutionalism.

5. The basis of local political power patterns is further troubled by the rise of larger units of an economic and jural order, which seriously occupy the interest and in many quarters the affection of mankind. It is true historically that the ancient sovereign was never wholly independent of outside attack and combination of enemies and even of destruction. But in the main there were types of isolation, made possible by the primitive nature of intercommunication and by the economic independency of the time. The modern author-

[11] Jacques Maritain, *Some Reflections on Culture and Liberty.*

ity is no longer able to dwell apart, or to live in economic self-sufficiency, however strenuous the effort may be to build up the autonomous political community. The trend is toward the larger unit, and toward the formation of new patterns of international order and of power, not modeled after the historic forms. While for the moment the enthusiasm of nationalism seems to be invincible, slowly growing forms of world order are gradually developing outside the state another center of interest. This may not be a competing center but complementary; yet in any case one that must be reckoned with in the formation of new power types and new styles in authority.

These tendencies are reenforced by two movements, the religious aspiration and organization directed toward the goal of universal church, and the proletarian movement directed toward the organization of a world-wide proletarian order, as well as by some of the international tendencies of business and finance. And the outcome is the opening out of new possibilities in power attitudes and authoritarian forms.

New Instrumentation of Power Process

The emerging trends of power may be considered in relation to the new instrumentation of authority in recent times and the apparent possibilities of the future. The usual forms of instrumentation are well known. Wealth, force, patronage, honors; these have been the stock in trade of rulers from time immemorial. The techniques of prestige, *empressement*, conference, adjudication, administration, of talk, humor, tact, rewards and punishments of appropriate types, of fear, tradition, routine; these and others, without attempting to catalogue them all at this point, have been among the chief historical devices for the instrumentation of power.[12]

The following from the Hindu manual of power shows how far back these devices date. The work of spies and

[12] I am not attempting to discuss at this time the methods of the organization or institutionalization of power as outlined in constitutions, customs, laws, decisions.

"sowing the seeds of dissension" are topics to which special attention is devoted as a part of the operation of statecraft. These intrigues

> . . . should characterize the enemy as an ordinary donkey towards skillful persons; as the branch of lakucha (Artocarpus Lacucha) broken to the officers of his army; as a goat on the shore to anxious persons; as a down-pour of lightnings to those who are treated with contempt; as a reed, a barren tree, or an iron ball, or as false clouds to those who are disappointed; as the ornaments of an ugly woman to those who are disappointed in spite of their worshipful service; as a tiger's skin, or as a trap of death to his favorites; and as eating a piece of the wood of pilu (Careya-Arborea), or as churning the milk of a she-camel or a she-donkey (for butter) to those who are rendering him valuable help.

New implements of power now begin to emerge; among these (as already discussed) are: (1) skills in mass organization, (2) the use of symbolism, (3) the growth of new types of social controls through the developing science of human behavior; through education, preventive medicine, mental hygiene, medical treatment, social work, guidance of leisure time, eugenics, semicustodial care and like methods far reaching in their implications for the social and political order.

As compared with the older situations in which armies, wealth, fear, custom, superhuman sanction played so large a part, the new world, politically speaking, displays quite a different form of power possibilities. The emerging combinations of social elements and processes, woven together to make the "political," are likely to vary widely from those of the traditional form.

Broadly speaking, the trends in instrumentation center around the application of scientific techniques to education and mass organization and to the inner individual personality, while wealth and arms tend to recede somewhat, incredible as this may appear for the moment, when these factors seem secure in their dominance.

The modern power holder might find it necessary to familiarize himself with more recent developments in the intellectual technique of mankind, admirable as many of the suggestions of the early inquirers are. He would find it important to know much about the extremes represented by the recent developments in social groupings on the one side and the individual personality on the other. More obviously than ever before, power is held by those who understand the action of masses of persons and the inner secrets of the human personality, whether knowing these data scientifically or artistically. Probably there is not a formally developed department of crowd psychology and another of human personality in the organization of the leader, but there is an informal specialization in these directions. There must be if the power pattern is to prevail, not only against the malcontents and rebels within the political system, but within the other members of the family of power, ready to snatch authority from the hands of an inattentive political power group.

What is the type of satisfaction the individual obtains through the crowd expression, or in his relations to rulers? And how are these manifestations most adequately organized for this purpose? Military art has studied armies for many generations, although it may well be questioned how scientifically in the light of modern knowledge, but the other governmental mass movements have not been so carefully scrutinized. Attention has been given to the organization of public administration as a special branch of governmentalism, but not to the whole situation.

In recent times there have been striking examples of the overthrow of established power systems through the use of the new techniques by Mussolini and Hitler. In each case the decisive role was played by the keener understanding of the mass psychology with which they were dealing and of the inner purposes of the human personalities making up the masses. This may well prove true in other coming changes of other power systems in the future. In any case the understanding of the basis of these situations as well as the accompanying techniques is necessary whether for purposes of attack or defense, and will be part of the equipment of the power holders, or the aspirants—a section in the "mirrors of princes."

The later branches of the power holder's technique of greatest importance in the present, although perhaps existing under other names in earlier times, are as follows: civic education; propaganda; organization; morale.

Civic education involves the shaping of the oncoming generation and the determination of its attitudes. True, attitudes will be formed from material other than that developed in the formal educational system, but much will be determined there; and it is one of the power centers in a political system. Soviets produce communists; fascists produce fascists; and democrats produce democrats.

In a sense the power that once was in religion or in the army passes into or is rivaled by the school. Universal education instead of special, compulsory education extending over a long series of weeks instead of a short tribal initiation—these produce conditions widely different from those obtaining in earlier periods and they now are closely related to the centers of authority. In earlier times the authority might be satisfied to have schools of the dominant language or the dominant religion, but now he demands schools producing attitudes upon political and economic affairs.

But this is a heady drink, and in it lurks danger for the power holder. The indoctrination may be so artificial and wooden that in a changing world it may be dangerous. What has been too rigidly taught may be hard to apply to a new situation unforeseen at the time of the indoctrination. The only safety would lie in a liberal education, leaving a wide range of adjustability as time went on.[13] Further, the authority who attempts to control the school situation may encounter opposition from other members of the family of power. Chief among them historically religion, and as a later comer the spirit of science itself with the independence of the professional group of teachers, resisting in each case the

[13] On this point see my *Making of Citizens,* in particular the last two chapters; and the other volumes of the Civic Education series, dealing with the problems of several states; also my *Civic Education in the United States.*

imposition of a propaganda program by a power group. Education is perhaps better adapted to a democratic régime than to one of more limited range, for in a popular system the attitudes developed may be those friendly to associated life, rather than in terms of a class or an idol. But it may be and has been applied to the glorification of a class or turned to the personal advantage of a dynasty or a small group of authoritarians.

Another element in the modern repertoire of power is that of propaganda, to which allusion has already been made in the consideration of power situations. The power system concerns itself with the manufacture and marketing of symbols of various sorts through which the community may be induced to collective action. The modern power holder must be as much concerned with his symbols as with his sword, with his propaganda as with his battalions. His army will not fight if the enemy propaganda or the rival propaganda undermines their will to battle; and he must therefore contend with the unseen enemy.[14]

Not only does the power holder deal with schools and propaganda, but he is concerned with organization on a large and unceasing scale. His political authority will be manufactured in a great factory where organization and specialization are the order of the day. It will not matter how good a swordsman he may be, or how fierce his moustachios. If he is not an organizer, he may lose to one who is. It is not merely the fighting spirit that prevails in these days of mass handling of men and materials, but facility in the manipulation of thousands of men and tons of material, finding the place and the time for them, in peace as in war. If he is not watchful, the political power holder will discover that the church or the labor union has surpassed him in the toughness of organization and facility in propaganda; and have stolen away his scepter while he slept, so to speak. The church has long been organized on a great scale, and the new groups of

[14] The Social Science Research Council's Committee on Pressure Group and Propaganda has compiled a bibliography of several thousand titles on this subject.

toil are fast developing their own special forms of organization.

Finally the power holder must be able to deal with the subtle quality of a community known as morale. An attitude may sweep through a group, bringing in a tide of good will and enthusiasm for the organization, or a cold breath of discontent and malaise. How shall this be produced, prevented, or controlled? This is a problem of first magnitude. In armies ways and means of inspiring the soldiers have been known for a long time, but on the civil side the tactics of enthusiasm are less familiar, although none the less important. The power group keeps its ear attuned to morale and strives as best it may to prevent the rise of the dreaded situations of ill will which are so disastrous to authority.

More important than the celebrated question raised by the Florentine, is it better to be feared than to be loved, is the later form of statement, is morale more important than money? For that is a form of rapport which may include the fear, the hate, and other interests or emotions applicable to the situation.

From time immemorial the question has been raised as to whether the influence of gold or that of the army is more useful for the holder of political power. Will the gold buy the necessary troops, or will the army usually be able to find and take the gold? Many interesting illustrations of the respective values of these factors might be given, and much ingenious discussion of the question is possible. In modern times the situation has materially changed, since the armies are now largely nationalistic, mass armies, not so easily purchased as were the older mercenary soldiers of fortune; and gold is a short way of saying an elaborate industrio-political system with wide ramifications into psychology.

Gold and armies are only claims to service, but there is no certainty that the claims will be honored when presented, unless the industrial and civic situations are favorable; and whether one can buy the other or take the other is always somewhat problematical. The title to the property or the value of the money claim may wither; and on the other hand the army may decide not to fight, or even worse, to fight on the other side.

Under modern conditions, the morale necessary for the successful army and the morale necessary for the operating industrial system are likely to spring from much the same basis. Any considerable number of soldiers and any considerable number of workers will come from the same ultimate mass of the population, upon whose good will both must in the long run rely. The power hungry, therefore, who reach the mass will be able to mobilize both gold and arms by the same logic. As between independent states, however, this might not be true, for one state might have wealth and the other numbers in differing degrees. Morale, in short, is the key to much of modern power, more significant than either property or armies.

In one way the concept of morale seems a vague and indefinite one, yet the results are immediate and directly perceptible whether in output or in terms of votes, taxes, or military volunteers. "Bread and circuses" was the old saying, but in modern times the situation is more complicated, though perhaps the general statement in its figurative sense is still substantially true, or at any rate on certain levels and in certain periods. Wars are won and lost through good and poor morale; laws are enforceable or not and public plans are accepted as the morale of the community in relation to the government is high or low.

Organizing power and showmanship are the devices most commonly observed, but deeper down are the more scientific devices in what may be called "constitutionalism,"[15] the knowledge of the physical-psychological basis of the personality, and on the other hand the knowledge of symbolism in its relation to individuals and masses. In this instrumentation civic education plays a larger and larger role, and research and technical intelligence along with it. Constitutionalism and symbolism are two keys to power instrumentation.

In a sense such devices have long been known and em-

[15] G. Draper, *Human Constitution, A Consideration of Its Relationship to Disease;* see also his *Man and Disease;* Bentley and Cowdry, *The Problem of Mental Disorder.*

ployed, but the more recent use of them is based on a wider mass participation, on a deeper knowledge of mass psychology and organization, and upon a more thorough understanding of mass advertising and appeal if not of artistic symbolism. One needs only to consider Mussolini, Hitler, Lenin, Gandhi to observe the effect of the new techniques in the power setting, and glimpse something of their meaning for modern political life.

Along with other agencies affecting the formation of power in the political system must be placed the instrumentality of science in its relation to social and political control. Science is no respecter either of law or of morals or of political systems if they cross its path. The scientific techniques of education, propaganda, organization have already been elsewhere discussed, but they may and indeed must be placed here in the center of the emerging forms and limits of social and political life. Medicine, psychiatry, constitutionalism, symbolism, these lie close to the centers of human life and conduct, and they enter into the development of the power holding system of the future. I do not know what they may bring with their enlarged and enriched comprehension of the secrets of human behavior, and it is idle to predict in so uncertain a phase of our knowledge. But we have solemn warning that revolutionary changes are on the way, more revolutionary than the most gifted imagination of the most inspired thinker has ever evolved.[16] We may set it down as one of the fundamentals of the study of emerging power patterns that the scientific techniques are moving toward the transformation of human political conduct and forms of association and authority.[17]

All of the above-described ideological and group movements are to be taken with great seriousness and even with reverence by their believers or beneficiaries; but they are overshadowed in ultimate significance by the coming evolu-

[16] Samuel Butler, in his *Erewhon,* made some remarkable anticipations, and H. G. Wells, in *The Shape of Things to Come,* and Aldous Huxley, in *Brave New World,* have produced challenges for those who wish the stimulation of their political imaginations.

[17] See my *New Aspects of Politics,* second edition.

tion of human behavior control in terms which will perhaps destroy the meaning of the present-day politics. Much of the political distress of the present time is based upon personality maladjustments which are preventible in large measure through the employment of the known instrumentalities of science; much of the futility of power struggles is based upon widespread ignorance and ill-trained attitudes to which power hungry aspirants appeal with success. But these attitudes may be conditioned under the control of science and with wiser and sounder instruction may give way to different standards and levels of intelligence, criticism, appraisal, appreciation. The shame of power is a reflection of the shame of the community, expressed in the tactics and maneuvers of those who weave their authority from the material they find on the surface of social attitudes and possibilities. The lot of the human race may be basically altered by readjustments in physical-psychic equilibrium and in civic education; and when these adjustments are once made the nature of the power struggle materially alters. The new holders of authority are conditioned in their activities by the new levels of appreciation and support.

These developments may seem remote and impractical to those who are not familiar with the recent trends in the field of social science and medical development, but a closer view of what is happening in these directions indicates striking possibilities, and, projecting forward the present trends of science at their present rate and in the present direction, probabilities. These controls are not based upon utopias but upon scientific developments, and their *leit motif* is neither an economic orientation, nor a religious point of view, nor a political attitude and tendency, but found in the possibilities unfolding in the form of personality adjustment and institutional developments corresponding. Under all the utopian and ideological systems proposed, the personality possibilities remain much the same, despite the institutional readjustments of power, and in point of fact there are vast opportunities in the reorientation of the personality patterns and their relations to the control situation in the given community.

The emerging instrumentation of power is then one of the

significant developments of the present and the immediate future, and will inevitably affect all the other factors in the power process. It may well be that the new patterns will vary so widely from the long-accepted types called political that the experts will find they are not political at all, and discover some other word to use when referring to them.

If we look at the emerging trends of political power, it is seen that the world out of deep unrest searches for a new and more valid principle of authority which does not seem to omit essential elements in life or block the way of the human spirit; which will not exclude an animating ideal, a principle of guidance which will transcend the economic motive, or the command-obedience phase of conduct, or the religious motive with its air of unreality. Furthermore, men search for an area or unit of power, desperately; and for a type or form of directing personnel, arising from mass control, resting upon confidence in the group, upon devotion to it, or upon belief in the reliability and rightness of its conclusions. Neither the economic class, nor the nation, nor the church at this time satisfies all of these elements, although each embodies and uses some of them. Each develops its soaring enthusiasms; but each displays its exclusiveness and its hates and fears of others.

Each principle leads to new power conflicts, unless it demonstrates its ability to effect a complete universalization; and this goal none seems to reach in centuries of struggle.

The older forms of power are crumbling, the older ideologies are losing their force, the older groups and units are falling apart or afoul of each other. The older gods of power are melting in the fierce heat of modern social forces, and men look to see what is to take their place in the reorganization of social forces, ideologies, symbolism. Government, industry, morality, art, and science are alike involved in the emerging scheme of things social.

What we observe around us is not ruin, but reconstruction. The great problem of the future is the construction of the new pattern of power, bringing together the scattered elements now often found far apart.

How shall we blend the skills of government, of industry,

of science, in a new synthesis of authority, uniting power and responsibility, containing a vivid appeal to the vital interests of our day, able to deal effectively with the revolutionary developments of our social, economic, religious, and scientific life, and yet without stifling liberty, justice, progress?

And how shall we make use of such an organization of power in the evolution, interpretation, and application of the new social ideals and attitudes which are on the way toward the transformation of our civilization into something we can now only dimly discern?

This problem transcends in importance the problem of the area of the emerging authority, whether local, or world-wide, centralistic or pluralistic; or whether the authority shall be found in the hands of the few, or the many, the learned, the warriors, the priests, the wealthy; the problem of class, or race, or religious domination.

But, it may be asked, will this power pattern be political, or economic, or scientific, or religious, or emotional-artistic in its essential nature?

The outstanding trend is (1) toward the *rapprochement* of the economic and the political, after a century of separation throughout the greater part of Western Europe; and (2) of the economic, the political, and the scientific. The sharp distinction between so-called "economics" and so-called "politics" tends to disappear, merged in the larger problem of what we may call, for lack of a better term, social engineering or management. The phase of an assumed separate and independent organization, or of ideologies postulating such a dichotomy, is passing away, and we may look forward to a fusion of these elements in such a manner as to make them indistinguishable, institutionally and as factors in social control.

In this combination, the new authority will be able to utilize what were earlier called economic sanctions or penalties with less of military or coercive sanction. Aspects of social activity, such as the unit cost of production of commodities and the terms upon which they are interchanged, and the price or other system employed for this purpose, continue to hold the color of the economic, but they tend to be assimilated to or with the political, and with difficulty operate in their respective vacuums. What has been happening in the last century is not the entire separation of these two elements, but the independence in large measure of the industrial system, and the tendency of the industrialists to dictate action to the government. But science and engineering and the growth of new social values put an end to this period, and we face a readjustment on an heroic scale of the elements once contained in the separate compartments of political and economic. The emerging power pattern will recognize and embody this new development in the patterns of life.

But the new power scheme must also reckon with the developing types of social controls made possible by the extension of the boundaries of modern science. Education, preventive medicine, psychology, psychiatry, psychoanalysis, psychobiology, "constitutionalism": these are evolving gradually new forms of emancipation and control which enter deep into the heart of the modern power problem. The future cannot be studied without them; for they condition the control systems that are in the next period of development. As modern machine technology has upset the categories and plans of economics, the new social technologies are upsetting the basic patterns of authority. And both the engineering technology and the social sciences are on the way toward an overturn of the categories both of government and of economics, sweeping along in such a fashion as to destroy or distort many of the earlier units, processes, and relations, and to compel the construction of new patterns of power and prestige. These controls may be called economic, political, medical, engineering in the social vocabulary of the moment. Their implications are compelling, regardless of the name they bear. If they revolutionize civic education, or undermine court procedure, or relegate capitalism or communism or fascism to the dust heap, or reorganize representation and responsibility, or make democracy or aristocracy or dictators useless; so it is. They sweep on with the rush of modern science toward an unknown goal. The new synthesis of political power must reckon then with the fusion of the economic and the political, and of both with the technological-scientific.

Neither jurists, nor economists, nor scientists may welcome this dénouement, but it moves on its way with inexorable solidity. That our traditions or our habits or our comfort or our special interests and privileges may be disturbed and reallocated will be important to us; but not controlling in the larger economy of the new era.

From the foregoing, it might seem that religion tends to disappear from the scene. In the sense that religion is magical, or credal, this may be true. But there is a larger world of aims and purposes in which values akin to religion continue to function and function for an indefinite period, if adjusted to modern conditions as well as they were to the earlier phase of human existence.

There is a world of dreams, hopes, appreciations, appraisals, apprehensions, anticipations, sensitivities shot through and through with artistic symbolism—a world of values not held within the law or the norms of ethics or the externalia of authority and discipline. And perhaps these constitute the inner core of the recurring phenomena of religion, from period to period of human experience. Perhaps these values are really the essence of an elaborate system of creeds and works and theologies. And perhaps they may be fitted into the power system of science, of politics, of economics in a new synthesis of authority, transcending that of the present time, and rising to greater heights than ever before in the story of the race.

Are these to be institutionalized under some name, as they have historically been, or shall they be "constitutionalized" in the psychobiological sense, or shall they be woven somehow into a new pattern?

The great idealisms that sweep men's souls, the mighty sacrificial enthusiasms that vibrate through life, and sometimes put to rout and shame the forms of gold and steel; what part do they play in the organization of the patterns of political power? Imprisoned they escape; burned they rise from the ashes; exiled they return, perhaps in triumph. To what role shall they be assigned in the emerging forms of authority?

Shall we omit all these elements from the scheme of power? Or can we allow them to enter without demoralizing the whole scene? How is it possible to rule either with them or without them? Shall we say that all roads lead to Rome? Or is it that Rome, religion, leads over all roads to every seat of authority?

"The great secret of the coming age of the world," says Benjamin Kidd, "is that civilization rests not on reason but on Emotion."[18] It is not the absence of emotion that is the mark of high civilization, but the control of it. He continues: "Other things being equal, the higher and more complete the individual or people, the higher and more complete the capacity for emotion. Power in the future civilization will be," he asserts, "the science of the emotion of the ideal in the collective mind."[19]

In times gone by some of these values have sought expression in one form of religion or another, finding shelter in the arms of the church since they were not welcomed elsewhere. These values and appreciations have been institutionalized in the church, which has protected the inner aesthetic emotional core with the harder forms and structures of ecclesiastical authority. And this authority in turn has become in many ways and at various times a replica and a rival of the political power itself. But in turn is overformalized and hardened.

We may raise the question, how far has this process been due to the failure of the governmental group to make an adequate place for these values, to a preference for types of violence, brutality, and like influences, to failure to reckon with the sacrificial basis upon which government itself rests,

[18] *The Science of Power*, Chap. VIII.

[19] Kidd finds the unifying principle in woman. "As distinct from man, *she is the creature to whom the Race is more than the Individual, the being to whom the Future is greater than the Present.*" *Ibid.*, p. 219.

"The type of civilization which first organizes itself around this central capacity of woman's mind will have a stupendous advantage over all others in the coming struggle of the world." *Ibid.*, p. 230.

to a dullness toward the artistic and aesthetic foundations of life?

Obviously, the artificial and forced subordination of the church to the state does not solve this problem to the satisfaction of either, but are there not other possibilities of unifying the essential elements in the situation, not the death of either but the higher and richer life of both?

In the new synthesis of authority may there not be found a recognition and embodiment of the value systems which have hitherto found a refuge only in other counter forms of institutionalization and order, such as the ecclesiastical, the artistic, the symbolic?

The new constellation may represent social authority, made up of integrated elements of power and prestige, brought together under the benign auspices of science and allocated to their respective functions in the social scheme of things. The aesthetic and emotional systems, the values with which they are surcharged, might thus become an integral part of the system of social control and social emancipation; and bring together the scattered fragments of the piece called life.

If what has been must always be, then there is little reason to anticipate a time when the values of life and the forms of power can dwell together in peace and unity. But if we may assume the continuing advance of social intelligence in the organization of human behavior, we may look forward to a closer union between the values and the skills of government, and the blending of the authority of the ideal with that of the real, to an integral organization of power in which the conflicting armies of the great social disciplines may be brought more nearly together and battle against the common enemy of ignorance, tardy adaptation, inertia, malfunctioning, rather than against each other.

Whether education and science can weave more closely together the scattered threads and bring about a new synthesis in which human values may be incarnated in the forms of authority, time will show. For the moment we may point to possibilities in this direction, but certainly not to widespread and distinctive achievement, in a moment such as this when intolerance and force testify to the present limitations of social intelligence as a means of human organization.

What then are the emerging trends of power, in the light of the data canvassed in the preceding paragraphs?

1. The transition to systems of control resting more directly upon recognized mass support, whether in democracy, fascism, sovietism.

2. The transition to the new functionalism of power, the politico-economic, technological network of services and functions.

3. The transition to the new instrumentation of the power process based upon deeper knowledge of mass psychology, upon mass organization, upon education, upon propaganda, upon "constitutionalism" and symbolism.

4. The transition to sanctions of power less closely allied to violence, and more nearly related to education, economic pressures, scientific controls and religio-aesthetic sanctions.

5. The transition to an integration of elements of authority now scattered through the state, the church, industry, science—into new syntheses of authority of quite another *genre*.

But we may also raise the same question of power from the under side of authority, on behalf of those upon whom power is exercised from time to time. We may inquire, what are the trends on this level of social and political organization?

What happens to the sense of human dignity, to the unconquerable domain of the inner spirit, in all this tightening of the mesh of mechanization and increasing subtlety of manipulation? Does the individual or the small group tend toward greater facility in self-expression in this new integration of authority, or toward closer and more insistent regimentation of conduct?

From the objective point of view the ideological struggle between "individualism" and "collectivism" is a sham battle, or if a real battle a struggle over narrow programs. Economic individualism in the old sense of the term is dead, but modern individualism reveals other aspects of the individual's place in society. And cultural individualism may find richer releases in the new type of world than in the old. Political and economic organization may prove the framework within which the inner life moves more freely than ever before. Individualism has far wider meanings than the economic alone, and may reach out into indefinite fields of self-expression in a world of leisure and opportunity within a general scheme of order, jural and economic.

The sharp antithesis between individualism and collectivism has little philosophical validity, if closely analysed. For the individual may find his highest satisfactions or some of them in relations with other persons, and he may rate these common experiences as highly as the isolated flight of fancy. He may be selfishly altruistic, or altrustically selfish. He may find himself agreeably intertwined in a whirling series of nebular loyalty systems which may at times compete but again coincide and reenforce one the other. And his own personality constellation may be one of these, one among many in which he lives and moves and has his being. He may even be more of a king in other domains than in his own personality. His own special occupation may yield to other associations in which his rank is higher yet:—and more agreeable.

In a power world organized in accordance with the changed conditions of human intelligence and control the individual and the smaller group, the minority, might well enjoy a richer and fuller life than has hitherto been possible for most persons and groups. The absorption with war externally and the local regimentation made necessary by the possibility of wars, might be removed or mitigated, and a vast fund of energy set free for other purposes. The local brutality arising from ignorance of better ways and the tradition which enthroned the incompetent administrator of force yield to another way of life in which these special perplexities and irritations would not so readily sway the course of human conduct.

Ignorance, brutality, traditionalism; these have been among the greatest foes of the human being who struggles to find a way through the vale of tears. War, pestilence, famine, slavery, insecurity, abasement are institutions in which much of life has been set. But these may yield in a different ordered world, and indeed the emerging trends of human association are signalling their departure even in an hour of emotional exultation.

The battle against disorganization may for a time prevent the full freedom which later periods will see, but one who wishes to exercise his imagination may dimly outline a type of society in which the antiauthoritarian of the new day may find for himself a freer field than ever before outside the world of dreams, a neoindividualism, a neoanarchism, if you please.

There are those who fear power, as there are those who fear life itself; who dread organization and even association in any form—perhaps from temperament; from some sad social experience; from some lack of aptitude in interrelations. But power may also be regarded not as a foe, a tyrant, an oppressor, a brutal hand upon the shoulder, a prison cell, the lash, but as a friend and guide, a companion, a special service, an instrumentation of personality, just as association may be the great flood into which one throws himself and rushes along in breathless delight perhaps, toward a goal not individually directed.

The power of the creative and constructive type is slowly being ground out with infinite pains and with vast and widespread accompaniment of effort, often with temporary disillusionment. Power functionally fitted to life is not oppression but release, not a limitation but an expansion of opportunity, a wider way to achievement, both for group and for individual. Power is positive rather than negative, creative rather than destructive. Maladjusted powers in nature and in social organization may devastate life and happinesss, and it has been found convenient, and for all I know useful, to have a demonology to which these wilder and less restrained powers may be consigned, as devils, evil principles, wicked spirits, until such time as the intelligence of mankind has found ways to tame and utilize them in social relations.

But power may also be fertility, creativeness, construction, growth, and in this meaning has always been recognized as beneficent and worshiped, and held to be the greatest friend of the race. Political power in the earlier stages of its existence was also recognized as something paternal in its origin and implications, and while feared for its brutality was also loved for its fatherly care. In the familial organization, still found to be sure in great ranges of the world's population, this idea lingers, but in the formation of the modern national state seemed to be lost in part at any rate. In the overthrow of absolutism, power was pictured as unwelcome and undesirable, while freedom from authority was set forth as the final desideratum in political association in many ideologies. The mighty advance in mechanization aided in this process of the maligning (diabolizing) of power, and thus there came to be unusual form of resistance to authority per se, quite without precedent in the historical development of government.

But just as the subordination of the mechanism and its application to the finer purposes of life become dimly evident in modern organization, so adaptation to the presence of vast authority and the recognition of its broad social purposes may be expected to unfold gradually in the consciousness and in the institutions and in the ideology of men. Authority may then appear as an instrument of mankind, not as its master, as a means of enlarging the capacities of the group, rather than as a brutal limitation. It would of course be fatuous to conclude that such a condition had already been reached in our day, or is to be expected in the very near future, but the slow development of the power process tends to advance in this direction, notwithstanding the many opposite evidences of momentary movement in another course.

The next phase may witness the flaming out of fascist revolutions, the armed clash of economic nationalisms, the bursting forth of communistic-capitalistic revolutions and counter revolutions, a world-wide struggle between conflicting racial types or economic interests, seen in the Orient and the Occident. Or it may be characterized by the adroit avoidance of catastrophic collisions and perhaps debacles;

and the slow emergence of jural order in the world as a whole and in the domain of the industrio-political.

The emerging trends of power are deeper down than nations, classes or other passing units and may reveal themselves through any or all of these struggles, as the new instrumentation of power comes into use, and as the new machine and social technologies make their way into social and economic and political life. There may emerge neither uniformity nor unity in authority, but a pluralism of political powers and of families of power with new techniques. The new patterns of thought and political behavior developed in the course of a generation may give us a world of coordinating powers of many stripes and types, finding an equilibrium and a steady course in the social cosmos.

I have now come to the end of the lane. What I began to write Unter den Linden in Berlin I conclude on the Midway in Chicago. I have observed the birth of power and looked at the family, including the outlaws. I have looked at the sacred credenda and the miranda of power; and the obverse side of the shame of power, and the poverty of power. I have analysed some of the more important ways and means by which the fittest survive in the world of political power; have considered the morbidity and mortality of power; have examined the role of abnegation as a road to authority; and finally I have endeavored to trace the emerging trends of power in the modern world.

I am not a propagandist for a particular power pattern, or a prophet moved to reveal the future forms of power. I do not share the complaisance of those who look forward to a world but little changed. Without undertaking the role of prophet, just disclaimed, it is perhaps appropriate to say that I myself look forward to fundamental changes in the political, the industrial, the religious, the scientific order, changes that will shatter many of the present-day and historic power structures beyond recognition and remake them in new forms that will be terrifying to those who love the *status quo*, either because it deals gently with them or because they fear the insecurity of change. That violence and passion will remake these patterns in the near future may well be, and indeed seems likely, for warnings are likely to fall on ears and eyes as indifferent as those who read in Babylonian days, *"Mene mene tekel upharsin."*

There is always the alternative of creating new power balances and patterns by utilizing the constructive intelligence of our time. The mold in which the modern state was cast a few centuries ago is broken, or breaking, but the way is open to the creative intelligence of our day to reorganize and reconstruct new forms of political and social life adapted to modern social forces. It may well be that violence will play a role in this remaking of the new world, but fearful periods of tension and suffering will be spared the human race if intelligence can shape forms and general understandings appropriate to the emerging order of things, and avert the grand catastrophes that from time to time have swept whole civilizations from the face of the earth.

It is a long road out of a slavery to inanimate nature, out of a slavery to human nature, up to the mastery of the dark and fateful forces around us and within; but the race is on its way. The future belongs to those who fuse intelligence with faith, and who with courage and determination grope their way forward from chance to choice, from blind adaptation to creative evolution.[20]

[20] Other aspects of this problem are presented in the companion volumes of this series (also published by Collier Books) by my colleagues: T. V. Smith, *Power and Conscience,* and Harold D. Lasswell, *World Politics and Personal Insecurity.*

Index

Index

A

B

Index

C

D

T

U

V

W

Z

IF YOU ENJOYED READING THIS BOOK, YOU'LL BE INTERESTED IN THESE OTHER COLLIER BOOKS ON

History

BS33	The Isolationist Impulse: Its Twentieth Century Reaction	*Selig Adler*	$1.50
BS97	Theodore Roosevelt and the Rise of America to World Power	*Howard K. Beale*	1.50
BS89	The American Spirit	*Charles A.* and *Mary R. Beard*	1.50
BS43	The End of Ideology: On the Exhaustion of Political Ideas in the Fifties	*Daniel Bell*	1.50
AS259V	The Origins of Modern Science: 1300-1800	*Herbert Butterfield*	.95
BS6	Tin Horns and Calico: A Decisive Episode in the Emergence of American Democracy	*Henry Christman*	1.50
AS29	The American Pilgrimage: The Roots of American History, Culture and Religion	*Cyclone Covey*	.95
BS132	The Compact History of the Civil War	*R. Ernest* and *Trevor N. Dupuy*	1.50
BS3	The End of the Russian Empire	*Michael T. Florinsky*	1.50
AS219Y	The Dilemma of Democratic Socialism: Eduard Bernstein's Challenge to Marx	*Peter Gay*	.95
BS140X	The Age of Ideas: From Reaction to Revolution in Eighteenth-Century France	*George R. Havens*	1.50
BS76V	Political Power and Personal Freedom: Critical Studies in Democracy, Communism and Civil Rights	*Sidney Hook*	1.50
AS1	The Great Rebellion: The Emergence of the American Conscience from Sumter to Appomattox	*Earl Schenck Miers*	.95
BS49	The Disruption of American Democracy	*Roy Franklin Nichols*	1.50
BS29V	The Greatness of Oliver Cromwell	*Maurice Ashley*	1.50
BS83	Woman as Force in History	*Mary R. Beard*	1.50
AS89V	European Background of American History: 1300-1600	*Edward Potts Cheyney*	.95